D0578303

# Corporate Decision-Making with Macroeconomic Uncertainty

# Corporate Decision-Making with Macroeconomic Uncertainty

*Performance and Risk Management*

Lars Oxelheim

Clas Wihlborg

UNIVERSITY PRESS

2008

# OXFORD
UNIVERSITY PRESS

Oxford University Press, Inc., publishes works that further
Oxford University's objective of excellence
in research, scholarship, and education.

Oxford  New York
Auckland   Cape Town   Dar es Salaam   Hong Kong   Karachi
Kuala Lumpur   Madrid   Melbourne   Mexico City   Nairobi
New Delhi   Shanghai   Taipei   Toronto

With offices in
Argentina   Austria   Brazil   Chile   Czech Republic   France   Greece
Guatemala   Hungary   Italy   Japan   Poland   Portugal   Singapore
South Korea   Switzerland   Thailand   Turkey   Ukraine   Vietnam

Copyright © 2008 by Oxford University Press, Inc.

Published by Oxford University Press, Inc.
198 Madison Avenue, New York, New York 10016
www.oup.com

Oxford is a registered trademark of Oxford University Press

All rights reserved.  No part of this publication may be reproduced,
stored in a retrieval system, or transmitted, in any form or by any means,
electronic, mechanical, photocopying, recording, or otherwise,
without the prior permission of Oxford University Press.

Library of Congress Cataloging-in-Publication Data

Oxelheim, Lars.
  Corporate decision-making with macroeconomic
  uncertainty : performance and risk management /
  Lars Oxelheim, Clas Wihlborg.
      p. cm.
  Includes bibliographical references and index.
  ISBN 978-0-19-533574-3
  1.  Risk management. 2.  Decision making. 3.  Management.
  I. Wihlborg, Clas. II. Title.
  HD61.O96 2008
  658.4'03--dc22—2008029861

9 8 7 6 5 4 3 2 1

Printed in the United States of America
on acid-free paper

# Preface

Within the last three decades, firms and organizations, regardless of size, have been subject to changes in the conditions for doing business including increased uncertainty about shocks and disturbances in the world economy. These developments require new strategies wherein management recognizes the interdependence of exchange rates, interest rates and inflation rates influencing the firm through a variety of channels not captured by conventional accounting systems. This book is aimed at providing the essential tools for managing risk and assessing the development of corporate performance and competitiveness in this new economic climate.

With our book *Macroeconomic Uncertainty: International Risks and Opportunities for the Corporation*, published by John Wiley in 1987, we opened up a new strand of literature emphasizing the impact of a volatile macroeconomic environment on corporate risk exposure. In 1997 we expanded the view by including a profit filtering process in the book *Managing in a Turbulent World Economy: Corporate Performance and Risk Exposure*, published by John Wiley. In that book, we also developed the Macroeconomic Uncertainty Strategy (MUST) analysis. In *Corporate Performance and the Exposure to Macroeconomic Fluctuations*, published by Norstedts Academic Publishers in 2005, we expanded the research reported in these two books by adding issues on performance measurement as an important ingredient of Value-Based Management (VBM), on corporate reporting of the impact of macroeconomic fluctuations and on the use of real options—investment in flexibility of operations—as a potential substitute for financial risk management. The current book is a further expansion of these three books. We have, among other things expanded on the role of the MUST analysis in a Cash Flow at Risk (CFaR) approach and on *ex post* evaluation of a chosen strategy in order to obtain feedback on its success. We emphasize that evaluation of strategies provides input for reward systems for management on different levels.

Since the publication of the previous books we have become all the more convinced that the MUST analysis's comprehensive approach to dealing with macroeconomic uncertainty is important and value enhancing for shareholders, and in the longer time perspective for management and other stakeholders in firms as well. In the shorter time perspective, management may prefer less transparency than what follows if MUST analysis is applied, but in the longer term, managers will benefit from fairer evaluation and bonus systems, as well as from greater transparency about the sources of uncertainty in the environment. Conceptual clarity about sources of performance and about what is hedging and what is speculation is useful for management as well as for external stakeholders trying to evaluate a firm's intrinsic competitiveness.

The academic readers we address are researchers and students in the field of international business and finance. In the business world, executives with strategic responsibilities, chief financial officers, and bankers who analyze corporate performance and advise on risk management will benefit from this book.

Finally, we are grateful for support and valuable comments from our colleagues at the Lund Institute of Economic Research, Lund; the Research Institute of Industrial Economics (IFN), Stockholm; and the Department of Finance, Copenhagen Business School, Copenhagen. The financial support from the Savings Bank Foundation Skåne, Sweden, is gratefully acknowledged.

# Contents

# Corporate Decision-Making with Macroeconomic Uncertainty

# Chapter 1

# Macroeconomic Uncertainty in a Corporate Perspective

## 1.1 INTRODUCTION

The last few decades have confronted managers with major changes in the macroeconomic environment of the firm and the conditions for doing business. The removal of the Iron Curtain had an immediate and strong impact on many Western European countries. The macroeconomic environment has changed permanently as a result of events in Eastern Europe, the formation of the European Economic and Monetary Union (EMU) on Jan. 1, 1999 (with the introduction of the euro) and the (re)appearance of China and India as important players on the global market. Increased openness to international trade and a higher degree of capital mobility between countries have made individual national economies more vulnerable to real and monetary shocks occurring in global markets. At the corporate level this can only trigger increased concern about exchange rates, interest rates, inflation, demand conditions, and competition.

The macroeconomy is by definition beyond control of even the largest firm's management. It is nevertheless of major concern to management, because changes in corporate performance from year to year are strongly affected by macroeconomic events and developments. Management and external stakeholders need to understand to what extent results depend on macroeconomic developments in order to evaluate how a firm's intrinsic or inherent competitiveness has developed. The macroeconomy is also a source of uncertainty. The rapid development of global financial markets has created new instruments for managing risk, and a firm's operations can be adjusted and structured with the objective of reducing the impact of unexpected fluctuations, and of profiting from them as well. On the other hand, the lack of transparency of some of these new instruments created macroeconomic turbulence and contributed to the subprime crisis in 2008.

It takes only a moment to understand that it is no longer relevant today to make a distinction between domestic and international firms in discussing macroeconomic exposure. Though the channels may differ, *all* firms are inevitably exposed to the shocks and disturbances of a global marketplace. Even a firm with production, sales, purchases, and financing concentrated at home and working only in local currency can still be exposed to, for example, exchange rate changes. A local firm serving as a supplier to a major exporter must see its fortunes rise and fall with the exporter's performance. Another local firm may face competition from imported products. Still another firm, which serves only the local consumer market, is affected when the general level of demand depends upon the international competitiveness of major export-oriented firms. These cases illustrate the point that confining the analysis of exchange rate effects to assets and cash flows denominated in foreign currency alone is bound to be misleading. This is true whether the firm is concerned about its current and future performance or about the future volatility of its earnings and cash flows.

It is easy to imagine the potentially dramatic effects that a 10% increase in a home country's real exchange rate[1] will have on the profits of a company. The exchange rate change will act as a subsidy to competitors producing elsewhere and will have an impact on both domestic and foreign markets. The large fluctuations in the real value of the U.S. dollar—implying a "subsidy" to U.S. producers of about 10% in the mid-1970s, a "subsidy" to foreign producers versus U.S. producers of about 50% in the mid-1980s, were followed by another round of large fluctuations before the decline of the dollar started again in 2002—illustrate the significance of the exchange rate as an important part of macroeconomic influences on the firm. Hence, to understand the intrinsic competitiveness of a firm, the impact of changes in the macroeconomic environment have to be understood. Such an understanding will also help management to identify, and to assess, both worst-case and best-case scenarios.

When analyzing performance, many firms still follow procedures more suitable for a world made up of "closed" economies. Even recently developed methods of analysing corporate performance such as Shareholder Value Analysis (SVA), Economic Value Added (EVA), Market Value Added (MVA),[2] and benchmarking in different forms, do not allow management to "filter" out influences from exchange rates and other macroeconomic variables in order to properly assess the development of the company's long-term sustainable profits. For example, when assessing the value of the firm by the use of price/earnings (P/E) ratios, the long-term sustainable earnings should be used. Hence, investors and financial analysts should be interested in knowing the impact of macroeconomic fluctuations on the firm, as should owners and labor organizations when it comes to the issue of salaries and bonuses. The latter should reflect the value-added created by management and not unanticipated fluctuations in the macroeconomic environment of the firm.

There are many reasons why all stakeholder groups of a firm should make an effort to comprehend the links between the firm and its macroeconomic environment. Yet, as late as in the mid-2000s, most annual reports provide no guidance (or very little) on this issue.

The understanding of macroeconomic effects can also be used in risk management. The approach we suggest in this book enables a firm to distinguish among different kinds of exposure and to separate the effect of a change in the macroeconomic environment from the effect of a change in its relative competitive position caused by factors that are more close at hand. This separation is useful not only in risk management and the evaluation of sustainable profits, but also for strategic management. The only circumstances under which a firm need not worry about macroeconomic exposure is when can be compensated immediately and fully in prices for cost increases of various kinds without losing sales volume. Such a firm hardly exists, but the point illustrates that pricing strategy and market position are important determinants of exposure.

It is worthwhile to note that increased financial and economic integration is not only a source of risk but also of tremendous opportunities. The trade-off between risks and opportunities in this new setting calls for new corporate strategies for the management of macroeconomic uncertainty. Now, all decisions concerning investment, marketing and finance depend on international factors. Firms working only in the local market must develop strategies for coping with the uncertainty generated in foreign markets as well. Multinational firms must improve their strategies on how to deal with the complex elements of macroeconomic uncertainty. One such improvement would be to eliminate the misperception that fluctuations in exchange rates, interest rates, and other macro price variables are of concern only to the finance division. The effects of these fluctuations on sales and other operations should be of equal, if not greater, concern. Management can actually take advantage of fluctuations by making operations flexible in different ways. Investments in flexibility or so-called real options in the face of uncertainty increase wealth by reducing the need to incur irreversible costs.

The major theme of this book is that a meaningful strategy for managing risk and exploiting opportunities requires that management recognizes the *interdependence* among a number of macroeconomic variables, and that these variables influence the firm through a variety of channels not captured by conventional accounting systems. The corollary of this point is that focusing on exchange rates in isolation may give a misleading view of the competitiveness of a firm and of the risks and opportunities to which it is exposed. Strategies based on a more comprehensive approach for managing exchange rate and "related" macroeconomic exposures are called for.

Consider as an illustration the formation of the EMU. By definition, exchange rate risk was removed from intra-EMU transactions. Did firms thereby become less exposed to macroeconomic risk? Not necessarily, since macroeconomic shocks occur under any exchange rate regime. The shocks affect the economy and firms through different channels, however, if exchange rates are fixed as opposed to flexible.

## 1.2 THE MACROECONOMIC ENVIRONMENT OF THE FIRM

In this section we put macroeconomics in a corporate perspective. We argue that in spite of the complexity of relationships in the macroeconomic environment, the important effects on the firm's performance can indeed be captured by the analysis of a limited number of variables. We emphasize the important role of exchange rates, interest rates, and inflation and that changes in these variables are reflections of changes in GDP, aggregate demand, monetary policy and other macroeconomic variables.

Figure 1.1 illustrates the link between macroeconomic disturbances and cash flow effects on the firm. Starting on the far left, we distinguish between domestic and foreign, as well as between policy- and non-policy-generated macroeconomic disturbances. In addition, there are firm- and industry-specific disturbances. To the far right in Figure 1.1, we find the cash flow effects on the firm that influence performance and risk. In between there might be policy reactions to disturbances in the form of monetary, fiscal, as well as industrial and trade policies, as in the third column of Figure 1.1. "Rules" for policy responses in the form of exchange rate regimes, money supply growth targets, etc., determine how a particular disturbance influences exchange rates, inflation rates, interest rates, and

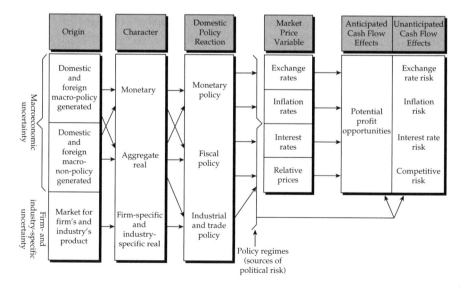

**Figure 1.1** Macroeconomic shocks and the cash flow of the firm.

relative prices in the fourth column. Uncertainty about such rules or regimes is one aspect of political risk. The corporate structure and strategy determine how macroeconomic disturbances affect cash flows on the far right in the figure.

An important part of identifying macroeconomic exposure is to distinguish it from exposure to firm-specific and industry-specific shocks. Macroeconomic disturbances, as well as firm- and industry-specific disturbances, affect the level of demand and the price of a firm's product. However, management implications of falling demand caused by, say, a restrictive monetary policy is different from the implications of falling demand relative to competitors in the stable macroeconomic environment.

The distinctions between policy- and non-policy-generated shocks and between real and monetary shocks are important in a corporate planning perspective. Both distinctions help management in forecasting, because the duration and impact of shocks usually depend upon their source. For example, the effects of monetary shocks tend to be more short-lived than the effects of real shocks.

Most periods of major shifts in business conditions in a country are associated with simultaneous changes in the exchange rate, the interest rate, and inflation within or outside the country. Behind changes in these variables we typically find macroeconomic shocks or disturbances as illustrated below.

One good historical example of a major macro disturbance with a worldwide impact was the expansionary policy of the United States during the late 1960s in connection with the Vietnam War. The government employed deficit financing. In contrast with later policy of the early 1980s, the Federal Reserve at the time allowed the deficits to be monetized, with inflation as a predictable result. These policies contributed to the breakdown of the Bretton Woods system of fixed exchange rates in the early 1970s. The United States, the United Kingdom, and a few other countries had conducted more expansionary monetary policies than countries such as Germany and Japan. With price levels diverging at fixed exchange rates, trade imbalances and pressures for exchange rate realignment grew inevitably until, in 1971, the United States devalued and cut the fixed price relationship between gold and the dollar. This realignment was insufficient, however, and in 1973 exchange rates were allowed to float to seek market equilibrium values.

The Bush administration followed a similar expansionary fiscal policy after the 9/11 attack on New York City. The Federal Reserve accommodated this expansionary policy to some extent and kept the interest rate level quite low. The subprime financial crisis in 2007 and 2008 has been partially blamed on this expansionary policy.

The breakdown of the pegged exchange rates within the European Monetary System (EMS) in 1992 offers a similar historical picture. Upward pressure on interest rates across Europe was created by the large fiscal deficits in Germany as it strove to rebuild East Germany. The asymmetric impact of the shock, in combination with the unwillingness of most other countries to follow Germany's strict monetary policy, contributed to the turbulence in Europe's foreign exchange markets, that is, to diverging interest and inflation rates ending with major realignments of exchange rates.

An illustrative example of a policy-generated shock of monetary character is the sky-rocketing of U.S. interest rates in the early 1980s. The initial increase was triggered by the shift in monetary policy in the United States in 1979, when the Federal Reserve Board set money supply targets. The restrictiveness of these targets led to higher U.S. interest rates. A wave of interest rate increases followed worldwide, together with a realignment of exchange rates. Abandoning interest rate targeting also led to higher interest rate volatility.

This switch in monetary policy was followed by a large alteration in fiscal policy in the United States. The fiscal deficit increased during the early years of Ronald Reagan's presidency while money supply growth targets remained restrictive. The U.S. dollar appreciated more or less continuously until early 1985 when it depreciated suddenly and dramatically. All firms competing with U.S. firms in the United States or elsewhere in the first half of the 1980s felt the impact. Other firms outside the United States were also hit by the worldwide interest rate increase in a direct way, as well as indirectly when many developing countries faced debt repayment problems.

Another prolonged appreciation of the dollar began in January 1999 after the EMU was launched. After an initial dollar price of Euro at 1.10, the Euro depreciated to a bottom of 0.85 dollars per Euro in the beginning of 2002. The dollar then depreciated to a level around 1.55 per Euro in June 2008.

Examples of policy-generated shocks of real character can be found by recalling the oil price increases in 1973, 1979, 1990, 2004 and in 2008. For industrialized countries these shocks can be compared with substantial decreases in the productivity of the labor force and the capital stock. They were accompanied by large fiscal and monetary policy adjustments in some countries, and gigantic flows in international financial markets as the oil producers' revenues had to be recycled. The combination of the productivity decreases and policy responses had drastic effects on the level of aggregate demand and employment, expressing themselves in inflation rates, interest rates, and exchange rates as well as in the relative prices among different commodities and services.

Illustrative examples of non-policy-generated shocks are harder to find because tracing the origin of a shock nearly always reveals the involvement of political activity. From the point of view of the industrialized countries the crumbling of the Soviet Empire in 1989 and 1990 can be seen as an external shock. It resulted in a substantial decline in demand for exports of several countries. The impact of the shock was asymmetric, meaning that some countries, like Finland and Germany, were affected more than others. Thereby, the fixed exchange rate system came under serious strain, resulting in realignments and increased exchange rate flexibility in the autumn of 1992.

The relationships among exchange rates, inflation rates, and interest rates are often discussed by academics in terms of market equilibrium relations among the variables and deviations from these relations. One relationship—Purchasing Power Parity (PPP)—refers to the equality of prices on a bundle of goods and services across countries when measured in one currency. Hence, the market price variables involved are changes in domestic and foreign price levels and in the exchange rate. When PPP holds, there are no unexploited macro-generated profit opportunities in international trade. The exchange rate is simply a rate for translation from one unit of account to another. The concept of exchange rate exposure changes meaning under these circumstances. It is also common to refer to the "Law of One Price" (LOP) for traded goods, implying the equality of prices on a specific product in two countries. A third relationship—International Fisher Parity (IFP)—refers to the equality of expected returns on similar securities denominated in different currencies. The market price variables involved in this relationship are the domestic and foreign interest rates, and the current and the expected exchange rate.

Deviations from PPP imply that there are profit opportunities in the fifth column in Figure 1.1 to be exploited in international trade if transactions costs are not prohibitive. Deviations from IFP imply profit opportunities in international financial markets, at least for the less risk-averse actors in the market. The last column in the figure shows macroeconomic risk concepts as they relate to uncertainty about exchange rates, inflation rates, and interest rates. Competitive risks caused by the possibility of unanticipated relative price changes that could result from firm- and industry-specific disturbances and industrial and trade policies are also shown here. A major problem for the firm is to identify and distinguish between the risks in the last column. Large parts of this book are devoted to this problem.

In a hypothetical world without information and transactions costs or other obstacles to immediate price adjustments, there are no deviations from the equilibrium relationships—PPP, the LOP for industrial goods, or IFP. In such a world there is no reason to believe that "extra" profits could be made by, say, investing in a particular currency or by making an investment in country A rather than country B. Then, too, for financial instruments with equal risk, 1 USD can be expected to generate the same return regardless of the currency in which it is invested. In the real world, however, there is a great deal of interference that contributes to deviations from these equilibrium relationships. At times the deviations may be considerably large and long-lasting. There is therefore every reason for a firm to formulate an explicit policy with respect to the risks and/or the opportunities they create (see Box 1.1). There is also every reason for the management to assess the impact of unanticipated deviations from these relationships on the historical cash flow or profit developments in order to comprehend and control the firm's competitive position.

In Figure 1.1 we abstract from stock market index as a macroeconomic price. Although it is a very important variable for explaining individual

## Box 1.1  The case of Volkswagen

One firm that has been severely affected by a turbulent macroeconomic environment is the German car manufacturer VW. The first shock came in the early 1970s, when the DEM was revalued against the USD.[a] At that time, VW, with its production based in Germany, relied heavily on one model, the Beetle, and U.S. market sales. When VW tried to compensate for the DEM appreciation by raising the Beetle's USD price, sales fell drastically. VW reported that net earnings dropped from DEM 330 million in 1969 to a loss in 1973 of DEM 807 million. The only measure taken to reduce exposure was covering receivables in the forward market.

On the basis of this experience, VW developed a new exposure management strategy. First, VW entered the Eurobond market and took a substantial USD loan in order to match USD commercial revenues with USD debt service expenses. Second, VW established a production site in the United States in order to match USD revenues with US production costs.[b] Third, the VW group introduced a new car, the Audi, which was to compete in less price-sensitive market segments.[c]

The exposure management strategy of VW was put to a test when the European Monetary System was broken up and the DEM again started to appreciate in 1992. In 1991, the VW group had reported an annual net income of DEM 1120 million. By 1993 profits had been eliminated and VW reported a loss of DEM 2000 million. Even though this loss could be partly blamed on problems with the newly acquired SEAT, a major part of the loss was caused by the DEM appreciation and a fall in demand for cars in Europe. Thus, the commercial operations of VW remained exposed to exchange rate changes. Its production costs rose relative to other countries when the DEM appreciated. In 1993 VW's break even-point was above 90% of capacity, while VW's stronger European competitors had break-even below 70%, and the high price sensitivity of the products made VW extremely exposed to falling sales volumes.[d]

There are two possible sources of failure in managing exposure to macroeconomic disturbances. First, a firm can fail to measure

[a]  The DEM was revalued in 1969, 1971 and 1972. By 1972 the DEM's revaluation amounted to 40% over the 1969 figure.

[b]  The strategy of diversifying production sites internationally has been pursued even further. VW now has production sites in, e.g., Mexico, Brazil, Spain (SEAT) and the Czech Republic (Skoda).

[c]  For the VW example from the seventies, see Srinivasulu (1981).

[d]  Wall Street Journal, 1 April, 1993.

---

**Box 1.1 continued**

exposure correctly. Second, exposure management can fail because the firm has adopted an inappropriate strategy to reduce exposure. VW's first crisis was caused by a combination of the two sources. It used a narrow exposure measure and an exposure management strategy that relied on external hedging.[e] The second VW crisis was precipitated by the company's failure to assess its exposure vis-à-vis production costs.

[e] The story of the limitations of external hedging has been told several times (Aggarwal and Soenen, 1989; Cornell and Shapiro, 1988; Lessard, 1986; Oxelheim and Wihlborg, 1987; Oxelheim et al., 1990; and Srinivasulu, 1981).

---

firms' equity prices, it is less directly linked to cash flows. On the macro level, uncertainty about equity prices at given interest rates can be thought of as uncertainty about the market risk premium. It captures changes in market risk at fixed levels of variables. There is no strong empirically substantiated link between the different macro shocks and the equity market risk premium. It is an empirical question whether an equity price index should be included.

It has been argued that exchange rates, interest rates, and inflation rates are the primary variables linking macroeconomic fluctuations and firm performance. It then remains for the individual firm to determine which variables are the most influential within each group. When it comes to exchange rates there are often many currencies to choose among for the individual company. For example, KLM, the Dutch airline company, uses 180 currencies in addition to the guilder in its operations. SAS, the Scandinavian airline company, is operating with a basket of 76 currencies. In general, many exchange rates move together. It is therefore sufficient to identify and focus on a few key rates. The same argument can be made with respect to interest rates and inflation rates.

## 1.3  WHAT LEVEL OF CONCERN?

We have distinguished between three sets of factors that determine a firm's exposure. First, the macroeconomic structure—as defined by, for example, capital mobility and the speed of price adjustments—determines the exchange rate, interest rate, and price effects of a disturbance. Second, the policy regime set by authorities influences the degree to which interest rates, exchange rates, and inflation, respectively, adjust to the disturbance and with what time-lag the adjustment occurs. Third, the sensitivity of a firm's value, cash flows, etc., to changes in macroeconomic conditions depends on firm-specific factors in its markets for inputs and outputs.

Some of these factors are under the control of management, others are not. In general, it can be expected that exposure declines with the time-horizon over which the effects of shocks are studied, because exchange rates, interest rates, and inflation tend to return to equilibrium as defined by Purchasing Power Parity and International Fisher Parity over time. Furthermore, management can create options for responding to shocks: they have, for example, the ability to shift production among countries in response to changes in relative labour costs. We return to such "real" options in Chapter 2.

Many firms are unclear about where the responsibility for analysis of macroeconomic exposure should lie. It is common that the finance function has a major responsibility for exposure management. This implies that many important aspects of the link between the macro economy and firm performance are lost. We argue that attention must be paid at all levels in the firm—strategic, tactical, and operational. Macroeconomic fluctuations potentially affect every stratum of the firm. Approaches of management to these effects must be determined at a high level and related to the overall objective of the firm. On the tactical level, the relative importance of macroeconomic, industry-specific, and firm-specific sources of risk should be determined and resources devoted to their management. Finally, policies are executed at the operational level.

The cube in Figure 1.2 is a visualization of the process that managers can use to systematize their approach to dealing with uncertainty. It consists of 27 combinations of levels of decision-making, character of shocks and disturbances, and of type of impact on the firm. In the top decision-making squares, each strategy implies a rule for managing risks, such as "do nothing" or "minimize cash flow variance." Any strategy can then be translated into tactical and operational decisions on the commercial or the real side, as well as on the financial side of the firm. In addition, the macroeconomic disturbances may influence the organizational side. In terms of Figure 1.2 we focus on the 9 (out of the 27) combinations lying to the left in the cube, although an important problem is to be able to draw the line between this macroeconomic part of the cube and the other parts.

## 1.4 MACROECONOMIC UNCERTAINTY STRATEGY (MUST)

Most of the chapters in this book deal with different elements of a "Macroeconomic Uncertainty Strategy" (MUST). Figure 1.3 distinguishes between a forward-looking and a backward-looking aspect of MUST. The forward-looking aspect of the strategy includes measurement and management of exposure to macroeconomic risk. The backward-looking part refers to analysis of sources of a firm's performance. In particular, the impact of macroeconomic developments can be "filtered out" in order to identify firms' intrinsic sources of changes in performance. The two aspects of MUST have in common the need to identify macroeconomic sources of changes in cash flows.

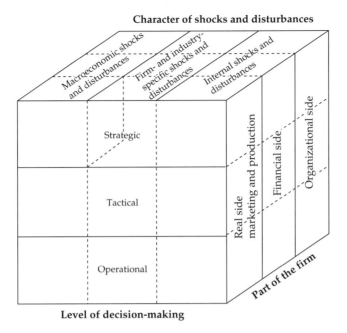

**Figure 1.2** Corporate decision-making under uncertainty.

## 1.5 THE CONTENTS OF THIS BOOK

The above four sections offer an overview of the problems of macroeconomic uncertainty. The structure of the remainder of this book is the following. In Chapter 2 we discuss the concepts of risk and exposure, and give reasons why management and shareholders should be sufficiently

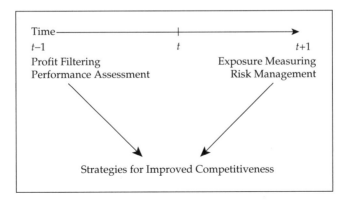

**Figure 1.3** Components of a MUST analysis.

concerned about exposure to devote resources to its measurement and management. This should be done to reduce risk, to increase profits and to analyze performance.

Chapter 3 is devoted to the traditional methods of defining and measuring macroeconomic exposures. These approaches are incomplete in the sense that they focus on exposures to exchange rates, interest rates, and inflation separately without taking interdependence among these variables into account. Nevertheless, the traditional measures are important since some are still in use, especially by accounting-oriented firms.

The macroeconomic approach is introduced in Chapter 4. Exposure measures are defined and factors influencing these exposures are identified. We discuss how the approach to measuring exposure depends on whether the measures are to be used in forward-looking risk management or backward-looking performance measurement.

Our suggested method for measuring macroeconomic exposures is illustrated in Chapter 5 for using Volvo Cars' cash flow exposure as an example. Exposure coefficients are identified as coefficients in a regression with important macroeconomic variables as explanatory factors and cash flows or economic value as the variable to explain. Thereafter, we show how the exposure coefficients can be used in scenario analysis, for risk management, and for performance analysis.

With exposures identified, management may choose to hedge these exposures. Approaches to hedging with various financial instruments are described in Chapter 6.

In Chapter 7 we ask how the objective of risk management a certain period can be achieved. We assume that the objective has been set in terms of an acceptable loss in cash flows caused by macroeconomic fluctuations within a certain time horizon, that is, the objective has been defined in terms of Cash Flow at Risk (CFaR).

The issue of whether or not to hedge and, if so, whether to hedge fully or partially, depend on the exposure management strategy. This strategy must be determined at a level high enough in the firm to take its overall objectives into account. Factors influencing the choice of exposure management strategy are discussed in Chapter 8.

In Chapter 9 we take common approaches to Value-Based Management (VBM) as a starting point for a discussion of performance assessment as input in managerial compensation schemes. We show how macroeconomic influences on corporate performance can be filtered out. Thereby managerial compensation packages can be more strongly linked to management efforts to enhance the firm's intrinsic competitiveness.

In Chapter 10 we discuss aspects of evaluation and organization of risk management strategies and operations. An often neglected issue is to evaluate whether the implementation of a strategy chosen by the top management has been successful relative to the objectives of the strategy. The chapter also elaborates on information requirements for rewarding and penalizing managers. Finally, the organization of risk management responsibilities is discussed.

Chapter 11 addresses management's need to communicate internally and externally about the effect of macroeconomic fluctuations on corporate performance. We look at current practices in reporting and hedging. These practices do not generally enable external stakeholders to disentangle macroeconomic effects on performance.

Finally, in Chapter 12 we summarize and return to the implementation of a Macroeconomic Uncertainty Strategy (MUST).

## NOTES

1  An increase in the real exchange rate occurs when the currency appreciates while price levels remain unchanged. The real exchange rate is often used as a measure of a country's competitiveness and attractiveness as production site.
2  The principle of measuring added-value in business has been around for at least 25 years. Currently there are a number of approaches in use. Among the most popular, EVA and MVA, have been developed by the New York consultants Stern Stewart & CO, and SVA by Rappaport (1986). (See also Chapter 8.)

# Chapter 2

# Concepts of Macroeconomic Risk Management

## 2.1 INTRODUCTION

In the previous chapter we concluded that an understanding of the link between corporate performance and fluctuations in the macroeconomic environment of the firm is important for both inside and outside stakeholders. In this chapter we proceed to discuss the concepts of risk and exposure, and to ask what role a risk management program for macroeconomic risk can play.

The concept of risk refers in general to the magnitude and likelihood of unanticipated changes that have an impact on a firm's cash flows, value or profitability. Academics and practitioners often mean different things by risk. The use of the concept in daily language is typically casual, but in order to derive principles for management of exposure to risk, stricter definitions are necessary.

Uncertainty is a concept closely related to risk and often used synonymously. In the following we use both concepts but with the view that uncertainty is a somewhat broader concept. Risk has a negative connotation, but uncertainty can be a source of opportunities as well as costs. We use the word *risk* to describe a situation in which there is an objective or subjective distribution of outcomes with respect to a variable such as the exchange rate or the interest rate. Only the gambler will find risk positive. Others may be neutral to risk or willing to pay to reduce it. Uncertainty, on the other hand, is a prerequisite for risk to exist, but uncertainty can also refer to the possibility that something completely unforeseen can happen. Furthermore, a firm or an individual may consider, for example, exchange rate uncertainty as something to be taken advantage of as a result of superior flexibility to changes in exchange rates.

We start this chapter by reviewing, in Section 2.2, concepts of corporate risk. In Section 2.3 we then ask who would and should care about corporate risks. In other words, we look at exposure from the point of view of different stakeholders. In Section 2.4 we provide a classification of macroeconomic risks. Section 2.5 contains a discussion about the costs and benefits of a risk management program taking into account that uncertainty creates opportunities as well as risk. A firm can actively influence its possibilities to benefit and avoid the costs of macroeconomic fluctuations by creating "options". Such creation is discussed in Section 2.6 while Section 2.7 provides a summary of arguments for risk management.

## 2.2 CORPORATE RISK: A BRIEF REVIEW OF THE CONCEPT

The concept of risk is used differently by practitioners and academics. This confusion of language frequently leads to misunderstandings. For example, one may read in the newspaper that "there is a substantial risk that the yuan will be revalued by 10% over the next few months". To a practitioner, this statement simply signals the strong likelihood that the chinese yuan will be revalued. To an academic, however, it means there is indeed a strong chance of revaluation, but "risk" would refer to the uncertainty about its timing and magnitude. It seems that many practitioners evaluate risk in terms of potential losses relative to today's values of variables, while in academic language "risk" is evaluated relative to expected changes in variables such as the exchange rate. Risk is then a measure of the timing and magnitude of unanticipated changes. When an academic states that "risk may be irrelevant" in the choice of currency denomination of a loan, he or she is not implying that the expected change should be disregarded, but only that some borrowers are acting as if there is no uncertainty about the change. In other words, the likelihood and magnitude of changes larger or smaller than the anticipated ones are being disregarded.

It is clearly essential that we define the concept of risk as it is used in this book. We largely follow the definition used in finance and economics since it enables us to better discuss how to design operational strategies for dealing with uncertainty in the macroeconomic environment. It is important to keep in mind that changes in variables may be anticipated or unanticipated and that risk is a measure of unanticipated changes. The anticipated change is measured by the expected change, which is normally a result of forecasting. In general, the management of uncertainty involves both the forecasting of variables such as exchange rates or inflation rates, and an evaluation of the likelihood that the forecast may be wrong, i.e. that unanticipated changes will occur. In finance, risk from an individual's point of view is defined as the variance of the rate of return on his or her portfolio. The variance is in turn a measure of how widely the return may deviate from the expected one. The risk to the individual of holding any one asset depends on the contribution of this asset to the variance of the portfolio return (see also Box 2.1).

---

### Box 2.1  Systematic and unsystematic risk

It is common in the finance literature to distinguish between the systematic and the unsystematic risk of an asset. The systematic risk cannot be diversified away by constructing a portfolio of assets, while the unsystematic (or idiosyncratic) risk can. By combining a large number of assets in the portfolio, the unsystematic risk of a particular asset becomes irrelevant. Thus, the individual or the firm holding an asset denominated in U.S. dollars is not exposed to the unanticipated changes in the value of the USD to the extent that these changes are unsystematic and generally compensated for by changes in the value of other currencies. Only those changes in the value of the USD that affect the value of the total portfolio are considered systematic risk. The individual or the firm is exposed to such changes in the value of the USD.

With these definitions, the systematic risk of holding USD, or the exposure of holding USD, depends on the contribution of unanticipated changes in the value of USD to the variance of the total portfolio. Thus, the covariation of the value of the USD and the portfolio return determines the exposure to unanticipated fluctuations of USD.

---

One often hears a distinction being made between "downside" and "upside" risk. In such terminology, "downside" risk refers to the possibility of unanticipated outcomes below the expected outcome. "Upside" refers to unanticipated outcome above what is expected. This distinction is especially meaningful when options are considered.

As previously mentioned, the presence of uncertainty is not necessarily negative. It can also present opportunities for both individuals and firms; especially those better able to forecast than others and those who remain flexible as circumstances change. A forecaster could naturally wish for the impossible, that is, that a forecast is certain, but if it is so certain that everyone knows about it, then it is unlikely that he or she could profit from it. Thus, in an uncertain environment, the firm looking for profit opportunities must also face the possibility that the outcome differs from the forecast. In essence, risk management deals with this possibility.

There are several classifications of risk. Most of this book is based on the idea that risk can be distinguished by its source—that is, either in the environment of the firm or in market price variables (exchange rates, etc.).

One way to classify risk is on the basis of how a firm's performance is measured. Accounting risk, for example, obviously refers to uncertainty about the book value of a firm, while economic risk refers to the economic value of the firm or some other measure of the firm's economic performance. In efficient financial markets the economic value equals the stock-market value of the firm. Accounting, as well as economic, risk and exposure can be broken down further depending on which assets or liabilities are affected. For example, it is common to discuss the exposure of the firm's commercial operations as opposed to its financial exposure. Assets devoted to producing the firm's output of goods and services are subject to commercial risk, while financial assets and, in particular, the firm's liabilities, are subject to financial risk.

Another way to classify risk is the method used by the Bank for International Settlements (BIS). It distinguishes between market risk, credit risk, operation risk, legal risk, counterparty risk, and liquidity risk. This classification is primarily oriented towards banks but it often applies as well to non-financial firms. Market risk is caused by uncertainty about the market value of tradable securities. Credit risk refers to the possibility that a borrower may fail to repay a loan. Operation risk is caused by possible deficiencies in the operational procedures for control inside the bank, while legal risk is caused by uncertainty about the interpretation of contractual terms. Intuitively, counterparty risk refers to the possibility that a counterparty to a transaction may fail to perform as agreed upon. Liquidity risk is caused by uncertainty about the ability to sell assets at market values.

Credit risk for a financial firm is the risk on non-tradable loans. Non-financial firms have few such assets, however. For non-financial firms the corresponding risk would be the risk related to firms' physical assets and their ability to produce value. This risk is often referred to as commercial or business risk. To further confuse matters, for non-financial firms commercial risk is often called operation risk. Liquidity risk for a non-financial firm is a term often used by practitioners to refer to the risk that the firm may face a lack of liquidity because, for example, its credit lines could be cut.

These different concepts of risk are clearly not independent. For a non-financial firm the primary risk would be its commercial risk—that is, its uncertainty about the value of cash flows that can be generated by its physical assets producing outputs. Its operation and legal risk, as defined by BIS, as well as its liquidity risk are secondary in the sense that they merely enhance or modify the primary risk. The importance of a specific kind of risk can shift depending upon the situation. For example, risk caused by lax internal controls is particularly important when the firm approaches distress as a result of weak primary business operations. Liquidity risk, in the sense that there is uncertainty about the time it takes to sell assets at market values, is critical when assets must be sold quickly but less relevant if the firm is obviously solid. However, if business operations are failing or some banks feel that such a possibility exists, then the firm could find itself unable to produce liquid funds.

In this book we focus on the primary risk, that is, on the commercial risk of a non-financial firm's business operations. The risk caused by a particular composition of the firm's liabilities is also of interest. The liabilities are important in risk management because their composition can be adjusted in order to balance the commercial risk. The other risks mentioned above are, to a large extent, affected by the firm's ability to manage commercial and financial risk.

## 2.3 CORPORATE RISK: WHO CARES?

Although it is obvious that shareholders prefer a diversified portfolio of securities in order to reduce risk of different kinds, this does not imply that individual companies should diversify their holdings of contracts as to different currency and country risks. The reason is that in efficient capital markets, corporate diversification is redundant, since individual investors can diversify risk themselves. The key to this argument is that in efficient markets, by definition, investors do not face higher transaction and information costs (e.g., currency exposure) than corporations.

Since investors can gain access to financial markets in many countries through, for example, investments in mutual funds, it is probably realistic to assume that the costs of diversification for individual investors are not generally higher than for firms. A manager's information about economic risk of different kinds is not necessarily superior to a shareholder's information. Managers' information about accounting measures of risk is superior, but we argue below that such measures say very little about economic risk. Thus, if shareholders were the only stakeholders in firms, then firms would have little reason to be concerned about risk in their decisions, unless we talk about risk of fines, theft, natural disasters, and the like. Instead they could focus on maximizing the expected return on investments. Each firm's contribution to shareholders' portfolio risk would nevertheless enter their investment decisions through the discount rate that is applied to projects of different kinds. The discount rate (the required rate of return on investments) would depend on the risk premium that shareholders demand on projects of different kinds.

The above argument for firms not concerning themselves with risk diversification in business decisions has been used to argue further that firms should be risk-neutral when choosing among, for example, assets and liabilities in different currency denominations. By a risk-neutral attitude, then, we mean that a firm always chooses the asset (liability) with the highest (lowest) expected return (interest cost), and that it does not consider the variance of the return (cost) in its decisions. Such a risk-neutral firm, observing speculative or arbitrage opportunities, would have an incentive to take advantage of them without the shareholders knowing much about them. Taking advantage means that the firm's risk exposure would no longer be constant or even known in the near term from a stockholder's point of view. Shareholders would not be able to obtain their desired diversification of different kinds of risk in financial markets.

In what follows we define as risk-neutral a firm that maximizes its profits, cash flows, value, or any other target variable in decisions within its normal area of business. If shareholders are the only stakeholders influencing management objectives, then the risk-neutral firm maximizes the market value of equity. The risk-averse firm, on the other hand, considers also the variance of its target variable.

Under what conditions do firms sometimes choose to be risk-averse? To answer this question we must consider who the other stakeholders in firms are. *Holders of the firm's debt* in the form of bonds and bank loans are one group of stakeholders. It is now widely recognized that if the costs of defaulting in the form of explicit bankruptcy costs (lawyers' fees and constraints on the use of assets) are substantial, then the rate of return variance becomes a management concern. This is true even if shareholders' interests are ultimately on the managers' minds. The reason is that this variance would be related to the probability of default and, therefore, to the probability that debt-holders and stockholders will suffer the direct costs associated with, for example, bankruptcy proceedings. This higher probability will reflect itself in higher fund-raising costs for the firm.[1] In Box 2.2 we introduce the concept of probability of ruin.

Another important group of stakeholders is the *employees*. Many people place a high value on earnings stability and especially job security. Accordingly, direct costs may be associated with unanticipated fluctuations in a firm's output level. A stable and predictable output level simplifies personnel planning as well. Fluctuations in a firm's optimal output level because of changes in sales price, demand or direct costs could, accordingly, induce it to take action that reduces the impact on output of these fluctuations. In cases where adjustment costs, that is, the costs of hiring and firing employees, are extremely high, firms may aim to keep output constant at the cost of lost customers or excessive inventories. In some cases a firm may avoid markets with large demand fluctuations, leaving those markets to competitors who have lower adjustment costs. In general, the higher the costs of adjusting output, the more we would expect the firm to avoid markets where there is substantial uncertainty about market conditions. Risk-averse behavior could take the form of a preference for long-term contracts that fix price and/or quantity or a lowered production level that shaves inventory costs (see, for example, Shapiro and Titman, 1984). The exact form of risk-averse behavior may differ among firms. It suffices here to establish that labor-related costs may induce a firm to avoid fluctuations in output and employment. Note that a risk-neutral firm with respect to a firm's value or cash flows could be risk-averse with respect to output fluctuations, because reducing such fluctuations could increase its expected value and cash flow by reducing labor turnover and costs. We return to this issue in the discussion of real options.

Relations to *suppliers* could induce risk-averse behavior in the same way with respect to the firm's commercial operations when these stakeholders consider a stable output level desirable. If so, they are willing to sell at a lower price to the firm offering a stable demand. However, reducing uncertainty about the future value of many financial assets and liabilities would not necessarily be in the suppliers' interest.

## Box 2.2  Probability of ruin

The factors that determine the "probability of ruin" can be understood by inspection of Figure 2.1, which shows two probability distributions for the firm's value, Pr(V). When the value reaches zero, "ruin," bankruptcy occurs. E[V] is the expected value of the firm. The probability of ruin depends on the variance of the probability distribution for V, reflecting how spread out the distribution is. In the figure the variance of the distribution $Pr(V)_2$ is greater than the variance of the distribution $Pr(V)_1$. The probability of ruin for each distribution is the area under each distribution to the left of zero, relative to the areas under the full distributions.

Taking the analysis one step further we may ask how the probability of ruin is affected by a risk factor, F, that affects the value, V. F may stand for an indicator of the central banks' monetary stance. First, the higher the variance $\sigma_F^2$ of the factor F, the higher the probability of ruin. Second, the more sensitive the value is to changes in the factor (dV/dF), in this case to changes in monetary policy, the higher is the probability of ruin (see Box 2.3).

In what follows we will emphasize the sensitivity coefficient dV/dF as a measure of exposure to the factor F. The factor's contribution to the probability of ruin depends on the exposure and the variance of the factor. The risk concept "value at risk" (VaR) captures both these contributions to the probability of ruin (compare Section 3.7 and Chapter 7).

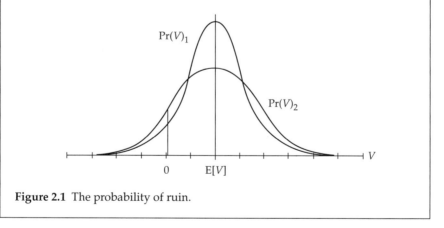

**Figure 2.1** The probability of ruin.

*Customers* often value predictability in the firm's pricing policy. Keeping the firm's market price stable over time in spite of fluctuations in demand conditions would increase or decrease the stability of output and profits. In either case, keeping the price constant in response to shocks implies deviations from short-term profit maximization. Such a pricing policy is not necessarily inconsistent with value maximization, however.

*Government authorities* may also be considered stakeholders. Authorities depend on corporate taxes and have a stake in their stability. Furthermore, the propensity of a government to deliver beneficial transfers and services to firms could be seen as a function of employees' satisfaction with the company as expressed politically through powerful labor organizations.

The final, but certainly not the least important, group of stakeholders is the firm's management. As is well known in the so-called principal-agent literature, managers' objectives are not always in line with shareholders' objectives. Managers that have invested time and resources in firm-specific knowledge can be expected to value job security and, therefore, aim to reduce the probability of default.

The compensation scheme for *management* influences its behavior as well. If shareholders are unable to distinguish between profit changes caused by temporary factors and those caused by management's long-term assessment of the firm's prospects, then the market value of the firm's shares may respond excessively to short-term factors. To the extent that risk-averse managers' compensation depends upon the market value of the firm or short-term earnings, they are induced to reduce the impact of uncertainty about short-term factors.

Managements' concern with job security could under certain conditions lead to risk-aversion in terms of the book value of the firm as opposed to its economic value. Specifically, if corporate law specifies conditions for bankruptcy in terms of book value rather than economic value, and the firm is unable to raise funds based on its economic value, then a manager of a firm approaching distress has an incentive to reduce the variance of the book value of the firm. In efficient markets with well-informed market participants, a negative book value would not be a hindrance to the issuance of new shares enabling management to prevent bankruptcy as long as the firm's economic value was positive. If, however, a firm is unable to improve its liquidity situation by borrowing (even if its economic value does not justify outright bankruptcy), then it may be in a situation of "liquidity risk." This would arise if the equity issue became excessively costly as a result of temporary low liquidity or lack of information in the markets. Such a scenario may lead to rational concern about book values.

Liquidity risk is also an argument for concern with uncertainty about cash flows. Froot, Scharfstein, and Stein (1994) argue that unexpected declines in cash flows reduce liquidity and threaten the firm's ability to take advantage of opportunities to, for example, invest in new capacity or an acquisition. In other words, the firm's financial flexibility can be reduced suddenly as a result of unexpected losses.

It is noteworthy that if the primary cause of risk-aversion is the probability of bankruptcy, then management's risk-aversion would depend on the value of the firm relative to the bankruptcy value. The degree of risk-aversion would tend to increase as the value approaches the bankruptcy value[2] (see Box 2.3). If the main concern is financial flexibility, then the firm's liquidity situation would affect the degree of risk aversion.

## Box 2.3 Exposure and risk-taking in option terminology

Figure 2.2 describes how the firm's value, $V$, changes with a macro-economic factor, $F$. The line $V(F)$ shows the dependence of value on $F$ alone. At $F^*$ bankruptcy occurs. Assume first that once bankruptcy occurs, the manager is indifferent among lower values of $V$. Thus, the manager's valuation (pay-off) at different outcomes for $F$ follows the path $0 \rightarrow F^* \rightarrow V(F)$. This implies that the manager can be said to hold call options on $F$ with an exercise price of $F^*$. The number of option contracts is described by the slope $\Delta V / \Delta F$ which describes the sensivity of the value $V$ to the factor $F$.

If the manager's incentive could be described by the call option alone, then the manager would be willing to take on more risk the closer $F$ is to $F^*$. The expected value of the pay-off on the options would be described by $E[V]$. Essentially, the manager expects to lose little by risking that $F$ falls to $F_3$ rather than $F^*$.

Consider instead in part (b) of Figure 2.2 that if $F$ falls below $F^*$ the manager faces a loss – $(B+C)$, where $B$ represents bankruptcy costs, and $C$ represents loss of reputation. Thus, the "pay-off" on the call options at $F^*$ and below is $-(B+C)$ rather than zero as above.

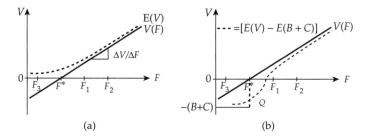

**Figure 2.2** Firm value and bankruptcy costs.

With the possibility of costs to the manager if $F$ falls below $F^*$, the expected pay-off to management as $F$ varies can be described by $E(V) - E(B+C)$ in Figure 2.2 (b). The slope of this function to the right of the point $Q$ indicates that management's risk aversion increases as $F$ falls from the right toward $Q$. The reason is that the probability of a large loss increases as $F$ falls. However, as $F$ becomes smaller than $Q$, the risk aversion declines because the probability of a big loss is already so high that a further fall in $F$ makes little difference. A number of put options on $F$ with exercise price $F^*$ would enable management to recoup the losses along $V(F)$ to the left of $F^*$. The number of contracts would depend on $\Delta V / \Delta F$. If the situation $(F_3, V_3)$ occurs, management

---

**Box 2.3 continued**

exercises the options and sells at $F^*$. Plowing back the pay-off, the firm avoids bankruptcy and management avoids the costs $(B+C)$.

If put options cannot be purchased or created, then management has an incentive to reduce the uncertainty about the impact of $F$ when $F > Q$, for example by contracting for a fixed $F$. The incentive to enter such a contract (a forward contract) is stronger at $F_1$ than at $F_2$. In this sense the risk aversion of management is stronger the closer $F$ is to $Q$. However, to the left of $Q$ in part (b) of Figure 2.2 as in part (a), there is no incentive to reduce risk this way.

---

Risk-averse behavior with respect to the variance of the firm's own cash flows or value is justified either by financial flexibility or by bankruptcy costs. Managers' concern with their own job security and compensations may also explain risk aversion. In either case, management will consider concerns other than shareholders' portfolio risk, as defined above, when developing risk management strategies. In particular, the "probability of ruin" or the probability of bankruptcy will influence the strategies. The risk concept "value at risk" (VaR) can be thought of as a measure of probability of ruin. Value at Risk is defined in Section 3.7, which discusses interest rate risk. In Chapter 7 we discuss a variation of VaR designed for the non-financial firm, namely Cash Flow at Risk (CFaR).

## 2.4 MACROECONOMIC RISK

In Figure 1.1 we distinguished between macroeconomic risk on the one hand, and firm-specific and industry-specific risk on the other. Macroeconomic risk depends on uncertainty in the environment of all firms in a country, though the impact on individual firms or their exposure is firm-specific. In addition, firms face the risks of crime, fire, weather changes, nuclear war, earthquakes, etc. We do not discuss risks of nature, terrorism, and war. They are sometimes handled by explicit insurance policies. Other risks are caused by uncertainty about the behavior of suppliers, customers, and lenders. Such risks are managed in more or less explicit contracts. The discussion here is limited to risks related to general and varying economic conditions in countries and globally. These risks are related to uncertainty about variables that are studied in macroeconomics and are often seen as business-cycle related. Several examples of unexpected events were discuss-ed in Chapter 1 to illustrate firms' exposure to macroeconomic conditions.

The following classifications are used to describe risks in the macroeconomic environment. The classifications capture the basic point that all

firms—multinational, exporting, import-competing or purely domestic—
are exposed to macroeconomic risk.

- *Interest rate risk* refers to the magnitude and likelihood of unanticipated
  changes in interest rates that influence both the costs of different sources
  of capital in a particular currency denomination and the demand for the
  product (see column 6 in Figure 1.1). These effects should be considered
  when measuring exposure to interest rate changes.
- *Currency risk* refers to the magnitude and likelihood of unanticipated
  changes in exchange rates and inflation rates, i.e. in the value of
  foreign and domestic money. We distinguish further between (real)
  *exchange rate risk* and *inflation risk* (see column 6 in Figure 1.1).
- *Country risk* refers to the likelihood and magnitude of unanticipated
  changes in a country's productive development. This concept is
  somewhat ambiguous and very broad. Country risk may refer to
  uncertainty about aggregate demand influencing sales,
  productivity, and/or the cost factors influencing production. The
  concept includes political risk capturing uncertainty about "the
  rules of the game," such as laws, regulations and political regimes
  selected by monetary and fiscal authorities. We emphasize this last
  aspect. In Figure 1.1 political risk refers both to uncertainty about
  disturbances in the two left columns, and to policy regimes in
  column 3 influencing how changes in exchange rates and other
  price variables affect cash flows.

These categories of macroeconomic risk could be distinguished from a
firm's *competitive risk*, which refers to the likelihood and magnitude of
unanticipated changes in firm-specific conditions as well as in industry-
specific prices and demand conditions (see column 6 in Figure 1.1).

In the above categorization, risks are not generally independent.
Interdependence arises because exchange rates, inflation rates, and interest rates adjust simultaneously to shocks of different kinds. Of the four
risk categories, currency risk and, specifically, exchange rate risk have
received the most attention. As noted, most current approaches to managing this risk presume implicitly or explicitly that exchange rate variability
is independent of the variability of other macroeconomic factors. In general, handling any risk category separately would seem to imply that the
changes emanating from unanticipated fluctuations in that source are
believed to be independent of other risk sources. Consider an illustrative
case in which a currency fluctuates only as a result of fluctuation in the
interest rate. In such a case, measuring exposure to exchange rate changes
and interest rate changes separately would lead to the same exposure being
measured twice. Here, the two variables are not two different risk factors.

In Chapter 4 we discuss at length how the firm's exposure to interest
rate and currency risks should be measured, recognizing the interdependence among interest rates, exchange rates, and inflation, and taking into
account that these variables are not the ultimate sources of risk.

A comprehensive risk management strategy requires more than a correct identification of risk, however. An understanding of the channels through which different sources of exposure affect the firm's cash flows and value is essential both for scenario analysis of exposure and for managing exposure by internal means, that is, by changing, for example, the currency of invoice, pricing and credit terms. Such internal means of influencing exposure are substitutes for forward contracts, options, and other financial contracts. Table 2.1 lists various channels through which firms are affected by changes in exchange rates, interest rates, and inflation.

Another important input in risk management is the pricing of risk in financial markets. Pricing of risk determines the firm's cost of reducing exposure in financial markets. Reducing exposure in financial markets—hedging—implies that other market participants are induced to bear the risk. They may not be willing to bear this risk without being paid a certain rate of return on a risky position. Thus, it is important to determine

**Table 2.1  Type of company and channels of risk.**

| Channels of risk | Type of company | | | |
| --- | --- | --- | --- | --- |
| | Multi-national with export and import | Domestic with export and/or import | Domestic with financial operations in foreign countries | Strictly domestic in all its operations |
| Value of monetary and negotiable securities in foreign subsidiaries | X | | | |
| Value of real assets in foreign subsidiaries | X | | | |
| Current and future remittances from foreign subsidiaries | X | | | |
| Export and import; volumes and prices | X | X | | |
| Value of claims and debts in foreign currencies | X | X | X | |
| Value of inventory | X | X | X | X |
| Domestic sales and purchases; volumes and prices | X | X | X | X |
| Value of loans and deposits in domestic currency | X | X | X | X |

whether a risk premiums is incorporated in the market price of a specific various financial contract. In later chapters we discuss the pricing of exchange rate risk in international financial markets. International Fisher Parity (IFP) is a relation between interest rates on similar securities in different currency denominations, implying that exchange rate risk is not priced. IFP holds if the interest rate differential between two currencies reflects only expected exchange rate changes. If it does, exchange rate risk can then be shifted in financial markets at zero cost, with important implications for risk management. IFP is explained in Appendix 3.3 (p. 65).

The time horizon of exposure is an additional dimension that needs to be addressed in risk management. Many macroeconomic disturbances tend to be temporary. In particular, exchange rate changes, as well as interest rate changes, have real effects that tend to dissipate over time. Over long periods, exchange rate changes tend to offset differences in inflation rates and interest rate changes in a currency tend to correspond to changes in inflation rates. Under these conditions, exchange rate and interest rate changes do not affect any real magnitudes. As noted, Purchasing Power Parity (PPP) is the concept used to state that exchange rate changes offset inflation differentials between countries. PPP is explained in Appendix 3.2 (p. 60). Fisher Parity conveys that the nominal interest rate changes with the expected inflation rate in a currency, while the real interest rate remains constant or independent of expected inflation. In general, exposure to exchange rates and interest rates occur for periods when PPP and Fisher Parity do not hold. We have reason to return to these concepts several times in the chapters below.

## 2.5  WHAT COULD BE GAINED FROM A RISK MANAGEMENT PROGRAM?

There is considerable interest among managers and academics in more detailed studies of the effects of launching risk management programs. So far this topic has received very little attention in academic journals. Admittedly, it is difficult to calculate precisely the effects on the bottom line. Nevertheless a cost-benefit analysis should be carried out before the program is launched in order to provide a solid foundation for the objective and scope of a risk management program.

Benefits could be the result of reduced risk in terms of probability of ruin and cost savings associated with this reduced probability, or of cost savings associated with reduced variance of firm performance and cash flows. The risk reduction may be translated into one or more of the following sub-benefits:

- Increased predictability of cash flows
- Lower expected bankruptcy costs, as noted in Section 2.2
- Reduced funding costs in credit markets
- Tax advantages (with asymmetric treatment of profits and losses, and through tax shields on higher debt-carrying capacity)

- Lower risk of hostile take-overs if the lower risk contributes to less confusion in equity markets between impacts of macro shocks and firm-specific shocks. Such confusion can be taken advantage of by relatively well-informed raiders.
- Reduced uncertainty about sales and employment levels, making the firm more attractive to employees and suppliers
- Less liquidity risk and thereby reduced risk that profit opportunities remain unexploited (see Section 2.3).

Implementing and running a risk management program means fixed as well as variable costs. The fixed costs are found in:

- Labor costs (staff of experts)
- Support systems (computers, etc.)
- Office space
- Possibility of higher risk of hostile take-overs, if the risk management serves primarily to enhance managers' job security or other personal objectives.

Variable costs are caused by:

- Transaction costs
- Costs of consultants
- Legal expertise (individual cases).

There is a danger that a risk management program serves only managers' objectives and that it focuses primarily on accounting based measures of exposure. It is useful to think through the potential costs of such a risk-management program and the benefits of implementing a more ambitious program based on economic objectives.

To benefit from risk management it is important to understand the sources of the exposure and whether the exposures can be measured with some confidence. Uncertainty about exposure is inevitable but actually manageable, as we will show in Chapter 6. The sensitivity of the firm's value to changes in risk factors provides the basic information in a risk management program. Conventional exposure measures—such as transactions exposures to exchange rate changes—capture only a fraction of the "true" economic exposure to exchange rate changes and these measures could be completely irrelevant. We return to these concepts of exposure in Chapter 3.

It may seem obvious that a risk-management program must be based on a clear and properly conceived objective. It is not always easy. A firm, for example, that focuses on reducing exposure in foreign currency payments in the near term cannot hope to achieve a substantial decline in the observed (ex post) variability of its domestic currency cash flows. The reason is that three-month forward exchange rates vary over time as much as do spot exchange rates. A firm with expected cash flows evenly distributed over time and a real discount rate of 10% will experience only a 5% drop in the present value variance as a result of relying on sequential three-month forward contracts. Thus, a distinction must be made between reducing the observed variability of cash flows over time and reducing uncertainty about cash flows on a particular future date. The two concepts of risk reduction are related to different risk management objectives. The determination of objectives for risk management is discussed in detail in Chapter 8.

## 2.6 RISK MANAGEMENT AND THE CREATION OF OPTIONS

Academic work on risk management incorporates to an increasing extent the theory of options pricing following the break-through in determining the price of an option in the early 1970s. Option theory is employed not only to determine the price of a financial instrument but also to evaluate management's strategic or tactical decisions.

The financial instrument called an option is a right to buy or sell a security at a future time at a predetermined price. An important characteristic of the option is that its pay-off follows the price of the underlying security only above or below a certain level, the "exercise price," while at the exercise price the pay-off is zero and the holder of the option is indifferent between exercising and not exercising the option. The option to sell a security at a predetermined price provides the owner of a security with an insurance that the cash flow to the owner will not fall below a certain level—the exercise price minus the price of the option.

Consider a firm planning to invest USD 100 million in plant and equipment generating future cash flows. The cash flows are uncertain and may in the end be larger or smaller than what is expected at the time of planning. If a part of the investment is not recoverable, then waiting to invest until uncertainty has been partially resolved has a positive value. Waiting to invest implies holding an option on the value of the project. It insures against losses under bad outcomes that are within the range of possibilities at the time of planning but will be known to occur or not occur at a later date.

If the planned investment were in an aircraft which can be sold at a market value independent of the source of uncertainty, then waiting to invest would not be valuable. The reason is that the investment can be recovered even if bad outcomes become a reality.

Options pricing theory has been applied to project evaluation under, for example, exchange rate uncertainty to evaluate the value of waiting to invest and the value of abandoning a project (see, for example, Dixit, 1989a, 1989b). Options theory has also been applied on foreign direct investment decisions, when there is uncertainty about real wage costs in the home country and the host country (see Kogut and Kulatilaka, 1994). Foreign direct investment effectively creates the option to move production from a home location to a foreign one if costs increase above a certain level in the home country. A good example of having production flexibility is a factory ship finding a harbor and working wherever real wage costs are the lowest.

The firm facing macroeconomic uncertainty once an investment in a project has been made can reduce exposure by creating options of different kinds, and the value of such options can be estimated. Abandonment of projects is clearly always an option and its value depends on the degree to which invested resources are "sunk," that is, non-recoverable, and on the costs of starting up again. The firm can abandon one market where cash flows are unfavourable without disinvestment, if sales efforts can be shifted to another market. Another real option can be created by being flexible with respect to suppliers of inputs (see Capel, 1997).

It has been noted that pricing strategy is an important determinant of exposure. A flexible pricing strategy can be thought of as creating an option reducing uncertainty about future cash flows, if changing the price allows the firm to reduce losses caused by adverse macroeconomic conditions. The costs of such an option could be associated with loss of customer loyalty caused by price uncertainty. Marketing efforts creating stronger customer loyalty could similarly be thought of as creating an option by making price responses to changing macroeconomic conditions possible.

When analyzing exposure to risk once an investment is in place, the firm's options to react to changing conditions are clearly important. Since the options generally are greater in number the longer the time horizon, this reasoning has the immediate implication that exposure to uncertainty over longer time horizons generally is less than the short-term exposure. On the other hand, uncertainty increases with the time horizon.

## 2.7  CONCLUDING REMARKS : THE CASE FOR RISK MANAGEMENT

Finance theory tells us that in efficient financial markets, investors and households can diversify risk by investing in a portfolio of securities, and thereby obtain their desired trade-off between risk and return on the portfolio. In this case, investors are not willing to pay more for the firm that is actively engaged in risk management than the firm focusing on maximizing shareholder value. On the contrary, risk management activity can increase the costs to investors of evaluating the risk associated with different securities. Thus, in order to make a case for active corporate risk management, we need to find arguments that explain why risk management increases shareholder value.

The general case for risk management with respect to any variable, macroeconomic or not, requires, first, that shareholders or other stakeholders face *exposure* to this variable. By exposure we mean that the wealth of shareholders or other stakeholders is sensitive to the future outcome for this variable. Second, the exposure to the variable must be *asymmetric* one way or another. In other words, the costs of an unanticipated change in one direction must not equal the benefits of an equal unanticipated change in the other direction. The asymmetry can be caused by a skewed shape of the frequency distribution for the variable; or, the costs associated with different outcomes are not a simple linear function of the outcome. For example, the farmer facing uncertainty about the rainfall during the season ahead has an incentive to conduct rainfall risk management if there is a particular high frequency that rainfall wipes out the harvest, or if the extra costs associated with abnormally high rainfall are higher than the benefits of abnormally low rainfall. The exposure of other stakeholders in the farm can be exemplified by the tractor driver, who requires compensation to face uncertainty about rainfall. The higher compensation associated with greater uncertainty reduces the value of the farmer's own stake in the farm. Thus the farmer has an incentive to conduct rainfall risk management, although the exposure is not *direct* but *indirect* through the tractor driver. Rainfall risk management could take the form of equipping the tractor with a heated cab in the last indirect exposure case or building high-capacity drainage systems in the direct exposure case.

We have discussed corporate risk in general and risk emanating from a turbulent macroeconomic environment in particular. Uncertainty about several policy and non-policy variables contribute to macroeconomic risk. It was argued that the macroeconomic impact on the firm can be captured by an analysis of the impact of exchange rates, foreign and domestic inflation, and foreign and domestic interest rates. We return to this issue in Chapter 4.

The many channels of influence from the macroeconomic environment to the cash flows of a firm imply that no company in the real world—small or large, domestic or foreign—is unaffected by macroeconomic uncertainty. All stakeholders—shareholders, lenders, employees, suppliers, customers, government authorities, and management—have an interest in an analysis of the sensitivity of the firm to macroeconomic fluctuations. Competitors also belong to this category. For example, a competitor that subscribes to "benchmarking" as a performance measure should aim at a comparison of "filtered" profits, that is, profits adjusted for influences of macroeconomic fluctuations.

Little has been written about the evaluation of what a risk management program can achieve. The breakthrough is still to come. A precondition for evaluation is obviously that a consistent strategy for dealing with risk exists. In Chapter 8 we discuss how such strategies can be developed.

The lack of good examples of real-world evaluations is evident and it could be a reflection of a lack of consistent risk management programs. We have not found any example of a company that assesses risk in a coherent way from an economic point of view. Admittedly, it is difficult to carry out a cost-benefit analysis of a risk management program by valuing potential benefits in monetary terms compatible with a firm's profit and loss statement. This difficulty is still no excuse, however, for making an opportunity cost analysis of individual cover or hedging decisions alone. As a step toward more comprehensive cost-benefit analysis we have discussed the different costs and benefits that may have to be considered in an evaluation of a risk management program.

## NOTES

1 See Froot, Scharfstein, and Stein (1994).
2 With limited liability of shareholders, there is an incentive for shareholders to take high risks at the expense of debt-holders when the value of equity is low. The reasoning here assumes therefore that managers have objectives different from shareholders, and that debt-holders have sufficient information not to be taken advantage of.

# Chapter 3

# Traditional Approaches to Measuring Macroeconomic Exposure

## 3.1 INTRODUCTION

After more than three decades of more or less flexible exchange rates the limitations of traditional approaches to exchange rate management have become obvious. Today managers are better educated to handle exposure of different kinds. Moreover, new approaches to exposure management are developing that make use of recent improvements in computer support and innovations in financial markets. These developments enable firms to be more ambitious in their management of exchange rate and related exposures. There are still reasons, though, to take the traditional approaches seriously, if for no other reason than that they are used by most firms. It is possible that after a comprehensive evaluation of risk, a traditional partial approach will be found sufficient for a particular firm.

In this chapter, traditional as well as more recent concepts of exposure to exchange rate and interest rate changes are reviewed and compared. The main focus is on exchange rate exposures but interest rate exposure measures, and to some extent inflation exposure measures, are also discussed. We show that all exchange rate exposure measures can be interpreted as coefficients of sensitivity to exchange rate changes although the coefficients are more or less limited in coverage and some are oriented only toward accounting.

In Section 3.2 we begin with a summary of conventional measures of transaction exposure and expand them to include the types of transactions incorporated in the economic measure. Thereby we define cash flow exposure and economic value exposure. In Section 3.3 we turn to accounting-based translation exposure measures. Section 3.4 contains a comparison of economic and accounting measures. Section 3.5 poses the question of the extent to which the choice of translation method matters. All the traditional exchange rate exposure measures are then compared in Section 3.6. Interest rate exposure is discussed in Section 3.7. Concluding remarks follow in Section 3.8.

## 3.2 FROM TRANSACTION EXPOSURE TO ECONOMIC EXPOSURE

Before the time of investment in plant and equipment, a firm is obviously able to influence exchange rate effects on future cash flows by its investment strategy. In this chapter we are however primarily concerned with the exposure when plant and equipment are in place. Even so, the nature of transaction exposure depends very much on the time horizon over which exchange rate effects are considered. One month into the future exchange rate changes would primarily affect contracted payments. One year into the future there are fewer such contracts. Accordingly, exchange rate effects on future prices and sales are the major concern over such horizons. Over the very long term, the firm can alter its investment strategy and its operations in so many dimensions that exchange rate exposure becomes meaningless, as noted in Chapter 2.

Before the time of receiving an order the firm has plant and equipment in place with the expectation to sell output and to buy inputs in the future, as shown in Figure 3.1, which describes stages of a sales or purchase transaction through time. Initially, neither the price nor the volume is determined in a contract. At this time the firm has a "non-contractual" commercial exposure, because the return on the investment in plant and equipment depends on future realized sales and purchases. Both the price and the quantity of these realizations may depend on the exchange rate, as well as on macroeconomic conditions in general.

Before the time of delivery, outputs and inputs may be ordered or contracted possibly at fixed foreign currency (FC) prices. After contracts are written there is a contractual exposure. This exposure becomes "financial" at time of delivery. Between the time of delivery and payment the firm may have extended or been given credit. Thus, to the extent that the invoice currency is a foreign currency there are FC accounts receivable

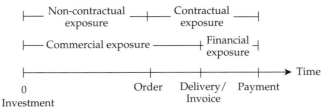

**Figure 3.1** Time aspects of a commercial transaction.

(A/R) and FC accounts payable (A/P) on the firm's balance sheet. At the time of delivery the responsibility for enforcement of the transaction moves from an operational department to the financial department.

In what follows we define different concepts of transaction exposure. All such exposures consist of actual and often expected FC cash flows in the future. After the discussion of transaction exposures we extend the exposure concept to include potential price and quantity effects of exchange rate changes on sales or purchases. This extended concept of exposure is called cash flow exposure. As a starting point, the cash flows of the firm in any period are divided into commercial and financial flows, as in Table 3.1. Commercial cash flows occur at the time of sales and purchases corresponding to the time of payment only in the case of cash transactions. If payment occurs at other times, then the flows are financial. Many firms denote payments of accounts receivable and payable as commercial flows because these payments originate in a commercial transaction.

**Table 3.1  Commercial and financial cash flows before tax.**

**Commercial cash flows**

|  |  |  |
|---|---|---|
| + Sources: | Sales revenues (as on income statement) | |
| – Uses: | Costs of goods sold (as on income statement) | |
| | Wages and salaries (as on income statement) | |
| | Depreciation and obsolescence (new investments to keep capacity unchanged) | |
| = Net commercial cash flows before tax | | |

**Financial cash flows**

**Excluding hedge contracts**

|  |  |  |
|---|---|---|
| + Sources: | Accounts receivable, payments | |
| | New accounts payable | |
| | New loans | |
| | Interest payments received | |
| – Uses: | Accounts payable, payments | |
| | New accounts receivable | |
| | Repayments of loans | |
| | Interest payments | |

a)      = Net financial cash flows before taxes and contractual hedging

b)      Cash flows on hedge contracts

±          Net of gains and losses on forward and futures contracts due

Net of gains and losses on options contracts

= Net financial cash flows before tax (a) + (b)

In Table 3.2 transaction exposures are illustrated. For simplicity only a subset of the flows in Table 3.1 are included. Instead both actual and expected flows in several periods are included. It is assumed that the observer is in time 0 with a time horizon of two periods for exposure measurement.

Among commercial flows only sales revenues and expected sales revenues for future periods are included. It is assumed that all customers obtain a one period credit—an A/R. Thus, at the time of sale the commercial flow is exactly offset by a financial outflow by the creation of the A/R. Payments of contracted A/R occur (with certainty) one period later. A/R payments more than one period into the future are uncertain and depend on expected sales of the period before payment.

The lower part of Table 3.2 defines different transaction exposure measures as of the middle of period 0. The lines show time periods of FC

**Table 3.2  An example of alternative FC transaction exposure measures. Two period time horizons from period 0.**

| Period | $-1$ | 0 | 1 | 2 |
|---|---|---|---|---|
| **Commercial flows in FC** | | | | |
| (+) Sales revenues | 70 | 80 | | |
| (+) Expected sales revenues | | | 90 | 100 |
| **Financial flows in FC** | | | | |
| (+) Contracted A/R payments | | 70 | 80 | |
| (+) Expected A/R payments | | | | 90 |
| (−) New contracted A/R | −70 | −80 | | |
| (−) Expected new A/R | | | −90 | −100 |

Exposures in period 0 with two period horizon.

**Transaction exposure 1:** Net contracted financial FC flows.

Contracted A/R in period 0; FC 80

**Transaction exposure 2:** Net contracted plus expected financial FC flows.

Contracted A/R in period 0; FC 80

Expected A/R payments in period 2; FC 90

**Transaction exposure 3:** Expected net commercial FC flows plus net contracted financial FC flows

Expected sales in period 1; FC 90

Expected sales in period 2; FC 100

Contracted A/R in period 0; FC 80

exposure using the different measures. It is assumed that the time horizon is two periods.

*Transaction exposure 1*: Net contracted financial FC flows. The narrow transaction exposure is simply contracted FC A/R due in period 1. In the example all purchases and A/P are, for simplicity, zero. Since the requirement for this exposure measure is that an FC payment is contracted, the firm has an exposure at time 0 of FC 80 for only one period—the maturity of the A/R.

*Transaction exposure 2*: Net contracted and expected financial FC flows. This broader transaction exposure measure equals contracted A/Rs plus expected A/Rs due in periods 1 and 2. In period 0 there is an existing exposure carried over from period –1 as expected payments in period 1 (FC 80). This exposure can be updated in period 0 based on new information about new A/Rs. The firm also identifies a new exposure equal to expected payment in period 2 for expected sales in period 1 (FC 90). This exposure can be updated with actual sales information in period 1.

*Transactions exposure 3*: Expected net commercial FC flows plus net contracted financial FC flows. This exposure measure consists of expected sales minus purchases through period 2 plus contracted financial exposures in period 0. In Table 3.2 it can be seen that there is an exposure equal to expected sales in period 1 (FC 90). There is a new exposure equal to expected sales in period 2 (FC 100) that can be updated in period 1. Furthermore, as a result of sales in period 0 there is a new contracted A/R exposure for one period. Total exposure for period 1 is 270.

Transaction exposure 2, including contracted and expected financial flows, is commonly used in business practice. (It is sometimes called "commercial" exposure because the financial flows originate in commercial transactions.) What difference does it make if the exposure measure is expanded to explicitly consider expected sales and purchases as in transaction exposure 3?

One difference between the two measures is that exposure measure 3 actually extends its reach one more period given the two year horizon. The reason is of course that sales occur a period ahead of payments. Extending exposure measure 2 to include three periods would add an exposure of FC 100 over three periods. If this is done, then the total of exposed positions in the first period would be FC 270 with both measures 2 and 3. The remaining difference between the two measures is that exposure measure 3 explicitly distinguishes between exchange rate effects on expected sales in FC, and exchange rate effects on contracted FC positions after sales are completed. Exposure measure 2, on the other hand, does not make the same distinction between commercial and financial positions but considers only exchange rate effects on expected payments. Nevertheless, it is clear that measures 2 and 3 capture the same exposures if time horizons are adjusted as mentioned above. Compared to exposure measure 1, both are more inclusive and informative, because they consider that sales values can be affected by exchange rates.

All transaction exposures suffer from one serious drawback: they take into account only valuation changes on given FC amounts in response to changes in the exchange rate between DC and FC. As a result, these measures cannot capture exchange rate effects on sales in the home country or exchange rate effects on sales abroad if the invoicing of all transactions is denominated in DC.

These drawbacks of transaction exposure can be seen if, for example, revenues are expressed in terms of the following three factors:

Revenues in DC =

Quantity sold $(Q) \times$ Price in FC $(P) \times$ Exchange rate $(S)$

In the formula an exchange rate change may affect quantity sold and the sales price. Transaction exposures treat both the quantity sold and the sales price as independent of exchange rate changes. Thus, transaction exposures include only the *valuation effects* of exchange rate changes, while *price and quantity effects* are neglected completely. If sales are contracted for in advance, the price and quantity effects of exposures may be considered negligible, but in general uncertainty about sales is an important component of exposure.

Exchange rate changes generally affect a firm's competitive positions in both the home and foreign markets. Thus, the quantity of sales can be affected for long periods. Similarly, the price the firm can charge in a market after the exchange rate change depends on the firm's competitive position. This determines the extent of "pass-through" of exchange rate changes in FC prices, as well as the ability of the firm to keep the home market price constant after an exchange rate change.

Many firms employ relatively broad transaction exposures. For example, Volvo Cars systematically covers their expected sales revenues in dollars with a one year time horizon adjusted for expected purchases in the United States (see Chapter 5). Thus, the possibility that the volume of the firm's commercial operations may depend on the exchange rate is not captured. For example, if Volvo Cars expects to sell for USD 10 million during one month in one year, then a change in the exchange rate between now and then will affect both the SEK value of the expected flow of USD, and the competitive position of Volvo Cars relative to competitors in the US markets. A depreciation of the Swedish krona during the year will enable Volvo to either raise prices in SEK without affecting USD prices, or to lower the USD price relative to U.S. competitors. In the latter case, the sales volume is likely to increase. In other words, depending on the pricing strategy of the firm, the exchange rate change will affect sales revenues through the quantity of sales and/or the domestic currency prices. This quantity effect is not restricted to foreign markets but occurs in the home market as well.[1]

From an economic as well as a practical point of view, a more fruitful approach to measuring exposure is to focus initially on commercial cash flows. These are generally not adjustable in terms of currency denomination for the firm committed to sales in a specific market. Financial flows, on the other hand, are often highly adjustable in the sense that their currency denomination can be switched at a very low cost, making them suitable as exposure management tools. For example, short-term loans can be taken in domestic or foreign currency. Accounts receivable and accounts payable can be influenced by leading or lagging payments and many firms can determine the invoice currency. The firm's exposure before hedging could be determined by the observation of commercial cash flows, while the financial flows could be considered instruments for exposure management, like forward contracts and options contracts. Therefore, net commercial cash flow is a more appropriate measure of exposure, while financial positions are considered adjustable in terms of currency denomination.

With this background we can now define an economic measure of exposure capturing valuation, price and quantity effects—the commercial cash flow exposure for period $t$.

The sensitivity of net commercial cash flows measured in domestic currency (DC) to exchange rate changes is equal to change in the domestic currency value of commercial cash flows in period $t$ caused by a one unit change in the exchange rate:

Commercial cash flow exposure =

Net expected commercial cash flows in FC in $t$ (valuation exposure)

+ Effect on FC cash flows in the foreign market in $t$ of a one unit exchange rate change (price and quantity exposure on FC flows)

+ Effect on DC cash flows in the home market in $t$ of the same exchange rate change (price and quantity exposure on DC flows)

The commercial cash flow exposure incorporates the exposure caused by uncertainty about the competitive position of the firm in the home market as well as the foreign market. This cash flow sensitivity measure consists, as can be seen, of three components: the first is the valuation effect of an exchange rate change on the expected foreign currency flows; the second is the effect of the same exchange rate change on the volume of the foreign currency flows caused by changes in the firm's competitive position in the foreign market; and the third is the effect on the volume of domestic currency flows in the domestic market caused by changes in the firm's competitive position in this market. An example in Chapter 4 will illustrate all these effects.

The commercial cash flow exposure shows the sensitivity of the domestic currency value of total commercial cash flows to exchange rate changes by measuring the change in the DC value of cash flows in response to a one unit increase in the exchange rate (unit of DC/FC). Alternatively, the sensitivity can be measured as the percentage rate of change in cash flows of a 1% change in the exchange rate.

All exposure measures discussed above are in fact measures of the sensitivity of cash flows. They are therefore additive. The difference between the last "cash flow exposure" measure and the more conventional "transaction exposures" is that the cash flow exposure includes price and quantity effects. Therefore, the sensitivity in this case is not defined by the exposed position alone. Over the last decades too many managers have learned this the hard way. While covering expected sales for the next one or two years they have nevertheless found themselves exposed to price and quantity changes (see Box 3.1).

Commercial cash flow exposure can be considered an economic measure as opposed to an accounting measure because it cannot be observed

---

**Box 3.1  Commercial cash flow exposure as a benchmark for risk management**

Using the transaction exposures as a basis for risk management is defensible if price and quantity effects are expected to be zero. We have argued that commercial cash flow exposure is the appropriate benchmark for evaluating the desired financial exposure. Not knowing the commercial cash flow exposure does not imply that it is reasonable to behave as if it is zero. It is possible to say something about the commercial cash flow exposure with some knowledge of the firm. Consider the following examples.

An exporter of very price-sensitive goods competing with foreign producers cannot change the FC price in response to changes in the DC value of FC. Thus, a depreciation (appreciation) of the DC will cause an increase (decrease) in DC cash flows. The valuation effect dominates if the firm is able to supply the market as before. Its costs relative to foreign competitors change, however, and therefore so do profitability and the supply to the market. Another firm with a subsidiary abroad using inputs from the home country and competing with foreign producers will see its cash flows in FC increase (decrease) as a result of the DC depreciation (appreciation). If the foreign subsidiary instead competes with producers in the depreciating (appreciating) country, then its cash flows will fall (increase). The reason is that the relative labor costs of the firms in the depreciating (appreciating) country fall (rise).

in accounting data or in projected cash flows. It must be estimated using information about determinants of cash flows. We return to issues of estimation in Chapters 4 and 5.

A truly complete measure of economic exposure would take into account the effect of an exchange rate change on all projected future cash flows. Since the economic value of a firm is the present value of future cash flows, the economic value exposure of a firm can be thought of as the sum of the exposures of future cash flows. Most likely, a current exchange rate change will affect near-term cash flows the most.

Defining the economic value exposure as the effect of an exchange rate change on the economic value, the magnitude of the economic value exposure depends on three factors:

1. The extent to which an exchange rate is expected to be permanent or temporary
2. The sensitivity of cash flows in future periods to exchange rate changes in the same periods
3. The sensitivity of cash flows in future periods to exchange rate changes in earlier periods.

Assume, for example, that there is an exchange rate change that is not expected to be reversed. Thus, it is a permanent exchange rate change. In this case, cash flows in each future period will depend on the exchange rate in the same period and possibly on the lagged effects of the exchange rate in the preceding periods. Clearly, cash flow exposures for individual periods constitute the building blocks of economic value exposure, but information of type 1 and 3 is required as well to estimate it. A short cut exists, however, if it can be assumed that the stock-market value of a firm is a measure of its economic values. If it can, the value exposure can be estimated using methods we discuss below.

## 3.3  TRANSLATION EXPOSURE

Translation exposure is most often an accounting concept, though one could theoretically define a corresponding economic concept. Accounting translation exposure in a particular currency (often called simply accounting exposure), can be defined as the net balance sheet position in a foreign currency translated at the current exchange rate. There are possibly foreign currency positions translated at historical exchange rates. These positions are not "exposed" because their domestic currency values do not change with the exchange rate. A firm's translation exposure in a particular currency usually refers to the consolidated balance sheet of a multinational corporation in quarterly or annual reports to stockholders.

Most trends in accounting standards are generated in the United States, predominantly by the Financial Accounting Standards Board (FASB). Two of their recommendations, FASB 8 and FASB 52, which have been of paramount importance during the last three decades, are useful benchmarks for this discussion of translation exposure. International accounting standards are discussed in Chapter 11 as well.

The accounting rules under FASB 8 specify that "monetary assets and liabilities" should be translated at the current rate, while non-monetary items (plant, equipment, inventories) should be translated at the historical rates quoted at the time of acquisition. Thus, FASB 8 can be considered a "monetary/non-monetary" (M/NM) translation method. In this method, translation gains (losses) for a period are equal to the average position in monetary items in FC multiplied by the appreciation of the FC. The translation gains or losses appear on the consolidated income statement under FASB 8. The rules for translating the income statement are consistent with the rules in the balance sheet in the sense that the historical rates are applied to the valuation of costs of goods sold and depreciation. Appendix 3.1 shows in detail how both income statements and balance sheets are translated using the M/NM method.

However, because of the short-run variability in measured profits caused by exchange rate fluctuations under the rules of FASB 8, considerable opposition was generated, culminating in the adoption of a new set of standards in 1981. Under the "all-current" (AC) method, the FASB 52, all assets and liabilities are translated at the current rate. Thus, all assets and liabilities in FC are "exposed." However, translation gains and losses do not appear in the income statement under FASB 52, but instead appear in a reserve account which is included in the firm's net worth. Exchange gains and losses appear on the income statement only when they are realized. An important provision in the FASB 52 is that the U.S. dollar can be chosen as a foreign subsidiary's "functional currency" under certain conditions.[2] Since assets and liabilities must be translated into the subsidiary's functional currency using the M/NM method, many U.S. corporations can choose to use a translation method identical to FASB 8. The accounting and economic concepts of functional currency are discussed in Box 3.2.

## 3.4  FROM TRANSLATION EXPOSURE
   TO ECONOMIC EXPOSURE

It has been argued here and in other places that exchange rate exposure should be evaluated in terms of unexpected exchange rate effects on the present value of future cash flows.[3] The economic relevance or irrelevance of accounting-based concepts of exchange rate exposure is illustrated in a few simple examples in Box 3.2. The common pitfall in exposure analysis is to equate the search for an economically relevant translation rate (i.e., current, historical or another rate) with the search for a method to evaluate exposure. The objective of the choice of a translation rate could be, for example, to obtain a measure of the (accounting) value of foreign assets that is comparable to the (accounting) value of domestic assets. Since the book values of domestic assets are not generally adjusted for inflation, true comparability requires that a translation provides a domestic currency

## Box 3.2 The functional currency: Accounting and economic definitions

The functional currency concept is established in accounting. Normally it refers to the currency of the country where a firm is located. According to U.S. accounting rules (FASB 52), any American firm can choose to use the dollar as the functional currency of a foreign subsidiary if, for example, most of its transactions occur in dollars. In general, the book value of the firm in the functional currency is more or less independent of exchange rate changes, because most transactions are denominated in the functional currency. In the same spirit, the functional currency in economic terms can be defined as the currency denomination in which profits or cash flows are independent of any exchange rate fluctuations. For example, if cash flows measured in USD change in the same proportion as the exchange rate USD/JPY, then cash flows measured in JPY must be independent of exchange rate changes and the JPY becomes the functional currency.

In the real world the functional currency in economic terms is generally a basket of serveral currencies. It depends not only on the company's pricing strategy, that is, its rule for adjusting price to exchange rate fluctuations, but also on the currency in which its competitors set prices, and the sensitivity of sales to price changes relative to the competition. Take the example of a pulp manufacturer in a small country. Pulp is a relatively homogenous product and international competition is strong. American and Canadian producers dominate the market and the world price is determined in U.S. dollars. The manufacturer must set its price in the home currency equal to the world dollar price times the home currency/dollar exchange rate. Companies may invoice in any currency, but the dollar is in any case going to constitute a large share of the functional currency.

For most producers of differentiated goods the sensitivity of sales to changes in prices relative to competition is rarely as high as for pulp manufacturers. Thus, the exposure to exchange rate fluctuations and the choice of functional currency is to some extent under the control of the company. During the strong dollar period of the early 1980s, many European car manufacturers adopted the strategy of keeping dollar prices nearly constant in the United States. Instead, home currency prices increased dramatically until 1985. Thereafter these prices fell when the dollar depreciated. The dollar therefore had a strong weight in the functional currency of the European firms. Japanese manufacturers, on the other hand, aimed at market shares when the dollar appreciated. They increased yen prices little and increased sales in the United States. Cash flows estimated in both yen and dollar changed substantially in response to exchange rate changes. Neither currency was an obvious functional currency.

value of foreign assets in comparable nominal terms. Exposure is properly defined in real terms, however. The sensitivity of nominal book values to exchange rate changes can be misleading from an economic point of view.

The above discussion indicates that there are two issues related to the choice of translation method from an economic point of view. One issue is the choice of exchange rate that provides the most informative economic valuation of foreign assets and liabilities or of foreign income. The second issue is to determine how the implied translation exposure compares with an economic concept of exposure. It is finally worth noting that the translation method determines the timing of gains and losses on the income statement and in the balance sheet. In the longer run, accumulated exchange rate effects on the book value of owners' equity are independent of the translation method.

## 3.5 DOES THE TRANSLATION METHOD MATTER?

The translation method determines when gains and losses caused by exchange rate changes are captured in income and owners' equity. Excessive gains in one period will be offset by losses or relatively small gains in subsequent or preceding periods. No method can capture the economic value changes of exchange rate changes under all circumstances. It is not appropriate, however, to ask this of an accounting rule. Since economic value depends upon expectations, which are quite uncertain and differ considerably among individuals, the purpose of an accounting rule is simply to provide the best possible information to market participants about events that have had an impact on the firm without attempting to reveal all factors. Given the information provided by accounting procedures, different individuals can form their own judgments and expectations about the impact of exchange rate changes.

For information value, the AC-method for balance sheet and income statement translation seems superior to other methods because market participants can easily infer from the income statement and the balance sheet in domestic currency the firm's position in foreign currencies. If balance sheet items are translated at the historical rates, the information value is less because different items are translated at different rates, and it is hard to disentangle what these rates are.

Ultimately, the actual choice of a translation rule may not be very important for market valuation once market participants grasp the particulars of it. Market participants can then reinterpret the accounting data in their own ways and form their own valuations. Views differ on this point, however (see Dukes, 1978). Studies from the late 1970s of the impact on the stock-market of the then-new FASB 8 indicate that the stock-market valuation of a firm is independent of the translation rule. However, the studies' are inconclusive on this point.

## 3.6  A COMPARISON OF EXCHANGE RATE
##      EXPOSURE MEASURES

Finally, we turn to the relationship between transaction and cash flow exposure on the one hand, and translation and economic exposure on the other. We ask: To what extent are different measures of exposure complements to, or substitutes for, one another? If they are complements they can then be added in order to give a measure of total exposure. If they are substitutes or partial substitutes, then obviously, adding them to obtain a total exposure measure will give a distorted picture.

Before answering these questions, we need to compare the exposure measures as shown in Table 3.3, which summarizes the discussion of exposure measures. Section A contains inputs for the comparisons. It is emphasized that all exposures refer to a measure of the sensitivity of DC value in period $t$ to a current change ($\Delta S_1$ from period 0 to period 1) in the exchange rate.

The conventional transaction exposure in Section B could be narrow or broad as discussed above. The broad measure includes commercial and contracted financial cash flows. The main difference between transaction exposure and the cash flow exposure of FC cash flows in Table 3.3 is that the cash flow exposure includes exchange rate effects on prices and quantities in FC. Cash flow exposure measures must also incorporate the effects of exchange rate changes on domestic currency cash flows, which are shown in Section B.

The economic value exposure in Section C represents the sensitivity of the present value of all expected cash flows. Most often management would be concerned with the change in the present value in the current period ($\Delta PV_1^{DC}$) of a change. Clearly, this exposure consists of a whole series of cash flow exposures. Since the present value in period 1 depends upon the present value of all expected cash flows after period 1, measuring a series of cash flow exposures is a substitute for measuring economic exposure directly, for example, by analyzing the stock-market value sensitivity to exchange rate changes. The series of cash flow exposures could also be used as input data for measuring the economic exposure of the present value.

The "economic translation exposure" in Section C views the subsidiary as a foreign entity and its present value is translated at the exchange rate on the value date. If the translation rate is a close proxy for a weighted average of future exchange rates at the times cash flows occur, then the economic exposure and the economic translation exposure in panel C are nearly identical for the foreign component of cash flows. The economic translation exposure is also a present value of expected cash flows and it is therefore a substitute for a series of cash flow exposures.

Section C shows also accounting exposure measured as the net book value of balance sheet items translated at the current rate. As a proxy for economic exposure or economic translation exposure, this measure suffers

**Table 3.3 Exchange rate exposure of flows and values at time 0.**

**A. Inputs**

| Time | $t = 1$ | $t = 2$ | ... | $t = n$ | Notes |
|---|---|---|---|---|---|
| Expected net cash flow earned in FC during period $t$ | $X_1^{FC}$ | $X_2^{FC}$ | ... | $X_n^{FC}$ | $X_1^{FC}=f(S_t)$ |
| Expected net cash flow earned in DC during period $t$ | $Y_1^{DC}$ | $Y_2^{DC}$ | ... | $Y_n^{DC}$ | $Y_1^{DC}=g(S_t)$ |
| Exchange rate | $S_1$ | $S_2$ | ... | $S_n$ | DC/FC |
| Real discount factor | $(1+d)^1$ | $(1+d)^2$ | ... | $(1+d)^n$ | |

**B. Flow oriented measures of exposure for a future period $t$ to an exchange rate change during period 1 (only t=1 included)**

| | | Valuation effect |
|---|---|---|
| Transaction exposure (the change in the DC value in t of an expected FC flow from a one unit current change in the DC price of FC) | $\dfrac{\Delta X_1^{DC}}{\Delta S_1} = X_1^{FC}$ | |
| Cash flow exposure of foreign currency flows in t (the change in the DC value in t of FC cash flows from a one unit current change in DC price of FC) | $\dfrac{\Delta X_1^{DC}}{\Delta S_1} = S_1\left(\dfrac{\Delta X_1^{FC}}{\Delta S_1}\right)+ X_1^{FC}$ | Includes valuation, price and quantity effects on FC flows |
| Cash flow exposure of domestic currency flows in t (the change in the DC value in t of DC flows from a one unit current change in DC price of FC) | $\dfrac{\Delta Y_1^{DC}}{\Delta S_1}$ | Includes price and quantity effects on DC flows |

**C. Value exposures for a future period $t$ to an exchange rate change during period 1**

| | | |
|---|---|---|
| Accounting exposure (the change in the DC book value from a one unit current change in DC price of FC) | $\dfrac{\Delta DC_t \text{ book value}}{\Delta S_1}$ | Net balance sheet position in FC that is translated at current exchange rates |
| Economic value exposure in t (the change in the DC present value of cash flows after t from a one unit current change in DC price of FC) | $\dfrac{\Delta PV_t^{DC}}{\Delta S_1}$ | $PV_t^{DC}$ $= E\left[\displaystyle\sum_{i=1}^{\infty}\dfrac{\left(X_{t+i}^{FC}S_{t+i}+Y_{t+i}^{DC}\right)}{(1+d)^i\,P_{t+i}^{DC}}\right]$ |
| Economic measure of translation exposure in t (the change in the DC value of FC present value of cash flows after t from a one unit current change in DC price of FC) | $\dfrac{\Delta PV_t^{DC}\left(\text{of } X^{FC}\right)}{\Delta S_1}$ | $PV_t^{DC}$ $= E\left[S_t\displaystyle\sum_{i=1}^{\infty}\dfrac{X_{t+i}^{FC}}{(1+d)^i\,P_{t+i}^{FC}}\right]$ |

from the same deficiency as the conventional transaction exposure. In other words, it does not take into account the possible effects of the exchange rate on the volume of commercial operations and, as a consequence, it cannot capture the idea that domestic assets can be exposed to exchange rate changes as well.

It is common that transaction and translation exposures are added as if they were complements. If we view the transaction exposure as a proxy for cash flow exposure, and accounting exposure as a proxy for economic exposure, then it is not generally appropriate to add exposures. However, it is possible to estimate transaction or cash flow exposures for the near term and translation or economic exposures capturing the exposure beyond the near term. For example, the transaction or the cash flow exposure for the current period can be added to the translation or value exposure at the end of the current period.

We note also that exposures as risk measures should reflect the sensitivity to unanticipated exchange rate changes, that is, those in excess of what was forecast. There is generally little difference between actual and unanticipated changes. Cash flows in the budget may be seen as anticipated cash flows based on exchange predictions. In the following chapter, we will discuss the problem that the exchange rate exposure, interest rate exposure, inflation exposure and possibly other aspects of macroeconomic exposure may overlap if the exchange rate is correlated with any other variable. Thus, if one wishes to measure not only exchange rate exposure but, for example, interest rate exposure as well, then the exchange rate exposure should be adjusted to the extent that the exchange rate varies systematically relative to the other variables. Traditional exposure measures generally neglect that the above mentioned variables are correlated.

Measures that cope with the shortcomings of the methods presented in Table 3.3 will be discussed in Chapter 4 in the form of an exposure measure to unanticipated changes in $S_t$, at constant levels of interest rates, inflation, and other variables.

Emphasizing that exposure coefficients should be seen as sensitivity coefficients, a number of authors have suggested that exposure should be measured as a regression coefficient.[4] Assuming that a firm is concerned with cash flows, the suggested exchange rate exposure measure is obtained as the coefficient $a_1$ in the following equation:

$$[\text{Cash flow in DC in } t] = a_0 + a_1 [\text{exchange rate, DC/FC}] + \text{error term}$$

(1)

Using historical data for cash flows, exchange rates for a number of periods, and standard statistical packages, $a_0$ and $a_1$ can be estimated. The error term captures variations in cash flows that are unrelated to the exchange rate. For example, if $a_1 = 200$, then a one-unit increase in the exchange rate in period $t$ causes a DC 200 increase in cash flows. In other words, the coefficient $a_1$ measures cash flow sensitivity to exchange rate changes. An important advantage of this exposure measure is that it includes commercial price and quantity effects, as well as valuation effects. It does not take into account the interdependence among macroeconomic variables, however.

The measure can obviously be applied to components of cash flows as well. For example, exchange rate exposure of business operations may be estimated separately from the exposure of financial cash flows. Similarly, different time horizons can be used to measure exposure to exchange rate changes over various periods on a monthly, quarterly, or annual basis. We return to these issues in Chapter 5.

## 3.7 INTEREST RATE EXPOSURE MEASURES

Most literature on corporate finance stresses the exchange rate as the key variable in commercial exposure. The interest rate is rarely mentioned. This is curious, since the correlation between interest rates and stock-market prices is well known, whereas the evidence of a systematic relationship between exchange rates and stock prices is much weaker.

The substantial effects of interest rates on demand conditions for many firms and the strong links between exchange rates and interest rates in financial markets, as emphasized in Chapters 1 and 2, imply that corporate exposure to interest rates cannot be neglected. If there is a case for analyzing commercial exchange rate exposure, the case for analyzing commercial interest rate exposure is at least as strong. The lack of direct book value effects of interest rate changes such as the valuation effects in the case of exchange rate changes is no argument for disregarding that interest rates can strongly affect a firm's commercial operations.

From an economic point of view, interest rate exposure can be defined in a way that is analogous to the economic definitions of exchange rate exposure above. Thus, focusing on economic value, exposure is measured by the following sensitivity coefficient:

$$\frac{\text{Change in economic value}}{\text{Change in the interest rate}}$$

Cash flow exposure to interest rate changes is similarly defined as:

$$\frac{\text{Change in real cash flows}}{\text{Change in the interest rate}}$$

Changes in economic value and cash flows generally come about for three reasons. First, interest rate changes affect the firm's cost of capital and, therefore, the discount rate applied to future cash flows and current interest costs. Second, the demand for many firms' products depends on interest costs, because the cost of credit influences demand. Durable goods demands of different kinds are particularly sensitive to interest rate changes. Third, other macroeconomic variables such as aggregate demand in an economy tend to be correlated with the interest rate.

As for exchange rate exposure, it is possible to distinguish between the exposure of the firm's commercial operations and the exposure of financial assets and liabilities. The total exposure is the sum of these two components. The firm tending to keep total exposure low could adjust the interest rate sensitivity of liability positions to offset the exposure of commercial operations. The logic is the same as for exchange rate exposure except that it is the maturity structure and the degree of adjustability of interest rates rather than the currency compositions that would be adjusted on the financial side. The problems of measuring the exposure of the firm's commercial operations, that is, its assets in production, are also analogous to the problems of measuring the commercial exposure to exchange rate changes. There is, as noted, one difference between exchange rate exposure and interest rate exposure: the former depends on both price and quantity effects and valuation effects, while there is no valuation effect of interest rate changes in the books. Traditional concepts of interest rate exposure are therefore less directly tied to accounting values.

Most traditional, as well as more recent interest rate exposure concepts, are oriented primarily toward the measurement of the exposure of financial assets and liabilities. The concepts have been developed in the financial sector where assets as well as liabilities are financial. Although several of the concepts can be applied to non-financial assets and cash flows, few firms go beyond financial positions when measuring interest rate exposure.

A brief review of traditional interest rate exposure measures includes the following concepts:

- Maturity gap
- Duration
- Modified duration
- Value at risk

After discussing each of these concepts that usually are applied to financial positions we turn to:

- Commercial interest rate exposure

## Maturity gap

This method of evaluating interest rate risk is particularly suitable for financial institutions, wherein both assets and liabilities are financial. The maturity gap describes the net interest rate sensitive positions in future periods. Consider, for example, a firm or a bank holding an asset providing DC 1,000 in fixed interest payments in each quarter over the next two years. This asset is financed with a revolving loan with an interest rate that is fixed in the beginning of each quarter. In this case, the interest rates on both the asset and the liability sides are fixed for the first quarter. As a result there is no maturity gap for the first quarter. The interest payments on the DC 1,000 revolving loan for each of the following seven quarters are uncertain, however. For each of these seven quarters the interest on the asset portion (DC 1,000) is known while the interest on the liability portion is uncertain. The net interest rate sensitive position is DC 1,000.

The data on gaps in different future periods can be used as a tool for managing interest rate exposure. Using various scenarios for interest rates in future periods, a maturity gap table is useful for calculating the gains and losses from various interest rate changes.

For hedging purposes, the maturity gap table indicates the position in each period that is exposed to interest rate changes. Interest payments in future periods are not necessarily completely fixed or completely flexible, however. Thus, the gap is an imperfect measure of exposure. Furthermore, if a firm is concerned with possible effects of interest rate changes on the present value of future flows, the maturity gap information does not directly provide information about value effects.

## Duration

The duration of an asset or a liability depends on the time pattern of future cash flows associated with the asset or the liability. The duration of an asset differs from the maturity. While the maturity is the time horizon of the last payment, the duration takes into account how payments are distributed between today and maturity. Duration is obtained by weighing each future period, when payments on the asset (liability) are due, using as weight the present value (PV) of the payment in the period relative to the total value of the asset (liability). Thus, assets with different payment patterns over time and the same value may have different durations. The following formula shows the duration of an asset with payments in three periods:

$$
\text{Duration} = \left[\frac{\text{PV of cash flows in period 1}}{\text{PV of asset}}\right] \times 1 + \left[\frac{\text{PV of cash flows in period 2}}{\text{PV of asset}}\right] \times 2 + \left[\frac{\text{PV of cash flows in period 3}}{\text{PV of asset}}\right] \times 3
$$

$$(2)$$

### Modified duration

The concern with the duration of assets and liabilities stems from the dependence of value sensitivity on duration. The change in the present value of future cash flows associated with an asset from a change in the

interest rate is the "modified duration". It increases with the duration of
the asset:

$$\text{Modified duration} = \left[ \frac{\text{Change in PV of asset (liability)}}{\text{Percentage point change in interest rate}} \right]$$
$$= \frac{\text{Duration}}{1 + \text{interest rate}}$$

(3)

Equation 3 shows the interest rate sensitivity of the value of an asset or a
liability defined in analogy with the exchange rate exposure coefficients in
the previous section. The interest rate sensitivity depends on the duration,
as well as on the level of the interest rate. The impact of the interest rate
level is relatively minor, however. It is a reasonable approximation to consider duration to be a proxy for the interest rate sensitivity of the value of
an asset (liability).

A firm holding an asset with a certain interest rate sensitivity (modified
duration) can hedge the interest rate risk associated with this asset by
obtaining a liability or a derivative instrument with the same interest rate
sensitivity. An important advantage of the modified duration measure of
interest rate exposure is that it is easily applicable to any kind of security,
including options. We return to hedging in Chapter 6.

## Value at risk

This exposure concept has been put to widespread use during the last few
years. Value at risk measures interest rate exposure (or any other exposure) as the maximum value that can be lost with a certain confidence. For
example, for a particular asset there could be a 95% probability that the
asset value falls DC 1,000,000 at a maximum. In this case, the value at risk
is DC 1,000,000 with a 95% confidence.

The value at risk concept is closely related to the concept of "probability
of ruin" discussed in Box 2.2. If the DC 1,000,000 is the maximum loss a
firm can take without "ruin," then the DC 1,000,000 at risk with 95% confidence implies a 5% "probability of ruin." Such a probability is unaccept-
ably high for most firms. Thus, if value at risk is to be used for evaluating
the probability of bankruptcy, the confidence that losses will stay below a
maximum acceptable level must be increased above 95% for most firms. Of
course, the acceptable confidence level depends on the time horizon.

The inputs to calculate value at risk to interest rate changes are the same
as the inputs used to calculate the probability of bankruptcy due to the
exchange rate changes discussed in Box 2.2. The two inputs are the interest rate sensitivity of an asset or a liability, and the probability distribution
for the interest rate. The interest rate sensitivity is simply the modified
duration measure discussed above. The probability distribution describes

the probabilities that the interest rate will achieve different levels. The probabilities of different interest rate changes are difficult to measure, but it is a useful exercise to try to assign probabilities to possibly large increases or declines that could affect a firm seriously.

Value at risk is applicable to portfolios of assets and liabilities as well as to individual assets. The additional input required to measure value at risk for a portfolio is the correlation among interest rates for the different assets and liabilities in the portfolio.

The firm concerned with cash flows in the near term rather than with economic value may choose to estimate Cash Flow at Risk (CFaR) rather than Value at Risk (VaR). Conceptually, CFaR is analogous to VaR. The probability distribution for cash flows substitutes for the probability distribution for value in the estimation of an acceptable loss with a certain probability.

## Commercial interest rate exposure

All the different interest rate exposure measures discussed here are usually applied to financial assets and liabilities. However, the modified duration measure, that is, the interest rate sensitivity, and the value/cash flow at risk measures are equally applicable to the non-financial assets of a firm generating commercial cash flows. As for exchange rate changes, the interest rate sensitivity of commercial cash flows can be estimated, as can the interest rate sensitivity of the value of a firm's productive assets generating commercial cash flows.

With information about the interest rate sensitivity of commercial cash flows, the value/cash flow at risk exposure for commercial cash flows and for assets generating these cash flows can be estimated with information about the probability distribution for the interest rate.

Information about exchange rate and interest rate exposures as measured by sensitivity coefficients or value/cash flow at risk to exchange rates and interest rates cannot generally be considered separately or, in the case of value/cash flow at risk, added. The reason is that exchange rates and interest rates tend to be correlated, as noted already in Chapter 1. Thus, in order to adapt value/cash flow at risk analyses to exchange rates and interest rates it is necessary to take account of the correlation between the variables. A key feature of the MUST analysis below is that this correlation issue is addressed. In Chapter 7 we illustrate the concept of CFaR as a measure of macroeconomic risk, building on the MUST analysis—and its use in risk management.

## Interest rate exposure with uncertain inflation

The assets of a firm may be financed by debt or equity. From the stockholders' point of view, uncertainty about the future (real) cost of debt is a source of risk. For a long time, two common rules of thumb were to (a) match the maturity of debt with the life span of the assets it was financing, and (b) match the currency of debt with the currency of cash flows from the sale of products. But by the mid-1960s in the United States, relatively high and uncertain inflation came to mean that the real cost of fixed rate, long-term debt was uncertain, while cash flows from sales were better protected against inflation. Then, too, by the 1970s, inflation rates among countries began to diverge under flexible exchange rates and became uncertain to different degrees. Accordingly, the task of choosing the cheapest source of debt in terms of maturity as well as currency became more complex.

An *ex post* analysis of effective interest costs in different currencies—costs including exchange rate changes—indicates that it is only over very long time periods that costs are equalized as IFP suggests (see Appendix 3.3). Similarly, the relative advantage of short- and long-term loan changes substantially over time. Whether markets are efficient enough so that expected interest costs will be equalized across currencies and maturities remains an open question. Still, there is little doubt that firms perceive profit opportunities in their choice. Even if no expected profit opportunities were to exist, risk-averse firms would be concerned with uncertainty about real interest costs.

The real interest cost on a loan is the nominal cost minus inflation. Thus, the real cost can be locked in *ex ante* only if the nominal interest cost can be linked to a relevant measure of inflation from the firm's point of view. Such a measure may differ substantially from the commonly used price indices to which interest costs in some currencies are linked.

When taking a non-indexed loan, a firm with a long time horizon for the use of its assets faces a combination of uncertainty about real sources of interest rate risk and the inflation risk associated with a particular currency denomination. When inflation is low and believed to be relatively stable, the major concern is only real sources of interest rate risk. Such risk can be avoided by issuing relatively long-term debt instruments on which the interest rate is fixed. However, when it is not known whether the inflation rate is going to be 5% or 10% on average over the next decade, real interest costs on even fixed interest rate loans become highly uncertain.

One response to high inflation uncertainty has been to increase the use of roll-over credits and flexible interest (floating or adjustable rate) loans. On these, the interest rate may be reset every six months or so based on short-term interest rates. Since inflation can be forecast rather well for a period of six months, borrowers and lenders can reduce their exposure to inflation risk by shifting to these flexible rate securities or to a series of short-term securities.

The drawback of flexible interest loans is that the six-month interest rate may change as a result of real sources of interest rate changes in the economy. In general, the more short-term interest rate fluctuations depend upon real factors, such as fiscal policy, savings propensity, or aggregate investment, the more favorable long-term loans are from a real interest rate risk point of view. On the other hand, when the basic real rate of interest is stable, and short-term nominal interest rate fluctuations reflect inflation expectations, short-term loans become relatively favorable. It should be noted that lenders would react in the same way as borrowers to both real sources of interest rate risk and inflation risk. Thus, increased risk of either kind induces both borrowers and lenders to shift maturity preferences the same way.

## 3.8 CONCLUDING REMARKS ON TRADITIONAL EXPOSURE MEASURES

We have discussed the inability of traditional exposure measures to capture macroeconomic exposure properly. They do not consider the interdependence among exchange rates, interest rates, and inflation rates. Since generally accepted measures of inflation exposure are not available, it can be claimed that the traditional measures of macroeconomic exposure actually consist of two sets: (a) measures of exchange rate exposure, and (b) measures of interest rate exposure. Both sets treat exposure as independent of changes in other macroeconomic variables.

In addition, several of these traditional exposure measures can also be criticized for being partial in scope. Most exchange rate exposure measures, for instance, do not capture exchange rate effects on domestic cash flows. The interest rate exposure measures emphasize financial assets and liabilities while neglecting commercial interest rate exposure.

A third drawback characterizing the commonly used traditional exposure measures is that they do not capture the dynamics of cash flows arising as a result of price and quantity effects caused by exchange or interest rate changes. Thus, they do not consider the competitive implications of these changes. The effects of, for example, higher cost of capital caused by macroeconomic fluctuations on sustainable profits and competitiveness are also neglected. Taken together these shortcomings should serve as a severe warning against too much reliance on traditional exposure measures as a support for hedging decisions in risk management, and for the analysis of the intrinsic competitiveness of the firm.

To pave the way for our broader macroeconomic approach, the MUST analysis, sensitivity coefficients were emphasized as exposure measures. The simple regression approach presented above will be extended in the next chapter to a multivariate framework in order to capture the interdependence of the different macro price variables discussed above.

Throughout this chapter, the terms "Purchasing Power Parity" and "International Fisher Parity" have appeared several times. They are key relationships in an analysis of macroeconomic influences on a firm. Deviations from these relationships are important preconditions for the existence of profit opportunities in international markets, and in a later chapter their roles in strategy choice will be examined. The relationships are discussed in more detail in appendices 3.2–3.3 in order to elucidate definitions and measurement problems.

# Appendix 3.1

# Measuring translation exposure under the monetary/non-monetary and the all-current methods

Table 3.4 shows the balance sheets at the end of year 0 of two subsidiaries of MNC USA, an American holding company. All foreign currency (FC) denominated accounts are translated at the rate USD 1/FC, which has been the exchange rate since the firm started its foreign operations.

Under the monetary/non-monetary method (M/NM) the translation exposure at the end of year 0 is the sum of all monetary items translated at the current rate:

FC[Cash +A/R] −FC[A/P + L.t. Dept]

which for MNC Home is FC 150 − FC 100 = FC 50 and for MNC Foreign is FC[50 + 100] − FC[50+400] = −FC 300. Thus, the total M/NM exposure is −FC 250.

Under the AC-method, the translation exposure at the end of year 0 is

FC[Cash +A/R + Inv.+ P/E] −FC[A/P + L.t. Dept]

**Table 3.4  Balance sheet year 0 of MNC Home and MNC Foreign.**

|  |  |  | MNC Home | | | | MNC Foreign | | |
|---|---|---|---|---|---|---|---|---|---|
|  |  |  | Conv. rate | Dollars |  |  | Conv. rate | Dollars |  |
| Cash | USD | 100 | − | 100 | FC | 50 | 1 | 50 |  |
| A/R | USD | 200 | − | 200 | USD | 100 | − | 100 |  |
|  | FC | 150 | 1 | 150 | FC | 100 | 1 | 100 |  |
| Inventory | USD | 300 | − | 300 | FC | 200 | 1 | 200 |  |
| P/E | USD | 1000 | − | 1,000 | FC | 600 | 1 | 600 |  |
|  |  |  |  | 1,750 |  |  |  | 1,050 |  |
| A/P | USD | 150 | − | 150 | USD | 100 | − | 100 |  |
|  | FC | 100 | 1 | 100 | FC | 50 | 1 | 50 |  |
| L.t. Debt | USD | 800 | − | 800 | FC | 400 | 1 | 400 |  |
| Owners' equity |  | (residual) | | 700 |  | (residual) | | 500 |  |
|  |  |  |  | 1,750 |  |  |  | 1,050 |  |

Note:    A/R = Accounts Receivable        P/E = Plant and Equipment
         A/P = Accounts Payable          L.t. Debt = Long-term Debt

**Table 3.5  Balance Sheet year 1 of MNC Home.**

|  |  |  | M/NM | | AC | |
|  |  |  | Conv. rate | Dollars | Conv. rate | Dollars |
|---|---|---|---|---|---|---|
| Cash | USD | 100 | – | 100 | – | 100 |
| A/R | USD | 200 | – | 200 | – | 200 |
|  | FC | 150 | 1.10 | 165 | 1.10 | 165 |
| Inventory | USD | 300 | – | 300 | – | 300 |
| P/E | USD | 1000 | – | 1000 | – | 1000 |
|  |  |  |  | 1765 |  | 1765 |
| A/P | USD | 150 | – | 150 | – | 150 |
|  | FC | 100 | 1.10 | 110 | 1.10 | 110 |
| L.t Debt | USD | 800 | – | 800 | – | 800 |
| Owners' equity |  | (residual) | | 705 | (residual) | 705 |
|  |  |  |  | 1765 |  | 1765 |

which for MNC Home is FC 150 – FC 100 = FC 50 and for MNC Foreign it is FC[50 + 100 + 200 + 600] – FC[50 + 400] = FC 500. Thus, total AC exposure is FC 550. The two methods result in accounting exposures with opposite signs! We turn next to the balance sheets at the end of year 1. Over the year the foreign currency has appreciated to USD 1.10/FC. MNC Home's balance sheet remains unchanged (Table 3.5). Only monetary items are FC denominated for MNC Home. Therefore, the two methods lead to the same result. Since MNC Home's balance sheet has remained unchanged before translation, net income for MNC Home must have been zero. The translation exposures similarly remain constant over the year. We can then explain the $5 increase in owners' equity as:

$$\text{Translation gain} = \text{average FC exposure over the year}$$
$$\times \text{exchange rate change}$$
$$= 50 \times (1.10 - 1.00) = \text{USD } 5$$

under both methods.

During the year, more substantial changes occurred in MNC Foreign. We present first the balance sheet at the end of year 1 for this subsidiary (Table 3.6).

Before showing the translation using M/NM, it is necessary to determine depreciation over the year in order to identify the P/E bought at historical cost. For that reason, MNC Foreign's year 1 income statement is shown in Table 3.7.

We are now in a position to translate MNC Foreign's balance sheet at the end of year 1, as well as its income statement. Table 3.8 describes balance

**Table 3.6 Balance sheet year 1 of MNC Foreign.**

| | | | |
|---|---|---|---|
| Cash | FC | 75 | |
| A/R | USD | 100 | |
| | FC | 125 | |
| Inventory | FC | 200 | (Bought evenly over year 1) |
| P/E | FC | 650 | (Additional non-depreciated P/E bought evenly over year 1) |
| A/P | USD | 100 | |
| | FC | 50 | |
| L.t. Debt | FC | 400 | |

**Table 3.7 MNC Foreign's income statement year 1.**

| | | | |
|---|---|---|---|
| Revenues | FC | 600 | (Evenly over the year) |
| Cost of goods sold (COGS) | FC | 200 | (FIFO) |
| Depreciation | FC | 125 | (Old P/E bought before year 1) |
| Other expenses | FC | 75 | (Evenly over the year) |
| Profits before tax | FC | 200 | |
| Tax (50%) | FC | 100 | (Paid evenly over the year) |
| Profits after tax | FC | 100 | |

**Table 3.8 Balance sheet year 1 of MNC Foreign translated into USD.**

| | | | M/NM | | AC | |
|---|---|---|---|---|---|---|
| | | | Conv. rate | Dollars | Conv. rate | Dollars |
| Cash | FC | 75 | 1.10 | 82.50 | 1.10 | 82.50 |
| A/R | USD | 100 | – | 100.00 | – | 100.00 |
| | FC | 125 | 1.10 | 137.50 | 1.10 | 137.50 |
| Inventory | FC | 200 | 1.05 | 210.00 | 1.10 | 220.00 |
| | | | (year average) | | | |
| P/E | FC | (600–125) | 1.00 | 475.00 | 1.10 | 522.50 |
| | FC | (650–475) | 1.05 | 183.75 | 1.10 | 192.50 |
| | | | | 1,188.75 | | 1,255.00 |
| A/P | USD | 100 | – | 100.00 | – | 100.00 |
| | FC | 50 | 1.10 | 55.00 | 1.10 | 55.00 |
| L.t. Debt | FC | 400 | 1.10 | 440.00 | 1.10 | 440.00 |
| Owners' equity | | | (residual) | 593.75 | (residual) | 660.00 |
| | | | | 1,188.75 | | 1,255.00 |

sheet translations using the M/NM and AC methods, respectively, whereas Table 3.9 shows the translation of the income statement.

We can now summarize the information and show how net income, translation gains, and changes in owners' equity are related in dollar terms. Under M/NM the change in owners' equity for MNC Foreign is $593.75 - 500 = 93.75$. Out of this amount, net income explains 121.25. The translation gain (loss) must be the difference, that is, loss equal to 27.50. We check this:

Translation exposure at the beginning of the year under M/NM = −300

Translation exposure at the end of the year under M/NM

$= FC[75 + 125] − FC[50 + 400] = −FC\ 250$

Average exposure under M/NM = −FC 275

Exchange rate change $= 1.10 − 1.00 = 0.10$

Translation gain (loss) $= 0.1 \times (−275) = −USD\ 27.50$

Under AC similar calculations can be made. The change in owners' equity under AC is 160. Of this amount net income explains 105. The translation gain must be 55. We check this by noting that exposure at the beginning of the year is FC 500, while at the end of the year it is

$FC[75 + 125 + 200 + 650] − FC[50 + 400] = FC\ 600$

Thus, average translation exposure is FC 550 and the translation gain is $0.10 \times 550 = USD\ 55$. In both cases the translation gain (loss) plus net income is the change in owners' equity.

Table 3.9  Income statement year 1 of MNC Foreign translated into USD.

|  |  |  | M/NM |  | AC |  |
| --- | --- | --- | --- | --- | --- | --- |
|  |  |  | Conv. rate | Dollars | Conv. rate | Dollars |
| Revenues | FC | 600 | 1.05 | 630.00 | 1.05 | 630.00 |
| COGS | FC | 200 | 1.00 | 200.00 | 1.05 | 210.00 |
|  |  |  | (inv. held 1 year) |  |  |  |
| Depreciation | FC | 125 | 1.00* | 125.00 | 1.05 | 131.25 |
| Other expenses | FC | 75 | 1.05 | 78.75 | 1.05 | 78.75 |
| Profits before tax |  |  | − | 226.75 | − | 210.00 |
| Tax (50%) | FC | 100 | 1.05 | 105.00 | 1.05 | 105.00 |
| Profits after tax |  |  | − | 121.25 | − | 105.00 |

*(P/E bought before year 1)

# Appendix 3.2

# Purchasing Power Parity and real exchange rates

The concept of Purchasing Power Parity (PPP) has long held a central position in economic theory. It can be traced back to the Spanish economists of the Salamanca school in the sixteenth century (Einzig, 1962). Over the years, many schools of thought have argued about this seemingly simple relationship. According to one school, equilibrium between prices for traded goods in different countries is maintained by variations in exchange rates, while the prices in themselves are determined internally. Another school argues that PPP should hold in the long run, emphasizing average price levels. According to Frenkel (1981), much of the controversy concerning the usefulness of the PPP doctrine is due to the fact that it does not specify the precise mechanism by which exchange rates are linked to prices, nor does it specify the precise conditions that must be satisfied for the doctrine to be correct. Rather, the PPP doctrine may be viewed as a short-cut; it specifies a relationship between two variables without providing the details of the process which brings about the relationship and, according to Frenkel, it should not be viewed as a theory of exchange rate determination. Rather, prices and exchange rates are determined simultaneously. The PPP theory has several appealing features:

> It is simple and intuitive. The ingredients of the theory are minimal and basic: price levels and exchange rates suffice to make calculations. Furthermore, whether or not the strict PPP theory holds, it is useful to know to what extent the theory is valid. For example, one can ask what proportion of relative-price changes between countries is likely to be offset by exchange-rate changes over various time horizons. (Officer, 1982, p. 289)

The PPP theory or doctrine exists in two forms, one relative and one absolute. As a special case there is a third version, "the Law of One Price" (LOP). PPP in its absolute version states that when the exchange rate is in equilibrium, a buyer at a random point in time should receive the same amount of goods for his money, regardless of which country he buys them from or in (Boyd, 1801). This can be written (4)

$$S = \frac{P^{DC}}{P^{FC}} \tag{4}$$

where

$S$ = Spot rate (DC units per unit of FC)
$P^{DC}$ = Price level domestically
$P^{FC}$ = Price level in the foreign currency

The revival of interest in the theory during the twentieth century has generally been ascribed to Gustav Cassel. According to him the PPP theory means that:

> When two currencies have undergone inflation ... the normal rate of exchange will be equal to the old rate multiplied by the quotient of the degree of inflation in the one country and in the other. (Cassel, 1922)

John Maynard Keynes found for the period 1919–21 that the method functioned satisfactorily. In his view the PPP theory tells us that

> ... the movements in the rate of exchange between two countries tend, subject to adjustments in the 'equation of exchange', to correspond pretty closely to movements in the internal price levels of the two countries, each expressed in their own currencies. (Keynes, 1923)

Both Cassel and Keynes refer to "relative PPP." Movements in internal price levels correspond to movements in the exchange rate. The relative version can be written as an approximation in the following way:

$$\hat{s} \approx \hat{p}^{DC} - \hat{p}^{FC} \tag{5}$$

The approximation states that the rate of change in the equilibrium exchange rate ($\hat{s}$) is proportional to the difference between the inflation rates ($\hat{p}^{DC} - \hat{p}^{FC}$) in the two countries.

More exactly, relative PPP implies the following relationship between relative exchange rate and relative price level changes:

$$\frac{S_t}{S_{t-1}} = \frac{P_t^{DC} / P_{t-1}^{DC}}{P_t^{FC} / P_{t-1}^{FC}} \tag{6}$$

The principle is simply that if goods or services of the same kind do not cost the same in all countries after adjustment for taxes, transport costs, and transaction costs, then there will be a flow of products and production factors which will force prices back to a state of equilibrium. Starting from a base year when the exchange rate between two countries reflects prices and costs correctly, this means that if prices rise x% faster domestically than abroad, then the domestic currency can be expected to depreciate by x%. Of course, the adjustment may take time depending on the exchange rate regime.

The PPP theory holds in the short run only if commodity arbitrage is perfect. In the long run, it should hold even without this condition.

Those who criticize the PPP theory in its relative form over the long run do so mainly because important real economic factors influencing relative prices between traded and non-traded goods and the terms of trade do not remain constant. PPP theory is, nevertheless, an essential ingredient in the analysis of long-term exchange rate changes. Most researchers will agree that:

> Under the skin of any international economist lies a deepseated belief in some variant of the Purchasing Power Parity theory of the exchange rate. (Dornbusch and Krugman, 1976)

There is now widespread agreement that PPP does not hold in the short run, or even for periods as long as two or three years. Substantial real exchange rate fluctuation, defined as fluctuations in the deviations from PPP, occurs. The debate around short-run PPP focuses instead on whether deviations (real exchange rates) follow a random process or whether the deviation is mean-reverting. Most researchers believe in a mean-reverting process, but some research presents empirical evidence that the rate of change of deviations from PPP is a random walk (see Roll, 1979, and Pigott and Sweeney, 1985). More recent evidence indicates that there are tendencies toward mean reversion but that the adjustment is slow (see, for example, Jorion and Sweeney, 1996).

## Measurement issues

Three technical problems must be considered whenever PPP measurement is to be performed:

- Choice of index for describing relative price level movements
- Choice of base period
- Choice between bilateral and multilateral measurements

*Choice of index*    A problem that has long occupied economists concerns the choice of an index to describe changes in relative inflation. The index numbers should be easily accessible, they should be frequently reported, and they should measure the relative movements in inflation for goods and services in foreign trade. The problem is complicated by differences in consumption patterns across countries. Choosing an index can be regarded as a problem of representativeness in the statistical sense. It should be noted that there is no index that is perfect for the purpose of PPP. When the structure of internal relative prices is stable, the choice among price indices seems to be less important. Internal relative prices—as measured by the relationship between the cost of living and the wholesale price indices—have not changed much in the United States and the United Kingdom. They have changed dramatically in the new European Union (EU) member countries and transition countries from the former Soviet Unions, however, which may account for more severe problems with the PPP equation when applied to these countries.

An index can be chosen among the GNP deflator, the consumer price index, the wholesale price index, the producer price index, the export price index, and the index for relative unit labor costs. The choice of index will depend on the intended use of the PPP data. The requirements are different when the PPP relation is used for managing the exchange rate compared, for instance, with a situation when it is used to compare living standards.

The *GNP deflator* is recommended by many as providing the broadest coverage of goods and services. But it is difficult to obtain figures more frequently than once a year. This implicit index contains a higher proportion of non-traded goods, which may or may not be an advantage for

PPP comparisons. It is a disadvantage if PPP is viewed as a commodity arbitrage relationship, but it is an advantage if PPP is seen as a monetary equilibrium condition.

The *wholesale price index* has a broad coverage of primarily traded goods. Empirically it has proved to be a good compromise choice. However, comparisons are complicated by statistical problems, since national index numbers differ in coverage and in the weights employed.

The *export price index* is criticized mainly on the grounds that it is narrow. It can be rejected on both statistical and conceptual grounds, since it covers too limited a range of goods and services and lacks direct information about prices. It may also be biased by dumping.

Compared with the wholesale price index, the *consumer price index* includes many more goods and services that do not form part of the trade between countries. PPP based on this index is, therefore, sensitive to price changes in non-traded goods. Furthermore, it refers to an index for expenditures rather than total production like the GNP deflator. The preference for either index would depend on whether expenditures or production is the most immediate determinant of real money demand.

The *producer price index* is similar to the wholesale price index. It has a smaller coverage than the consumer price index. *Unit labor cost measures* suffer from their limitation to one factor of production and from the difficulty of measuring production volume. It is useful for evaluating changes in attractiveness among countries as production site, however.

There is little general agreement in the literature when it comes to recommending any one of these index categories. As mentioned before, the choice is dependent on the intended use. In the monthly publication *International Financial Statistics*, the International Monetary Fund (IMF), presents six different estimates of PPP indices or real effective exchange rate indices. These indices are based on relative unit labor costs, relative normalized unit labor costs, relative value-added deflators, relative wholesale prices, relative export unit values, and relative consumer prices.

*Choice of base period*   To provide a good picture of real exchange rate developments, it is important to find an appropriate base period when the exchange rate is assumed to be at PPP, reflecting an equilibrium based on the relative competitive positions of two countries. A starting point or an equilibrium point can be identified by analyzing the behavior of a country's attractiveness, its trade balance, and the foreign exchange market. Price competitiveness is often measured in terms of relative international market shares. Therefore, a possible starting point is that when the exchange rate is in equilibrium, a country does not gain or lose market shares, and firms' profit margins are constant. There are other ways in which a base period for PPP can be chosen and it is difficult to say whether a certain choice is the best for all purposes. However, it is possible to obtain important information about the variability of deviations over time even if the level of deviations cannot be assessed with certainty.

*Choice between bilateral and multilateral measurement*   Bilateral and multi-lateral measures are both interesting in their own ways. A multilateral calculation of relative PPP requires weighting of a number of bilateral real exchange rates. If we want to assess the likelihood of a devaluation in the near future, it is useful to analyze changes in an index reflecting deviations from PPP for a whole currency basket. On the other hand, if, for example, we are trying to find principles for evaluating claims and debts in various currencies, we need to make bilateral comparisons.

## Real exchange rates, 1979–2007

Figure 3.2 shows real exchange rate developments for Japan, the United States, and Germany. For all three countries, "effective" real exchange rates are measured. In other words, the real exchange rate index for each country shows the average rate on a basket of foreign currencies in a particular period relative to a base period. The average is calculated using bilateral trade weights. In other words, if in the case of the United States the exports plus the imports from a country correspond to 10% of all U.S. exports plus imports, then the bilateral trade weight is 0.10.

In Figure 3.2 the period average is used as reference and set to 100. It can be seen that real exchange rate changes can be large, and that the adjustment towards PPP (to index 100) is slow. Deviations are long-lasting. It is

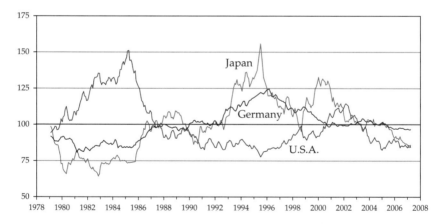

**Figure 3.2** Real effective exchange rates: Major OECD countries 1979–2007.
Note: The real effective exchange rate refers to changes in exchange rates adjusted for changes in unit labor costs. The development in each country is compared with the 17 OECD countries; average 1979–2007 = 100. An index below 100 indicates that a country's "competitive" position has been strengthened or the country's currency is undervalued. An index above 100 indicates a probable overvalued currency or a weakened "competitive" position. Germany is represented by the Euro as of January 1, 1999.

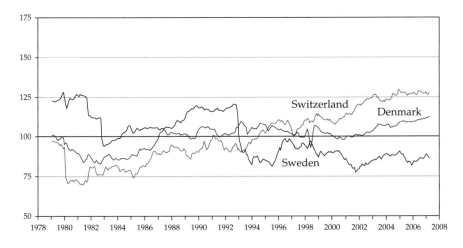

**Figure 3.3** Real effective exchange rates: Small and relatively open economies 1979–2007. See note to caption for Figure 3.2.

also clear that, among the three countries, the United States faces the largest fluctuations in its average real exchange rate.

Comparing Figure 3.2 and Figure 3.3, it is clear that real exchange rate fluctuations are larger for the larger countries with relatively little international trade in percent of GPD.

# Appendix 3.3

## International Fisher Parity

International Fisher Parity (IFP) refers to one concept of equilibrium in international interest rate differentials after adjustment for expected exchange rate movements.[5] The relationship, sometimes called the uncovered interest rate parity, can be written in the following way:

$$\frac{S^*_{t+1}-S_t}{S_t} = \frac{i_t^{DC} - i_t^{FC}}{1+i_t^{FC}} \tag{7}$$

where:

$S_t$ = spot rate at time $t$; units of DC per unit of FC
$S^*_{t+1}$ = market expectations at time $t$ regarding future spot rate at time
    $t + 1$
$i_t^{DC}$ = domestic currency interest rate for one period at time $t$
$i_t^{FC}$ = foreign currency interest rate for one period at time $t$

According to IFP the expected exchange rate change is reflected in the interest differential for two assets that differ only in terms of currency denomination. When IFP holds, the expected returns on domestic and foreign currency assets are the same. For IFP to be an equilibrium relationship, the risk premia on the foreign currency and the domestic currency assets must be the same. In other words, there is no currency risk premium. Tests of IFP include the testing of hypotheses about expectation formation. Therefore, the tests are never conclusive. The main debate surrounding IFP is whether there is a systematic deviation that could reflect a risk premium on holding a particular currency. We cannot review the massive amount of tests that have been performed (see, for example, Oxelheim, 1990). The evidence that there are systematic deviations has been mounting, but there is little agreement on whether the deviations represent risk premia, market inefficiency, or a learning mechanism (see, for example, MacDonald, 1988).

IFP is sometimes tested by an analysis of the ability of the forward exchange rate to serve as a predictor of the future spot exchange rate. The equivalence between this test and direct IFP tests depends on Interest Rate Parity (IRP). IRP implies that the forward premium on a currency relative to another reflects the interest differential between the currencies or

$$\frac{F_t - S_t}{S_t} = \frac{i_t^{DC} - i_t^{FC}}{1 + i_t^{FC}} \tag{8}$$

where $F_t$ is the forward rate at time $t$ for delivery of currency at time $t + 1$.

Comparing Equation 8 for IRP with Equation 7 for IFP shows that if both hold, then $F_t = S_{t+1}^*$, that is, the forward rate is the expected future spot rate. In the information-efficient society of today, IRP holds if covered arbitrage between currencies is feasible without large transaction costs and exchange controls. This arbitrage operation is between currency positions with identical currency risk. Therefore, we would expect IRP to hold, and there is overwhelming empirical evidence that it does within the Euromarkets, but to a lesser extent between, say, T-bills issued in different countries. In the latter case, differences may be explained by political risk premia (see Oxelheim, 1996). The test of IFP that compares forward premia with exchange rate changes is therefore equivalent to comparing interest differentials in Euromarkets with exchange rate changes.

The empirical issue of whether IFP holds is impossible to settle, because it requires knowledge about expected exchange rate changes, as noted above. Nevertheless, a few characteristics of tests can be illustrated in Figures 3.4–3.6.

Figures 3.4 and 3.5 show that the variation in actual exchange rate changes by far exceeds the variation in expected exchange rate changes as measured by interest rate differentials. The three currencies represented in

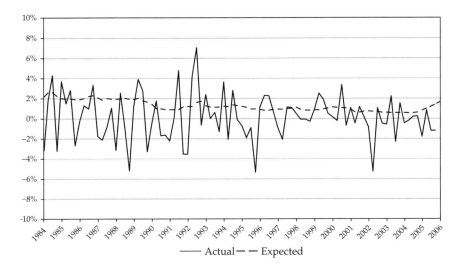

**Figure 3.4** Actual exchange rate changes and expected exchange rate change according to the three-month interest rate differential DKK–CHF 1984–2007. Note: quarterly observations, quarterly percentage: —— actual exchange rate changes; – – – – expected exchange rate changes according to the difference between Euromarket rates in London.

the exhibits are Danish kroner, Swiss francs and U.S. dollars. The Danish currency has been fixed to the Deutsch mark for most of the period.

The difference between actual and expected exchange rate changes is *ex post* deviations from IFP, that is, the forecast error in the interest rate differential. For IFP to hold *ex ante*, the forecast error must be zero on the average, and the error should be random. It is hard to judge these properties by viewing a diagram, but clearly the forecast error in the interest rate differentials fluctuates around the actual change with large magnitudes in both directions.

Figure 3.6, finally, shows whether the forecast errors tend to zero on the average. If they do, then there is no average gain from holding funds or borrowing in one currency instead of another. The figure shows the accumulated gains or losses for a Danish borrower who, in 1974, borrowed in Danish kroner (DKK), U.S. dollars and Swiss francs (CHF), respectively. Three months' revolving loans are used. The accumulated gains from borrowing in dollars amount to the accumulated differential between the lines in Figure 3.5. If the deviations from IFP in Figure 3.5 were random we would expect the accumulated gains in Figure 3.6 to fluctuate around 0 (=100 in Figure 3.6). The figure shows that there are clear and rather long-lasting trends in the deviations from IFP. The Danish firm borrowing in Swiss francs in 1974 accumulated losses for four years. Thereafter IFP held fairly well on average for about seven years. Then, there is again a

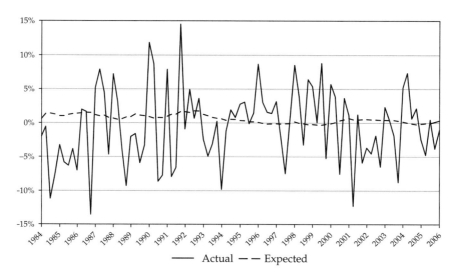

**Figure 3.5** Actual exchange rate changes and expected exchange rate change according to the three-month interest rate differential DKK–USD, 1984–2007. Note: quarterly observations, quarterly percentage: ———— actual exchange rate changes; – – – – expected exchange rate changes according to the difference between Euromarket rates in London.

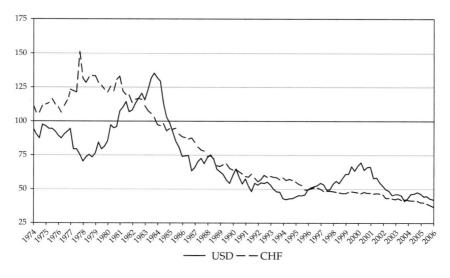

**Figure 3.6** Index of additional costs to a Danish borrower of borrowing in USD and CHF as compared with DKK, 1974–2007. Note: quarterly observations of prime loan rates: ———— USD: – – – – CHF.

weak trend from 1978 and onward. During this time the firm accumulated gains by having a loan in Swiss francs.

The firm borrowing in dollars accumulated gains from 1974 through 1978. Thereafter, the dollar appreciated far in excess of the interest rate differential, leading to losses for the borrower in dollars through 1984. The opposite happened from 1985 to 1992. Thereafter, IFP has held rather well *ex post* as well.

What conclusions can be drawn? Clearly, there are gains to be made by having forecasting expertise. Is it possible to gain by analysing the time pattern of *ex post* deviations from IFP? There is clearly a time pattern to the deviations but it is hard to judge how regular the pattern really is and how risky it is to exploit the time pattern. Just as there are gains to be made from forecasting correctly relative to the interest rate differential, there are losses to be made from being wrong. Finally, the firm borrowing (investing) for periods up to several years faces a substantial likelihood that borrowing costs (investment returns) will depend strongly on the choice of currency denomination. Currency risk is a reality.

## NOTES

1 An early extension of the exposure concept to include price and quantity effects can be found in Stonehill et al. (1982). They applied simulations to measure "economic exposure" of operations.
2 The main condition for USD being considered as the functional currency of a foreign subsidiary is if a large share of its payments is denominated in USD.
3 Major textbooks on international financial management agree on this point but operationalize the concept in different ways.
4 See, for example, Adler and Dumas (1980), Hodder (1982), and Garner and Shapiro (1984).
5 IFP takes its name after Irving Fisher, whose results were published in 1896 (Fisher, 1896).

# Chapter 4

# Measuring Macroeconomic Impact on the Firm: A Comprehensive Approach

## 4.1 INTRODUCTION

Most firms have implemented one method or another for measuring and hedging risk caused by exchange rate, interest rate, and inflation uncertainty, although in efficient financial markets shareholders do not stand to gain from attempts by management to reduce the variability of earnings. We have noted that most exposure measures used by firms are based on accounting information and as such they are seriously flawed from an economic point of view. Conventional measures of transaction and translation exposures capture direct effects on accounting values of changes in exchange rates and interest rates without taking into account that changes in these variables influence the firm's cash flows in a variety of ways that are not immediately observable in accounting data. Furthermore, in most countries accounting practices do not include inflation adjustment. We have also discussed that most conventional exposure measures disregard that exchange rates, interest rates, and inflation are often not independent. These variables are simultaneously influenced by changes in macroeconomic conditions and policies.

As we discussed in Chapter 2, firms have good reasons to be concerned about the impact on competitiveness from exposure to changes in macroeconomic conditions. The approach we propose here directly addresses the impact of changes in macroeconomic conditions on cash flows. It does so by measuring the sensitivity of commercial cash flows to unanticipated changes in macroeconomic conditions as captured by exchange rates, interest rates and inflation. The advantage of this approach is the information it provides about how liability positions and financial contracts can be effectively used to achieve the desired exposure of total cash flows.

In principle, it is possible to define economic exposure in terms of the sensitivity of economic value to macroeconomic shocks, but we argue below that a suitable starting point for measuring economic exposure is to use cash flows. Most of the discussion of measurement of cash flow exposure applies to value exposure as well.

Increasing attention to the exposure of the firm's commercial cash flows to exchange rate changes in particular is one way to overcome the deficiencies of conventional exposure measures. It should be noted that modern textbooks discuss this approach to exposure using either the concept of competitive exposure or the concept of economic exposure.[1]

To understand sources of exposure and profit opportunities arising as a result of macroeconomic disturbances, it is necessary to discuss in more detail how cash flow and value depend on exchange rates, price levels, interest rates, and relative prices. In this analysis we face the problem of choosing the proper level of aggregation and the time period over which cash flows are forecast. Cash flows can be broken down into many dimensions. There are, for example, cash flows from operations (commercial flows) versus financial flows, domestic versus foreign, contractual versus non-contractual, and adjustable versus non-adjustable.

In Chapter 1 we claimed that in order to understand what is going on with the competitiveness of a firm, managers should "filter" out the macroeconomic influences on cash flows. If they are also risk-averse, they should invest in getting good exposure measures. The bulk of this chapter will focus on the exposure measurement. However, the same base model that is used to estimate the exposure coefficients will be used in Chapter 9 to estimate the relationship between the performance of a firm and changes in the macroeconomic environment.

In Section 4.2 a scenario analysis is outlined to discuss the exposure for a hypothetical firm selling in home and export markets. Thereafter, in Section 4.3 cash flow measures of exposure are defined, taking into account the interdependence among macroeconomic variables. The possible decomposition of cash flows before estimation of exposure is described in Section 4.4. Exposure coefficients and the sizes of shocks are discussed in Section 4.5. In Section 4.6 the relationship between share prices and macroeconomic fluctuations is discussed. Concluding remarks are given in Section 4.7. Implementation aspects of the proposed method are discussed in the next chapter.

## 4.2 DETERMINANTS OF CASH FLOW EXPOSURE

Which factors determine the effects of macroeconomic shocks on a firm? This question is raised here to illustrate the fallacy of focusing on exchange rate exposure in isolation. By taking a broad view of the macroeconomic impact on the firm it is possible to see how the firm's behavior in product markets is as much a determinant of exposure as is the choice of currency denomination of financial contracts. We begin by considering the case of a real exchange rate change. In a second case it is assumed that this change

**Table 4.1  Base case for determination of exposure.**

| Sales: 100 units | | |
|---|---|---|
| Domestic @ GBP 1 | GBP | 50 |
| Exports to the US @ 0,6 x USD 1.67 | GBP | 50 |
| | GBP | 100 |
| Production costs: 100 x unit costs | | |
| COGS domestic @ GBP 0.20 | GBP | 20 |
| COGS imported @ GBP (0.33 x 0.6) | GBP | 20 |
| Wages @ GBP 0.20 | GBP | 20 |
| | GBP | 60 |
| Operating cash flows: (GBP 100 – GBP 60) | GBP | 40 |
| After-tax operating cash flows (50% tax rate) | GBP | 20 |
| Depreciation tax shield 50% of GBP 20 | GBP | 10 |
| After-tax non-financial cash flows | GBP | 30 |

Note: Conversion rate GBP/USD = 0.6

is caused by a specific macroeconomic shock. The exposure, which looks at first glance like exchange rate exposure, is very different when the macroeconomic source of the exposure is considered.

Consider a company that produces 100 units in the United Kingdom, of which 50 are sold domestically and 50 are exported to the United States. Major competitors are located in the United States and Japan. The firm uses a simple mark-up pricing strategy that sets the invoice price at (10/6) × [COGS (cost of goods sold) + wages] per unit.

The base case in Table 4.1 shows that some inputs are imported and others are produced domestically. Now assume an exchange rate change amounting to a 5% appreciation of the pound, while everything else remains as in the base case and the same mark-up pricing strategy is applied. The effects on cash flows are seen in Table 4.2.

The price of imported inputs will fall and, therefore, with a constant mark-up the pound price falls, while the dollar price increases. With unchanged sales volume, non-financial cash flows after tax fall by GBP 0.35.

An important consideration is what happens to the sales volume. If American and Japanese producers' costs are not directly affected by the exchange rate change, then it can be assumed that the price of competitors' products in the United Kingdom falls by 5% while the dollar price remains unchanged in the United States.

In both markets, the price of our firm's product will rise by about 3% above that of its competitors, and sales volume will fall unless demand is totally insensitive to price. Table 4.2 shows that with moderate price sensitivity (price elasticity = 1) cash flows will fall by another GBP 0.60 as a result of the reduction of sales.

**Table 4.2  How the base case is affected by an exchange rate change (after roundings).**

| | |
|---|---|
| Unit price: (10/6) x (COGS imported + COGS domestic + wages) | |
| In the UK | GBP 0.983 |
| In the US | USD 1.725 |
| Sales unchanged: | |
| Domestic @ GBP 0.983: 50 units | GBP49.15 |
| Exports to US @ GBP (1.725 x 0.57): 50 units | GBP 49.15 |
| | GBP 98.30 |
| Production costs: 100 units | |
| COGS domestic @ GBP 0.20 | GBP 20.00 |
| COGS imported @ GBP (0.333 x 0.57) | GBP 19.00 |
| Wages @ GBP 0.20 | GBP 20.00 |
| | GBP 59.00 |
| After tax operating cash flows: 100 units | GBP 19.65 |
| Depreciation tax shield | GBP 10.00 |
| After tax non-financial cash flows | GBP 29.65 |
| Competitor's unit price | |
| In the UK: 5% appreciation of GBP | GBP 0.95 |
| In the US: unchanged | USD 1.67 |
| Cash flow effects of 3% fall in sales for 3% price differential (3% of GBP 19.65) | −GBP 0.60 |
| Exposure coefficient: [(− .35 − .60)/(.57 − .60)] = 31 2/3 | |

Note: The pound (GBP) appreciates by 5% relative to the base case (from 0.60 to 0.57).

Price sensitivity is generally greater in foreign markets where the position of competitors is stronger. If sales volume is very sensitive, then the mark-up strategy can be costly (see, for example, Marston, 1990). Cash flows can be made less sensitive to exchange rate changes if prices are adjusted to follow a constant market share strategy in countries with a high price sensitivity of demand.

Tables 4.1 and 4.2 can be used to measure the exposure coefficient for non-financial cash flows. As shown in Chapter 3, an exposure coefficient tells us the effect on cash flows in domestic currency of a one unit change in the exchange rate: In the case described here the exposure coefficient equals:

($\Delta$ Cash flows in GBP/($\Delta$ GBP/USD)).

As shown in Table 4.2, the fall in cash flows is GBP −.95. The exchange rate change is GBP (.57−.60)/USD = −.03. Thus, the exposure coefficient is

31 2/3. This coefficient is denominated in USD and comparable to translation and transaction exposures. It corresponds to a regression coefficient as in Equation 1 in Chapter 3. The coefficient tells us that if the price of dollar increases by one pound, the non-financial cash flows increase by GBP 31 2/3. Thus, an appreciation of the dollar causes an increase in cash flows. In Chapter 6 we will see that the coefficient tells us exactly the required hedge contract to remove exposure, except that the hedge contract exposure has the opposite sign of the exposure.

The non-financial cash flow exposure is usually neglected by firms. It can be compared to the conventional transaction exposure. In the example the transaction exposure can be observed in Table 4.1. This exposure consists of the difference between USD Accounts Receivable and USD Accounts Payable. It can be assumed that at any time the firm has receivables equal to one period's export revenues. In this case these export-based receivables are USD (50 × 1.67) = USD 83.50. The payables would be one period's dollar purchases or USD 33 corresponding to COGS imported in Table 4.1. Thus, the transaction exposure is USD 50.5. Clearly, the transaction exposure underestimates the cash flow exposure for one period substantially.

So far the analysis in the example has followed a traditional partial approach. As mentioned, it does not take into account the fact that exchange rate changes often are caused by shocks that affect the firm through several channels. Exchange rate changes that are independent of other variables may occur over short periods such as weeks or months, but changes over longer periods are generally the result of macroeconomic shocks such as shifts in aggregate demand, fiscal or monetary policy, and in productivity shifts.

Assume for illustrative purposes that the 5% appreciation of the pound was due to a monetary expansion in the United States. This initially causes a 3% inflation in the United States and a 2% increase in the demand for all products in the United States.

Table 4.3 shows the effects on cash flows with the same constant mark-up pricing strategy. Costs of domestic inputs and wages remain unchanged per unit. Costs of foreign inputs in dollars rise 3% due to inflation and costs fall by 2% in pounds as compared with the base case, to 0.196 per unit. With the same relative mark-up, the unit price in pounds becomes GBP 0.933 while the U.S. competitors' price becomes GBP 0.981.

The price relative to competitors changes very little in this case because U.S. inflation and the exchange rate changes partially offset each other. If Japanese producers had dominated the market, their prices in the UK market would have fallen to GBP 0.95 since the inflation occurs only in the United States. Naturally, pricing strategy and demand sensitivity to competitors' prices become important in this case.

Considering only a 2% increase in sales volume in the United States, revenues become GBP 100.293 on 101 units. The cost of goods sold plus wages become GBP 60.17 and after-tax operating cash flows become GBP 20.06. Price and volume effects nearly offset each other as long as we assume that demand does not respond to the relative price change.

**Table 4.3 How the base case is affected by changes in the exhange rate, interest rate, inflation and demand.**

| Unit price: (10/6) x (COGS imported + COGS domestic + wages) | | |
|---|---|---|
| In the UK | GBP | 0.993 |
| In the US | USD | 1.74 |
| Sales | | |
| Domestic @ GBP 0.993: 50 units | GBP | 49.65 |
| Exports to US @ GBP 0.993: 51 units | GBP | 50.64 |
| | GBP | 100.29 |
| Production costs: 101 units | | |
| COGS domestic @ GBP 0.20 | GBP | 20.20 |
| COGS imported @ GBP 0.1957 | GBP | 19.77 |
| Wages @ GBP 0.20 | GBP | 20.20 |
| | GBP | 60.17 |
| After tax operating cash flow: 101 units | GBP | 20.06 |
| Depreciation tax shield | GBP | 10.00 |
| After tax non-financial cash-flows | GBP | 30.06 |
| Competitor's unit price | | |
| In the UK: 1.03 / 1.05 | GBP | 0.981 |
| In the US: 1.03 x 1.67 | USD | 1.72 |
| Cash flow effects of 1% fall in sales for 1% price differential | GBP | – 0.20 |
| Exposure coefficient: [(–.20 + 0.06)/–.03] = $4\frac{2}{3}$) | | |

Note: The pound (GBP) appreciates by 5%. US prices increase by 3% and US demand increases by 2%

Since the firm's product price changes less relative to that of its competitors in this case, the negative effect of using a mark-up strategy becomes less pronounced even if demand is sensitive to the firm's price relative to competitors' prices.

Although it is not quite appropriate in this case to consider the total change in cash flows as a consequence of exchange rate exposure, we can estimate the exchange rate exposure in the same way as in the previous case when the exchange rate was the only variable affecting cash flows. The exposure coefficient $4\frac{2}{3}$ is calculated as $((-.20 + .06)/-.03) = 4\frac{2}{3}$. This coefficient is smaller than in the previous case, but it incorporates exposure to inflation and aggregate demand.

A comparison of the cases in Tables 4.2 and 4.3 demonstrates that even though the exchange rate change was identical in the two cases, the cash flow effects are very different.

In Table 4.2 the mark-up pricing strategy would have increased exposure dramatically if foreign demand had been very price-sensitive, while in the second case the pricing strategy played a smaller role, since relative prices were affected to a lesser extent. If in the second case a producer from a third country had dominated in foreign or domestic markets, the firm's competitive positions would have been influenced more strongly by the shock.

Many macroeconomic scenarios can be analyzed in a similar fashion and in each case the effects would be different. Similarly, scenarios for alternative pricing strategies can be constructed and the cost structure varied.

If our hypothetical company had measured its competitive or business exposure to exchange rate changes alone, it might have performed the analysis in Table 4.2 and found that dollar debt would partially hedge its exposure. The remaining exchange rate exposure could have been reduced either by a change in pricing strategy or by taking positions in forward markets. However, if the exchange rate had changed as a result of the change in monetary policy abroad, then the firm's cash flows would have been affected very little. The hedging operations performed against exchange rate changes would have been counterproductive. No one in the company would necessarily have discovered this problem, since it was hedged against exchange rate changes and reporting systems do not capture the interdependence among different cash flow changes. The management might have been under the impression that they were managing exposure well in the United States.

This example tells us that pricing strategies, foreign competition, and price-quantity effects are vital elements of the exposure, and that pricing strategy can serve as a substitute for hedging in financial markets if the company has some leeway in its pricing decision. A company that can immediately pass on all macroeconomic disturbances to customers or to sub-contractors without any volume changes or cost effects is unexposed to macroeconomic uncertainty. However, to find such a company in the real world is not easy.

## 4.3 ESTIMATING CASH FLOW EXPOSURE

Exposure is now defined as the sensitivity of cash flows to changes in different macroeconomic variables. Since the net present value depends on future expected cash flows, it is simple–at least conceptually—to take the additional step of defining exposure in terms of the net present value.

In Chapter 3 we presented a measure of exchange rate exposure in terms of cash flow (X) sensitivity:

$$\frac{\text{Change in DC Cash flows}}{\text{One unit increase in units of DC/FC}} = \frac{\Delta X^{DC}}{\Delta DC/FC}$$

This measure (squared) multiplied by the variance of the exchange rate gives us the contribution of the exchange rate to the variance of cash flows. This exposure can be obtained by analyzing the relationship between cash flows and the exchange rate but, as noted, this measure has drawbacks under some circumstances:

- It is not independent of exposures to variables related to the exchange rate, such as interest and inflation rates; by disregarding the influence of these variables, the above exposure measure may provide a strongly misleading impression of exchange rate exposure.
- It may not be stable over time. If it is not, then exposure coefficients obtained from historical data may not provide a good guidance for the future.

The first point can be seen by considering a firm's other exposures. For example, if exchange rate exposure is defined as above, then the firm would measure interest rate exposure in a consistent manner by estimating

$$\frac{\text{Change in DC Cash flows}}{\text{One unit increase in the interest rate}} = \frac{\Delta X^{DC}}{\Delta i^{DC}}$$

If the exchange rate and the interest rate are correlated, as we would expect, then the two exposures would be partly overlapping. Similarly, if the firm measures inflation risk, and inflation and exchange rates are correlated, then inflation exposure and exchange rate exposure would be overlapping. To resolve this overlap problem, the exposure coefficients should be estimated under the assumption that the other variables are constant. Otherwise the exchange rate exposure includes interest rate and inflation exposures, but it would not be known how much. A *multiple regression* of the cash flows on the exchange rate and variables suspected to be correlated with this variable would resolve the problem of overlap. We return to this method for estimating exposure.

An important reason for instability in a simple exchange rate exposure measure is that exchange rate changes may, in reality, be real or nominal, and their causes may be real or monetary disturbances. In our terminology a real exchange rate change is a change in the exchange rate in excess of the inflation differential.[2] Real and monetary disturbances may affect both real exchange rates and inflation rates to different degrees. Thus, if cash flow exposure to only real exchange rates without considering inflation is estimated, then the exposure coefficient would capture the effects of inflation as well.

We suggest below two ways in which improved exposure measures can be obtained from historical data by means of regression analysis. In the first, exposure to exchange rates, interest rates, and inflation is estimated simultaneously. In the second, we discuss the possibility of estimating exposure to actual macroeconomic shocks in terms of exposure to monetary and fiscal variables.

## Exposure to market price variables

The firm trying to evaluate its exposures could measure the coefficients for a number of market price variables. Among such variables we include: price levels ($P$), exchange rates ($S$), interest rates ($i$), and firm- and industry-specific variables ($r$). The exposures would be identified by the following equation, which is described in both symbols and words:

| | |
|---|---|
| $\dfrac{X_t^{DC}}{P_t^{DC}} - E_{t-1}\left[\dfrac{X_t^{DC}}{P_t^{DC}}\right] =$ | Unanticipated change in real DC cash flows = |
| $a_1(P_t^{DC} - E_{t-1}\left[P_t^{DC}\right])$ | $a_1 \times$ (unanticipated DC inflation) |
| $+ a_2(P_t^{FC} - E_{t-1}\left[P_t^{FC}\right])$ | $+ a_2 \times$ (unanticipated FC inflation) |
| $+ a_3(S_t - E_{t-1}\left[S_t\right])$ | $+ a_3 \times$ (unanticipated exchange rate change) |
| $+ a_4(i_t^{DC} - E_{t-1}\left[i_t^{DC}\right])$ | $+ a_4 \times$ (unanticipated change in DC interest rate) |
| $+ a_5(i_t^{FC} - E_{t-1}\left[i_t^{FC}\right])$ | $+ a_5 \times$ (unanticipated change in FC interest rate) |
| $+ a_6(r_t - E_{t-1}\left[r_t\right])$ | $+ a_6 \times$ (unanticipated change in firm-specific relative price) |
| $+ \varepsilon_t$ | $+$ error term |

$$(9)$$

where

$X_1^{DC}$ = total cash flows in DC

$P_t^{DC}$ = domestic price level / (shareholder's habitat)

$E_{t-x}$ = expectations operator in period $t-1$

$P_t^{FC}$ = foreign price level

$S_t$ = exchange rate

$i_t^{DC}$ = domestic interest rate

$i_t^{FC}$ = foreign interest rate

$r_t$ = relative price (of relevance for firm's profitability)

$\varepsilon_t$ = error term

Equation 9 has the unanticipated change in real DC cash flows on the left-hand side, measured as actual minus expected real cash flows. Thus, nominal accounting data should be deflated with a price index if inflation is a serious concern. Expected cash flows would depend on the expected levels of the different variables incorporated in the firm's budget (if the budget is based on forecast of the market price variables). It must be said, as an understatement, that we have not generally found that budgets are carefully developed forecasts.

Looking in more detail at the exposure coefficients, the coefficient for the nominal exchange rate $(a_3)$ captures the effects of real changes, because the exposure to changes in price levels are captured separately in the coefficients for the domestic and foreign price levels $(a_1$ and $a_2)$. It is important also to distinguish between the impact of those relative price changes that are *independent* of exchange rates and inflation, and those that occur in a macroeconomic adjustment causing exchange rate, interest rate, and price level changes. The former impact is captured by the coefficient for a relative price $(a_6)$ and the latter by the coefficients for macroeconomic price variables $(a_1$ through $a_5)$. Without using this kind of approach to measuring exposure, a firm could easily be misled by a change in its output price, believing the source to be a fundamental change in business conditions rather than a temporary effect of macroeconomic disturbances.

Each $a$ coefficient is an exposure measure, that is, a sensitivity measure to each price variable *holding other variables constant*. In general, several of the price variables change at the same time in response to macroeconomic shocks. The total effect of, for example, a fiscal policy disturbance is, therefore, the sum of the effects of changes in price variables caused by the disturbance. We illustrate this idea in the Volvo Cars case presented in Chapter 5 and in the Electrolux case in Chapter 9.

One method of estimating all the exposure coefficients is to employ multiple regression analysis, using time series of all the variables in Equation 9. If regression analysis cannot be conducted, then it becomes necessary to form judgment based on an understanding of macroeconomic relationships and the cash flow effects of changes in different variables. In Oxelheim and Wihlborg (1987) scenario approaches to measuring exposure are presented as an alternative to the regression approach. Conceptually, the coefficients of the multiple regression provide the information we are looking for in scenario analysis as well.

Here we illustrate the potential result of an estimation of Equation 9 and interpret the exposure measures. In Equation 9 all variables are levels, but we could equally well express all variables as either changes or rates of change.

Equation 10 shows the percentage change ($\Delta$) in the DC purchasing power of cash flows from a 1% unanticipated change in each of the market price variables on the right-hand side, holding the other variables constant.

The left-hand side in Equation 10 is the actual change in real cash flows minus the expected change. The figure for the last term must be obtained from budgets. Next, we see that a 1% unanticipated change in the DC

| | |
|---|---|
| $\Delta\dfrac{X_t^{DC}}{P_t^{DC}} - E_{t-1}\Delta\left[\dfrac{X_t^{DC}}{P_t^{DC}}\right] =$ | Unanticipated percentage change in real DC cash flows = |
| $-0.1(\Delta P_t^{DC} - E_{t-1}\left[\Delta P_t^{DC}\right])$ | $-0.1 \times$ (Unanticipated DC inflation in percent) |
| $+0(\Delta P_t^{FC} - E_{t-1}\left[\Delta P_t^{FC}\right])$ | $+0 \times$ (Unanticipated FC inflation in percent) |
| $-0.5(\Delta S_t - E_{t-1}\left[\Delta S_t\right])$ | $-0.5 \times$ (Unanticipated exchange rate change in percent) |
| $-0.005(\Delta i_t^{DC} - E_{t-1}\left[\Delta i_t^{DC}\right])$ | $-0.005 \times$ (Unanticipated percentage change in the DC interest rate) |
| $+0(\Delta i_t^{FC} - E_{t-1}\left[\Delta i_t^{FC}\right])$ | $+0 \times$ (Unanticipated percentage change in the FC interest rate) |
| $+0.6(\Delta r_t - E_{t-1}\left[\Delta r_t\right])$ | $+0.6 \times$ (Unanticipated percentage change in the firm-specific relative price) |

$$(10)$$

price level (inflation) leads to a 0.1% fall in real cash flows. Real cash flows are insensitive to changes in the foreign price level and the foreign interest rate, while a 1% unanticipated depreciation of the local currency causes a 0.5% drop in real cash flows, holding other variables constant. A 1% unanticipated DC interest rate change (i.e., from 10% to 10.1%) causes a 0.005% fall in real cash flows. The firm-specific relative price $r$ may be captured by the firm's output prices relative to a price index. A 1% increase in this ratio induces an increase of 0.6% in real cash flows.

To obtain the magnitude in dollar terms we need to know the *level* of expected cash flows. Assume this is USD 30 million as in Table 4.4. Then we can calculate cash flow effects in DC as in the table. Examples of changes that would cause effects of the kind described are given in the right-hand column. It is important to note that all exposure coefficients are "clean," that is, they refer to the sensitivity of real cash flows to changes in each variable, while other variables are held constant. For example, the exchange rate coefficient indicates the effect of an exchange rate change at a constant domestic price level, a constant domestic interest rate, and a constant relative price. The relative price coefficient is the sensitivity of cash flows to purely commercial disturbances in the relative price.

Table 4.4 Cash flow effects in million DC of a 1% (unanticipated) change in each market price variable, holding other variables constant. Expected real cash flows are USD 30 million.

| | Exposure coefficient (%) | Real DC effect (million) | Example |
|---|---|---|---|
| Domestic price level | − 0.1 | − 0.03 | Consumer price index (CPI) goes from 100 to 101 (unanticipated) or a rise in inflation from 10% to 11% |
| Foreign price level | 0 | 0 | |
| Exchange rate | − 0.5 | − 0.15 | DC/FC from DC2 to DC2.02 |
| Domestic interest rate | − 0.005 | − 0.0015 | Interest rate from 10% to 10.1% |
| Foreign interest rate | 0 | 0 | |
| Relative price | 0.6 | 0.18 | Output price index relative to CPI increases from 1 to 1.01 |

Consider as an illustration that an increase in the DC fiscal deficit causes a 3% appreciation and a 10% (one percentage point) increase in the DC interest rate. In this case the total effect of the unexpected fiscal policy shift to the company in our example is a [−3 × (−0.5) + 10 × (−0.005)] = +1.45% change in real cash flows. In DC terms this amounts to 0.435 million.

## Exposure to macro policy changes

Real exchange rate changes may occur for a number of reasons. An unanticipated monetary disturbance such as a money supply increase would, according to many macroeconomic models, lead to an immediate real depreciation, a fall in the interest rate, and an *increase* in the demand for goods. A fiscal contraction—an aggregate real disturbance—on the other hand, could lead to a real depreciation, a fall in the interest rate, and a *decrease* in the demand for goods.

These considerations suggest that macroeconomic exposures could be expressed as sensitivities of cash flows to macro policy changes. In terms of Figure 1.1, we are now defining exposures to changes in the policy variables in column 3 as opposed to exposures to market price variables in column 4. We may, for example, define exposures as the coefficients $b_1$ to $b_5$ in Equation 11, where the macroeconomic disturbances include only domestic and foreign money supply (M) and domestic and foreign fiscal (D) shocks. Other formulations can be tested based on the analyst's vision of what constitutes fundamental policy responses to macroeconomic shocks.

$$
\begin{array}{l|l}
\Delta\dfrac{X_t^{DC}}{P_t^{DC}} - E_{t-1}\Delta\left[\dfrac{X_t^{DC}}{P_t^{DC}}\right] = & \text{Unanticipated change in real DC} \\
& \text{cash flows} = \\[2mm]
b_1\left(M_t^{DC} - E_{t-1}\left[M_t^{DC}\right]\right) & b_1\times(\text{unanticipated change in DC} \\
& \qquad \text{money supply}) \\[2mm]
+ b_2\left(M_t^{FC} - E_{t-1}\left[M_t^{FC}\right]\right) & + b_2\times(\text{unanticipated change in FC} \\
& \qquad \text{money supply}) \\[2mm]
+ b_3\left(D_t^{DC} - E_{t-1}\left[D_t^{DC}\right]\right) & + b_3\times(\text{unanticipated change in the} \\
& \qquad \text{DC fiscal deficit}) \\[2mm]
+ b_4\left(D_t^{FC} - E_{t-1}\left[D_t^{FC}\right]\right) & + b_4\times(\text{unanticipated change in the} \\
& \qquad \text{FC fiscal deficit}) \\[2mm]
+ b_5\left(r_t - E_{t-1}\left[r_t\right]\right) & + b_5\times(\text{unanticipated change in} \\
& \qquad \text{firm-specific relative price}) \\[2mm]
+ \varepsilon_t & + \text{error term}
\end{array}
$$

$$(11)$$

where

$$
\begin{aligned}
M^{DC}, M^{FC} &= \text{the money supply domestically and} \\
&\quad \text{in the foreign country(ies), respectively} \\
D^{DC}, D^{FC} &= \text{the budget deficit domestically and} \\
&\quad \text{in the foreign country(ies), respectively} \\
r_t &= \text{relative price(s) of relevance for} \\
&\quad \text{firm's profitability} \\
\varepsilon_t &= \text{error term}
\end{aligned}
$$

Each exposure coefficient represents the unanticipated change in cash flows caused by a one unit unanticipated change in the disturbance, holding other variables constant.

If macroeconomic shocks can be identified, then the exposure coefficients for policy changes would provide information about the vulnerability of the firm to such shocks. Various macroeconomic scenarios could be evaluated using the coefficients $b_1$ through $b_4$. The exposures to these macroeconomic shocks would incorporate the exposures to the market price variables discussed above to the extent that fluctuations in these variables are explained by macroeconomic shocks.

It is possible that exchange rates, interest rates, and inflation rates change without clearly depending on changes in policy variables. For example, exchange rates and interest rates react quickly to changes in expectations about future events. Thus, the "policy coefficients" may have to be complemented with exposure coefficients for, for example, exchange rates, to capture exchange rate exposure over and above that incorporated in the exposures to monetary and fiscal policy changes.

## Market price exposure and macro policy exposure compared

Which formulation for macroeconomic exposure is preferable: Equation 9, focusing on exposures to market price variables, or Equation 11, focusing on exposure to macro policy changes? The answer to this question depends on the purpose of the attempt to estimate exposures, and on the observability of the exposure variables.

If the purpose of the exposure analysis is to obtain a measure of performance in hindsight, independent of events in the macroeconomic environment (with the ultimate purpose of evaluating management performance), then it is relatively important to use a formulation with high explanatory power. It is of less concern whether exactly the same relationship applies in the future, and whether the exposure variables are observed immediately when shocks occur.

However, if the objective of the exposure analysis is risk management, then it is important that sources of exposures, or risk factors, in the macroeconomic environment are observable at the time changes occur. It is also desirable that the risk factors can be linked to risk management instruments. Furthermore, for risk management purposes the exposure coefficients should be forward-looking. In other words, if exposures are identified using historical data, then the same exposure relations should be valid for the time horizon of the risk management program. One particular problem to take into account is that disturbances are sometimes temporary, sometimes permanent, and the exposure coefficient would be expected to differ in the two cases. This issue is discussed in the next subsection.

The great advantage of market price variables—exchange rates, interest rates, and prices—is that they are observable at all times. The exception is the general price level and inflation. There is some lag before data on average price levels are obtainable but most prices of relevance for the firm, when evaluating the real impact of exchange rate changes, are observable. Macro policy changes such as, for example, money supply changes are not observable until data have been collected and published by national statistics offices. Even then it is notoriously difficult to know the exact source of changes in market price variables. For these reasons it is likely that management responds mostly to market price variables when making decisions about production, pricing, and sales in the belief or hope that changes in the market price variables bear a systematic relation to actual shocks.

An additional advantage with market price variables in risk management is that financial hedge instruments such as forwards and options are defined in terms of exchange rates, interest rates, and commodity prices. In some countries there are financial instruments valued in real terms, that is, their nominal values are linked to changes in the price level.

The above considerations imply that there is a strong case for measuring macroeconomic exposure to market price variables as in Equations 9 and 10. This does not mean that measuring exposure to macro policy variables is without value. If the primary focus of risk management is on worst-case scenarios, then it may be advantageous to analyse various macroeconomic scenarios as defined by the actual policy changes that may occur. Exposure coefficients for macro policy changes of different types would be useful inputs for such scenario analysis.

As noted above, the main objective of measuring exposure could be to evaluate management performance after correcting for the impact on profits and values of macroeconomic events beyond the control of management. Also for this purpose, the exposures to macro policy changes could be useful.

In conclusion, for risk management there are clear advantages of using coefficients of exposure to market price variables like exchange rates and interest rates. However, there are circumstances when the coefficients of exposure to macro policy changes are useful.

### Temporary versus permanent shocks

Exchange rate changes, interest rate changes, and inflation, as well as changes in the money supply and other variables, can be expected to be either temporary or permanent. If the changes are expected to be temporary, then current changes cause expectations about reversals and the firm is likely to respond less than if current changes are expected to be irreversible.

The distinction between these two cases can be captured in the exposure coefficient equations by adding terms for expected changes.[3] For example, the forward premium in each period can be added to the list of right-hand-side variables in Equation 9. Using the forward premium as a measure of exchange rate expectations, this variable gains significance if management reacts differently to expected temporary and permanent shocks.

### 4.4 DECOMPOSING CASH FLOW EXPOSURE

To implement the exposure analysis, a decision must be made regarding the *level of aggregation* of cash flows. Total cash flows evaluated after tax may consist of flows from a number of products as well as from several subsidiaries in different countries. Total cash flows include both operations cash flows generated by real assets (plant and equipment), and cash flows related to the financing of the firm. Financial cash flows are typically quite adjustable in terms of both currency denomination and timing. By "adjustable" we mean that the costs of changing currency denominations and maturity structures are low.

The adjustability of commercial cash flows is low. Most firms commit substantial resources to a particular market according to product and country. The responsiveness of prices to exchange rate changes and other macroeconomic events is often determined by competitive considerations. For these reasons, a suitable starting point for exposure management is to estimate the exposure of commercial cash flows. Given the coefficients of exposure to exchange rates, interest rates, and inflation, the financial structure can then be adjusted in terms of currency and maturity structures to obtain the desired exposure of total cash flows. If the cost of adjusting the structure of liabilities is high in the short run, then financial derivatives can be used.

This reasoning does not imply that commercial cash flows should never be touched for purposes of risk management. There are, for example, firms with substantial flexibility in terms of, let us say, pricing behavior and choice of supplies. In such cases, pricing may be considered risk management tools. Flexibility in business operations was defined as real options in Chapter 2. The firm can invest in such options, and their existence can affect exposure coefficients. Their role in risk management is discussed in Chapter 8.

Naturally, commercial cash flows can be decomposed further by subsidiary, product group, country, and so on. In general, commercial cash flow exposures need to be estimated in such a way that there is stability over time in the exposure measures. For example, if the firm has made an acquisition recently or added or deducted a product group, then these changes must be reflected in the decomposition of cash flows. The changes may also be captured by adding so-called dummy variables on the right-hand side of Equations 9–11.

## 4.5  EXPOSURE COEFFICIENTS AND SIZES OF SHOCKS

Can it be assumed that the exposure coefficients measured by scenario analysis and regression analysis are independent of the magnitude of shocks? The answer is no if the firm has invested in flexibility. The flexibility may be the result of price adjustments or the effects of switched sales and purchases. We discuss in Chapter 9 that flexibility kicks in when the exchange rate reaches specific trigger points. At these points the exchange rate has moved sufficiently for it to be profitable to adjust the price, to switch supplier or to switch sales among countries. If the firm makes any of these adjustments the sensitivity of cash flows declines. In other words, the exposure coefficient declines. We will discuss implications of such nonlinear relationships between cash flows and exchange rates in Chapter 9.

## 4.6  THE SHARE PRICE AND MACROECONOMIC FLUCTUATIONS

The stock-market value of a firm is generally considered to be a measure of the economic value of a firm's assets minus the value of debt. Thus for individual firms, exposure can be analyzed by estimating the relationship between stock prices and macroeconomic fluctuations.[4]

There are many studies of the effects of exchange rate changes on stock returns.[5] Most studies indicate that stock-market effects of contemporaneous exchange rate changes at the firm level tend to be weak for most firms, even if they are large exporting firms (see Jorion, 1990; Amihud, 1993, and Bartov and Bodnar, 1994). There are exceptions, however, even in a country as large as the United States. In general, the results are sensitive to the inclusion of other macroeconomic variables, as well as to the estimation period. In studies with the overall stock-market return included, the exchange rate has very little power to explain fluctuations in share prices even for firms that have substantial exposure. This finding indicates that in the investors' perspective exchange rate risk is diversifiable in many countries.[6]

One controversial result found in the literature is that lagged exchange rate changes affect stock-market returns for individual firms (see Bartov and Bodnar, 1994). This is an indication of market inefficiency. If this result holds up to further scrutiny, then it would indicate that stock-market valuation is not a proper indicator of economic value. Then macroeconomic exposure is not correctly evaluated by an analysis of the stock-market value effects of macroeconomic price variables.

A serious drawback of using stock-market values for exposure analysis is that these values are not independent of financial decisions and hedging decisions. In other words, the exposure of a firm's stock-market value does not reflect the commercial exposure of the firm. Stock-market values can nevertheless be used for analysis of the exposure of the firm's cash flow-generating assets if values and returns are corrected for the effects on financial positions in different currencies, and for the effects of interest rate changes on financial positions with different maturities. With knowledge of the currency composition and the maturity structure of financial assets and liabilities, capital gains and losses caused by exchange rate changes, interest rate changes, and inflation can be estimated. These capital gains and losses can be deduced from changes in stock-market values. Changes in the market value of the assets generating commercial cash flows are thereby obtained. Annual reports do not generally provide sufficient information to adjust stock market values this way (see Chapter 11). The information about financial positions is obviously available inside firms, however.

## 4.7 CONCLUDING REMARKS ON THE COMPREHENSIVE APPROACH

Exposure may be defined in terms of market price variables, such as exchange rates, interest rates and prices, or in terms of macro policy changes. The advantage of one approach over the other depends upon the use of the exposure coefficients. For risk management, exposures to market price variables are generally preferable because these variables are directly observable and because of the existence of financial instruments defined in terms of these variables. The exposure coefficients for macro policy changes may be useful for scenario analysis, however.

To obtain stable coefficients, we suggest that before the estimation procedure is started, cash flows should be disaggregated by, for example, product, subsidiary, and country. For the purposes of risk management, commercial cash flows that are not easily adjustable in the short term should be distinguished from financial cash flows. Then, the exposure of commercial cash flows can be estimated separately. Financial positions can thereafter be adjusted until the desired exposure for total cash flows is obtained.

The approach we have suggested assumes that relevant historical data are available. When coefficients are estimated for risk management purposes, "yesterday's" company should represent "tomorrow's" company in major respects. In practice, there will sometimes be problems in the estimation of coefficients when running regression models. These problems are obvious in the case of a company that has just started its business or of a company that recently has entirely changed its business. The existence of estimation problems does not imply that the firm must revert to traditional exposure measures. The coefficients can be assessed and updated by means of information available internally. Scenario analysis can be very useful for this purpose.

## NOTES

1 The discussion started in the mid-1980s. See Lessard and Lightstone (1986). For the multivariate approach, see Oxelheim and Wihlborg (1987).
2 A real exchange rate change implies that there is a change in the relative price between countries' bundles of goods. Formally:

$$S_t / S_{t-1} \equiv [(P_t^{DC} / P_{t-1}^{DC})/(P_t^{FC} / P_{t-1}^{FC})] \times (u_t / u_{t-1})$$

where $S_t$ is DC per unit of FC, $P_t^{DC}$ and $P_t^{FC}$ are the domestic and the foreign price levels, respectively, and $u_t$ is the deviation from PPP—the real exchange rate.
3 Jorion (1990) suggests that current exchange rate expectations should be included when analyzing exchange rate exposure coefficients. Note that interest rates include similar information.
4 Campbell (1987) and Solnik (1984) emphasize the presumed negative relationship between interest rate and stock-market prices, whereas Fama and Schwert (1977) analyze the influences of inflation. Others, such as Fama (1981), Geske and Roll (1983), Solnik (1983), Keim and Stambaugh (1986), and Pindyck (1988), take into account the links between interest rates, inflation, real activitiy, and stock-market returns.
5 See, for example, Bhandari and Genberg (1989), Goodwin et al. (1989), and Ibrahimi et al. (1995). The three papers find that the stock market effects of real exchange rate changes are not stable over time.
6 There is a literature on the pricing of exchange rate risk in stock markets. Most often this literature indicates that exchange rate risk is not priced in stock-markets, although the result is controverisal; see Adler and Simon (1986), Jorion (1991), and Dumas and Solnik (1995).

# Chapter 5

# Measuring Macroeconomic Exposure:
# The Case of Volvo Cars

## 5.1 INTRODUCTION

In the previous chapter we defined macroeconomic exposure as a group of coefficients that register the sensitivity of cash flows or value to either (a) market price variables such as exchange rates and interest rates, or (b) macro policy changes such as monetary and fiscal policy shifts. For risk management purposes we argued in favor of market price variables that are easily observable and of particular significance to the firm. A major advantage of this view is that it captures the exposure to each individual variable while recognizing that they are often related. As will be shown below, the exposure coefficients jointly allow the estimation of the exposure to various macroeconomic disturbances that simultaneously affect exchange rates, interest rates, inflation rates, as well as firm-specific prices.

In this chapter we discuss how the exposure coefficients can be measured using the statistical method of multiple regression analysis and illustrate how the coefficients can be used.[1] The basic inputs in an analysis of exposure to cash flows are time series of monthly or quarterly observations of (a) different types of cash flows, and (b) a group of macroeconomic and firm-specific variables that are capable of explaining the changes in cash flows over time. If such time series cannot be created, then exposures must be measured by means of scenario analyses.

We emphasize here issues of implementation when using the seemingly simple multiple regression method to measure exposures. Regression coefficients are exposure or sensitivity coefficients. They can easily be translated into information about required hedging operations in financial markets or about the currency composition of liabilities. They can also be used as input for the determination of a pricing strategy, that is, as a rule for the response of price to changes in exchange rates and other variables.

Finally, the exposure coefficients can be used to separate the effects on firm performance of macroeconomic variables (i.e., beyond management control) from effects of changes in competitive conditions that are susceptible to influence by management. To specify regression equations, it is necessary for management to think about the role of exposure management within the overall objective of the firm, and about the relevant sources of information for identifying exposure that are more complete than conventional financial accounting data. In other words, it is necessary to carefully consider what the exposure coefficients should show.

Regression coefficients as exposure measures are presented in Section 5.2. Possible choices and specifications of dependent and independent variables are discussed and put into the context of the firm's objective in Sections 5.3 and 5.4. A case study of Volvo Cars is presented in Section 5.5. Regression results, interpretations and the practical uses of coefficients are discussed and illustrated in Section 5.6, where we show how the coefficients can be used to analyze macroeconomic scenarios and also the cash flow effects of inflation under different exchange rate systems. We also consider capital gains and losses on long-term liabilities in different currency denominations in the picture of exposure. In Section 5.7 we show how Volvo Cars' cash flows might have developed over time had the firm used estimated coefficients for forward-looking risk management. Section 5.8 provides concluding remarks.

## 5.2  EXPOSURE COEFFICIENTS

Regression analysis of time series data for cash flows in any domestic currency on exchange rates, interest rates, inflation, and other macroeconomic variables, as well as on firm- or industry-specific variables, enables management to identify the exposure coefficients in an equation of the following type:

| | |
|---|---|
| $(CF_t^{SEK} / P_t^{SEK}) =$ | (Real cash flows in period $t$) = |
| $A_0$ | constant |
| $+A_1(SEK/FC)_{t-i}$ | $+A_1$ (exchange rates in period $t-i$) |
| $+A_m V_{t-i}$ | $+A_m$ (a group of other macroeconomic price variables in period $t-i$) |
| $+A_z Z_{t-i}$ | $+A_z$ (a group of firm-spefic variables in period $t-i$) |
| $+\varepsilon_t$ | +error term |

$$(12)$$

where

$CF_t^{SEK}$ = nominal cash flows during period t in SEK
$P_t^{SEK}$ = price level in Sweden in period $t$
$(SEK/FC)_{t-i}$ = vector of exchange rates in period $t - i$
          (period averages)
$V_{t-i}$ = vector of other macroeconomic variables in period $t - i$
          (period averages)
$Z_{t-i}$ = vector of firm- and industry-specific disturbances
$A_1, A_m$ = vectors of coefficients as measures of exchange rate
          and other macroeconomic exposures
$A_z$ = vector of coefficients for variables in Z
$\varepsilon_t$ = error term

Any delayed effects of change in exchange rates and other variables can be discovered by using lagged independent variables. If there are no lags, $i$ is zero in Equation 12. The exact specification of Equation 12 depends upon econometric considerations, the firm's exposure, management objectives and the observability of macroeconomic disturbances at the time management's decisions are made with respect to, for example, hedging. These issues are discussed in Section 5.3.

It is important for management to understand exactly how exposure coefficients are interpreted. The way the equation above is written, any $A_1$ coefficient tells the analyst about the change in a period's cash flows in real SEK when there is a one unit (SEK 1) change in the price of a foreign currency (FC) from one period to another, while other variables in the equation remain constant. Considering that we later in this chapter will be using a Swedish company as case company, we use SEK as domestic currency (DC).

Regressions on exchange rates alone do not take into account the fact that the several macroeconomic price variables to which a firm is exposed are often correlated when they adjust simultaneously to macroeconomic shocks. If two variables are highly correlated, then multicollinearity arises and, in extreme cases, none of the coefficients can be identified. In sum, the two variables compete in expressing the same information. A further elaboration would be, for example, if the local currency always appreciated when the interest rate rose; then either the exchange rate or the interest rate coefficient should be included in the estimation procedure. One variable is also sufficient for risk management in this case because hedging exchange rate risk would be the same as hedging interest rate risk.

## 5.3 THE CHOICE OF DEPENDENT VARIABLE

### The objective of the firm

Cash flows, economic value, and book value are among the possible dependent variables in a regression on macroeconomic variables. The choice of which to use depends on the firm's overall objective and sub-objective for exposure management. This choice was discussed in Chapter 2, and we return to it in Chapter 8.

It suffices to note that management's choice must depend upon the success measure it deems most useful, its attitude toward uncertainty about this measure, and its preferred time horizon. Some firms are more concerned with market share or volume of output or sales simply because variability in these causes labor adjustment costs. It is possible that such a firm is risk-neutral with respect to total cash flows while being willing to incur costs to reduce variability in employment. Exposure management for such a firm would obviously not include financial hedging but would focus on pricing, marketing, or geographical sales strategies. The time horizon of exposure management would be reflected in the frequency of observations. We return to this issue when discussing independent variables.

## Adjustability of investments, cash flows, and budget periods

A firm's concern for risk management begins at the investment stage. If a planned investment has not been carried out, then the firm has "a timing option" that can be exercised after some resolution of uncertainty. This timing option is more valuable if uncertainty about important determinants of performance is high. The exposure coefficients for such variables are therefore already of importance at the planning stage of an investment when no historical data for a project exists. It is possible, however, that the firm has experience with similar projects or that data can be obtained about the performance of other firms that have similar projects. In the latter case the analysis may have to be carried out with such publicly available information as stock-market values or cash flow estimates based on data in annual reports.

Once investment decisions are made, the firm is committed to generate cash flows from the investment. Still, it may be possible to vary such elements as the marketing and sales efforts among national markets, the price and output responses to changes in economic conditions, and/or aspects of the financial structure (see Chapter 8). Market conditions force firms to specify pricing strategies. These strategies are often relatively long-term and costly commitments. The currency denomination and other aspects of long-term liabilities could similarly be costly to adjust, although the development of swap markets has created tremendous flexibility in the financial structure. The most adjustable financial positions are obviously short-term loans and investments, and positions taken in forward, futures, and options markets.

The choice of dependent variable for which sensitivity coefficients are estimated should be based on the firm's costs of adjusting positions and strategies. It is common in the financial management literature to assume that the financial positions are adjustable, but that the firm is committed on the commercial side to markets and suppliers, as well as to pricing responses to changes in economic conditions. If so, the objective is to estimate the sensitivity of real commercial cash flows to changes in macro-economic variables. The estimated coefficients can then be used to determine the more adjustable financial positions that would reduce or eliminate the commercial exposure.

For the purpose of estimating commercial exposure, the specification of the regression should be based on the firm's budget periods and on its ability to adjust operational decisions. Even a highly flexible firm would not be able to substantially adjust its budgets for operational expenses from one quarter to another in response to, for example, exchange rate changes. Financial positions, on the other hand, can be used to hedge uncertainty on a quarterly basis. In this case, the dependent variable could be quarterly cash flows.

For risk management purposes, it is the deviations from the budget in a previous quarter that are of concern, assuming that budget figures properly represent expected cash flows. If so, the independent variables in Equation 12 would refer to the unanticipated part of the exchange rate, the interest rate, and other variables relative to anticipations included in the budget.

A firm with operations that are less flexible may consider important operational decisions non-adjustable for a year and budget every quarter for the corresponding quarter one year into the future. To be most informative in this case, the exposure coefficients ($A_1$ and $A_m$ in Equation 12) could be made to refer to the sensitivity of quarterly cash flows with respect to unanticipated changes in right-hand-side variables relative to the budget one year earlier.

## Levels or rates of change

When specifying a regression equation it is necessary to decide whether variables should be measured in levels or rates of change. From an informational point of view, the choice is irrelevant. Information from a regression in one dimension is easily recalculated in another dimension. Analysis of autocorrelation in the error term and stationarity of variables are what determine the appropriate dimension. (A stationary variable fluctuates around a constant value.) If cash flows are increasing over time, then either the rate of change or the change may be stationary. In general, it is desirable to estimate exposure coefficients for stationary dependent and independent variables. It may also be necessary to specify variables in log form, squared, or otherwise adjusted.

## Level of aggregation and coefficient stability

It is possible to analyze exposure for either aggregated cash flows (for a whole firm), or for parts of cash flows, for example, for a product or a market. Regression coefficients should offer information for decision-making. Therefore, the coefficients should be stable and not depend much on the period over which they are estimated. One source of instability of coefficients is possible changes in the product or in the market mix of the firms.

A large acquisition, new competitors, and the release of new products on the market are examples of structural changes that could influence the sensitivity coefficients substantially and therefore the approach to estimating exposures.

A second source of instability in coefficients is changes in governments' policy regimes with respect to exchange rates and interest rates. If, for example, the price of an important currency is pegged in some years and floating during others, then the firm is exposed to a kind of political risk. The firm's response to specific exchange rate changes, as well as the existence of links between the exchange rate and general economic conditions, is likely to be influenced by regime shifts. A 1% depreciation is likely to have a very different impact during a floating period than it would during a period of exchange rate realignment that followed a long period of pegging. Interest rate exposure may also vary over time. This implies that coefficient instability may remain even if all important determinants of cash flows are taken into account. In this case the analyst must complement exposure measures with knowledge about the sources of instability. It is important to remember that uncertainty about the correct exposure is no reason to refrain from measuring exposure. Risk management strategies can be adjusted depending on the degree of uncertainty about coefficients (see Chapter 6).

The analyst may face a dilemma seeking to obtain data for as long period as possible in order to increase the reliability of results, because the longer the period, the less likely it is that the structural characteristics of both the firm and the macro economy have remained unchanged. Thus, it is often necessary to break down cash flows into structurally stable parts of the firm, and to estimate regression for both subsections and subperiods. The estimated coefficients can then be aggregated using knowledge of the firm's current structure and applied currently with consideration of changes in the macroeconomic policy regime.

## 5.4  THE CHOICE OF INDEPENDENT VARIABLES AND TIME HORIZON

### The choice of market price variables

Changes in exchange rates, interest rates, and other price variables generally depend on policy or non-policy shocks in monetary conditions, fiscal policies, and business cycle and industry-specific conditions. The choice of independent variables depends naturally on the purpose of the exercise, but there are econometric considerations as well. If the purpose is to explain as much variability as possible, then the analyst would want to use any combination of relevant *a priori* determined variables that might give a high explanatory value.

The most common purpose for running a regression analysis is to identify exposure coefficients for a group of variables so that management can observe and use them as inputs for various decisions. As noted, exchange rates, interest rates, and other price variables are easily observable. Considering theories of exchange rate and interest rate determination, exchange rates, domestic and foreign interest rates, and domestic and foreign price levels seem *a priori* to be the most important price variables.

It is also necessary to consider variables capturing industry- and firm-specific conditions in markets in the group $X_t$ in Equation 12. Such conditions may be correlated with macroeconomic variables and lead the analyst to misjudge the impact of macro shocks, as well as of firm- and industry-specific shocks.

Some easily observable measures of industry- and firm-specific conditions are relative product prices. These are likely to depend both on macroeconomic conditions and on market conditions that affect output. In combination with macroeconomic variables, the coefficients for firm- and industry-specific conditions allow the analyst to evaluate management's ability to adjust to industry- and firm-specific conditions without contamination from macroeconomic conditions.

### The role of lags

It was noted above that if the firm is not able to adjust its commercial operations to changes in macroeconomic conditions within, for example, a year, then the exposure can be measured as changes in cash flows over one year in response to changes in exchange rates over the same period. The same information can be obtained if variables are specified over shorter time periods and lags of independent variables are included. For example, half-yearly cash flows can be specified as depending on macroeconomic variables in the same and in the previous half year (this is shown in Box 6.3). With this specification the sensitivity of cash flows in the current period to macro variables in the current and the previous periods is obtained. This information enables management to hedge exposure every six months with a one-year time horizon.

Lagged independent variables can be introduced to capture expectations as well. If the regression equation is specified as in Equation 12 without a distinction being made between anticipated and unanticipated changes, then lagged independent variables could be introduced to capture expectations. Expectations about, for example, inflation in a period are then assumed to be dependent on inflation in the previous periods. Lacking direct observations of expectations, this assumption is often both reasonable and practicable.

### 5.5 VOLVO CARS

In 1927—the year when Ford ceased production of the T-model after selling 15 million cars—the first Volvo car left the factory in Gothenburg (Volvo is Latin for "I roll"). Assar Gabrielsson, a former director of SKF, the Swedish ball and roller bearing multinational, was the force behind the creation of Volvo. SKF provided financial support for Assar Gabrielsson's venture.

During the first three years, 996 cars were produced, compared to around 400,000 cars per year in 1995. Initially there were two models, compared to nine models that year. The first step towards becoming a multinational was taken in 1928 when a subsidiary was established in Finland. The first foreign assembly plant opened in Halifax, Canada, in 1963. This factory was followed by an assembly plant in Gent, Belgium, in 1965, and a small plant in Malaysia in 1968. In 1972, Volvo acquired 33% of the failing DAF's car operations in The Netherlands. The plant in Gent was in 1995 comparable in size to the one in Gothenburg. In The Netherlands, Volvo and Mitsubishi formed a joint venture with the Dutch government in 1991, NedCar, replacing Volvo's subsidiary in the country.

The American market was approached in 1955 with the PV444, and in 1973 the United States became the largest market for Volvo Cars. Volvo was the fourth largest imported brand at the time.

Volvo's niche as a prestige family car characterized by high safety standards is well established. The cars and the company have received many international awards for safety features and safety work. The cars were the first on the market with three point safety belts as standard equipment.

Until the 1970s, Volvo focused on cars, trucks, and buses. After starting truck production in 1928, the production of trucks and buses actually exceeded the production of cars during the first decades. In the 1970s and the 1980s, the company gradually developed into a conglomerate incorporating pharmaceuticals, airplane engines, sports equipment, food products and financial services.

After an aborted alliance and an attempted merger with Renault, the strategy was reassessed in 1993. The planned merger was rejected by the shareholders with the result that the leadership of the company was changed. A divestment process was initiated and by 1996 Volvo was again focusing on transport equipment.

With its high dependence on export, an important question for Volvo on the "agenda year 2000" was the location of production sites. An assembly plant in the United States was seriously considered. If that became a reality, Volvo would follow major competitors like BMW and Mercedes. For Volvo, it was the second time that assembly in the U.S.A was considered.

Volvo faced problems similar to those of SAAB, the other Swedish producer of prestige cars. Although Volvo is larger than SAAB, there were doubts that Volvo would be able to manage the larger development costs for new models on its own. SAAB's solution was to become a part of General Motors, who purchased 50% of SAAB's car division in 1990 and later the remaining 50%. Volvo's strategy was to develop alliances like the one with Mitsubishi in the Dutch joint venture. However, in 1999, Volvo Cars was acquired by Ford.

1989, the last year of our data period, one-third of the employees of AB Volvo were involved in car production within the separate subsidiary, Volvo Cars. Total car production in 1989 was 410,000 cars of which 180,000 were produced in Sweden, 91,000 in Belgium, 115,000 in The Netherlands, and 14,000 elsewhere.

The distribution of sales (number of cars) in 1989 was the following:

| | |
|---|---|
| Sweden | 66,600 |
| North America | 108,900 |
| Great Britain | 81,700 |
| Rest of Europe | 76,200 |
| Other markets | 97,000 |

On the input side, Germany and the countries with major production units dominated as suppliers.

As noted, the company competes mainly in the market for relatively prestigious and expensive cars, comparable in price to the low end of BMW and Mercedes. Major competitors during the 1980s were the above-mentioned cars, as well as Audi from Germany, and the high end of Japanese and American cars. During the first years of the 1990s the Japanese added models and production capacity in the firm's range. This shift in the competitive situation, as well as the fact that in the 1990s both BMW and Mercedes outlocated production to the United States, may probably have influenced exposure coefficients from that decade on.

Initially, we obtained cash flow data from Volvo Cars from the middle of 1981 through 1989. Annual reports do not provide sufficient information for exposure analysis, as we will see in Chapter 11. Although the parent firm of the car manufacturer went through some structural changes during the period, the geographical structure of car production and sales remained largely unchanged. A new model was introduced during the period we analyze but according to our analysis it did not represent a substantial change in the firm's product strategy. Pricing policies did not undergo major revisions according to company spokesmen. The pricing strategy was described as "what the market can bear." This implies that prices respond to exchange rate and interest rate changes which influence the competitive position.

We also obtained data for sales revenues for the period 1990–1992. These data were used to conduct an out-of-sample evaluation of regression results for the period 1981–1989.

Figures 5.1–5.3 show quarterly data (1981–1989) for the percentage change in the car manufacturer's cash flows of different kinds relative to the previous quarter. The cash flow data in local currency (SEK) were deflated to obtain changes in real (inflation adjusted, or constant SEK) cash flow.

Total cash flows in Figure 5.1 include commercial and financial flows before tax, while Figure 5.2 shows commercial flows before tax. Sales revenues or gross commercial cash flows are shown in Figure 5.3.

The data have been obtained from the manufacturer and represent management's cash flow data rather than flows approximated from income statements. Commercial flows are defined as operating revenues from sales of cars minus costs before forward contracts are entered. Depreciation is not included. Financial flows include interest payments and new borrowing minus repayments of loans. Exchange rate gains and losses appear only if they are realized.

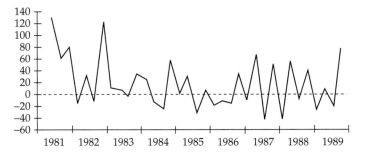

**Figure 5.1** Volvo Cars: Total cash flows (percentage change from preceding three months).

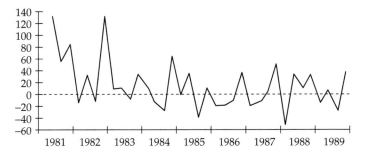

**Figure 5.2** Volvo Cars: Commercial cash flows (percentage change from preceding three months).

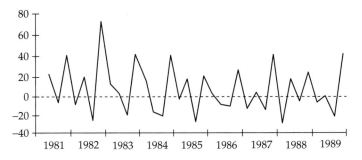

**Figure 5.3** Volvo Cars: Sales revenues (percentage change from preceding three months).

Ideally, we would have liked to know cash flows at an unchanged financial structure. Capital gains and losses on long-term liabilities due to exchange rate changes, interest rate changes, and inflation in every period should be considered, because a firm may hedge commercial cash flow exposure with long-term liabilities in different currencies. In the annual report, data on the currency composition of long-term debt are reported. We use this information below to complement the cash flow data in order to evaluate the extent to which capital gains and losses on long-term debt contribute to the hedging of exposure of commercial cash flows.

The reason for analyzing the exposures of cash flows with different coverage is to compare exposure coefficients for commercial and total cash flows. It is thereby possible to assess whether or not short-term financial positions contribute to a reduction in the sensitivity of total cash flows to exchange rate changes. Volvo's management claimed they generally hedged commercial exposure by taking one-year forward positions in amounts equal to expected sales revenues in the United States.

Figures 5.1–5.3 show that quarterly fluctuations in cash flows were quite substantial and that a seasonal component could be detected. The similarity of the patterns indicates that fluctuations in sales revenues were a major source of fluctuation in commercial and total cash flows.

In Table 5.1 we present results for regressions with the different cash flow variables as dependent variables. Sensitivity coefficients for sales are, as noted, of particular interest for the firm that seeks to reduce uncertainty about sales volume. The independent variables in the regressions on quarterly cash flows are macroeconomic price variables and industry-specific prices in the same quarter. The distinction between anticipated and unanticipated changes is not made. The main reason is that the car manufacturer could not deliver data for budgeted cash flows at anticipated exchange rates, interest rates, inflation, and so forth. It is likely that the difference between anticipated and unanticipated exchange rate and interest rate changes over quarters is negligible.

In all regressions the dependent as well as the independent variables are measured as percentage rates of change from the preceding quarter. As Table 5.1 shows, we focus on market price variables: exchange rates, interest rates, and price levels in the home country, the United States, Germany, and Japan. The United States was the largest market, while Japan's role was as the home country for competitors. Germany had a mixed role. Germany itself was a small market for the corporation but countries with currencies pegged to the DEM at that time were not unimportant. Germany was also a major supplier of inputs, and the home country of major competitors. The relevant independent variables have been identified by first finding the answers to the following questions:

(a) Where do Volvo Cars produce?
(b) Which are Volvo Cars' major competitors and where do they produce?

**Table 5.1  Sensitivity coefficients for Volvo Cars, model 1. Percentage change in cash flows in response to a 1% change in macroeconomic variable.**[a]

| | (1) Nominal total cash flows | (2) Nominal commercial cash flows | (3) Nominal sales revenues | (4) Real total cash flows | (5) Real commercial cash flows | (6) Real sales revenues |
|---|---|---|---|---|---|---|
| Home country real effective exchange rate (FC/SEK) | -5.2 | -6.2 | -2.5 | -4.6 | -5.6 | -2.0 |
| German real effective exchange rate | | | | | | |
| US real effective exchange rate | | | | | | |
| Swedish nominal effective exchange rate | | | | | | |
| Exchange rate SEK/DEM | | | | | | |
| Exchange rate SEK/USD | | | | | | |
| Exchange rate SEK/JPY | | | | | | |
| Swedish short-term interest rate (3 months) | -0.3 | -0.3 | -0.1 | -0.3 | -0.1 | -0.1 |
| Swedish long-term interest rate (5 years) | | 0.2 | | | 0.2 | |
| World short-term interest rate (basket) | | | | | | |
| World long-term interest rate (basket) | | | | | | |
| Real oil price development | | | | | | |
| Real prices of non-energy commodities | | | | | | |
| Consumer prices in Sweden (inflation) | | | | | | |
| Consumer prices in the United States (inflation) | | | | | | |

*continued*

**Table 5.1** continued

| | (1) Nominal total cash flows | (2) Nominal commercial cash flows | (3) Nominal sales revenues | (4) Real total cash flows | (5) Real commercial cash flows | (6) Real sales revenues |
|---|---|---|---|---|---|---|
| Consumer prices in Germany (inflation) | | | | | | |
| World consumer prices (inflation/basket) | | | | | | |
| Producer prices in Sweden | | | | | | |
| Producer prices in the United States | | | | | | |
| Producer prices in Germany | **23.5** | **26.7** | **5.9** | **22.0** | **25.3** | **4.7** |
| Industry-relative prices | | | | | | |
| Adj. $R^2$ (incl. seasonal dummies) | 0.83 | 0.87 | 0.90 | 1.90 | 0.84 | 0.87 |
| D.W. | 1.76 | 1.56 | 1.46 | 1.77 | 1.57 | 2.53 |

[a] Coefficients in **bold** indicate that the hypothesis that the coefficient is equal to zero can be rejected at the 5% level (one-sided test).

    (c)  From where do Volvo Cars buy inputs?
    (d)  From where do Volvo Cars' competitors buy inputs?
    (e)  Which are Volvo Cars' major geographical markets?

For financial cash flows we also ask: Which are the major currencies among Volvo's financial positions?

    All data for exchange rates, interest rates, and price levels are quarterly averages obtained from International Financial Statistics.

    In addition to the macroeconomic price variables, a few industry-specific relative price variables are introduced, as shown in Table 5.1, in order to distinguish between industry shocks and macroeconomic disturbances to the extent they are correlated. The oil price variable is measured as the percentage rate of change of the real USD price of Brent quality oil. The raw material price is the percentage rate of change in real USD terms of an international index for non-energy raw materials. Finally, the industry-relative price is the percentage rate of change of a producer price index for the engineering sectors of the manufacturing industry in Sweden relative to the Swedish consumer price index.

## 5.6  RESULTS, INTERPRETATIONS, AND THE USE OF COEFFICIENTS

### Explanatory factors

Regression results for cash flow data are presented in Tables 5.1 and 5.2. As a result of high correlation among the exchange rates, as well as among other variables, a step-wise regression approach is used to determine which exchange rate(s) capture exchange rate effects to the greatest extent. The same reasoning applies to interest and inflation rates. We present in Table 5.1 the best regressions in terms of explanatory value (adjusted $R^2$) for each of the six different specifications of the dependent cash flow variable. In Table 5.2, the best regressions when the effective exchange rate is excluded are presented in order to show which bilateral exchange rate is most significant for the company. Lagged variables are not included because they did not add explanatory value.

    Before turning to the interpretation of the results it can be noted that seasonal fluctuations explain a large part of fluctuations in cash flows. For example, 25% of fluctuations in commercial cash flows are explained by seasonal factors. A strong upturn can be identified for the fourth quarter following from the sales start of the annually modified model. The seasonal component weighs even more heavily in sales revenues. The adjusted $R^2$s between 0.8 and 0.9 indicate that macroeconomic factors were important for all definitions of cash flows, while oil prices and an industry-relative price seemed unimportant for Volvo Cars, although the last result may have been caused by relatively small fluctuations in the price.

    The exposure coefficients for total cash flows and for commercial cash flows are substantially larger than the coefficients for sales revenue.

**Table 5.2  Sensitivity coefficients for Volvo Cars, model 2; no effective exchange rates.**[a]

|  | (1) Nominal total cash flows | (2) Nominal commercial cash flows | (3) Nominal sales revenues | (4) Real total cash flows | (5) Real commercial cash flows | (6) Real sales revenues |
|---|---|---|---|---|---|---|
| Exchange rate SEK/DEM | 5.2 | 6.0 | 2.7 | 4.7 | 5.5 | 2.4 |
| Swedish short-term interest rate (three months) | − 0.4 |  | − 0.2 | − 0.4 |  | − 0.1 |
| Producer prices in Germany | 28.2 | 32.0 | 8.4 | 26.3 | 30.1 | 6.9 |
| Adj. $R^2$ (incl. seasonal dummies) | 0.85 | 0.85 | 0.95 | 0.83 | 0.83 | 0.92 |
| D.W. | 1.63 | 1.29 | 2.01 | 1.65 | 1.30 | 2.10 |

[a] See footnote to Table 5.1.

This result is easily explained by sales revenues being a larger gross figure, while the other cash flows are net figures and closer to zero. A certain change in sales revenues has a much larger effect on the rate of change in sales minus expenses than it does on sales alone.[2]

Are the signs and the sizes of coefficients realistic? A real appreciation of the SEK has a negative effect on cash flows. The same is true for an increase in the local interest rate. These results correspond to intuition. A similarly intuitively reasonable result is that an increase in German producer prices at a constant exchange rate and interest rate leads to an increase in the cash flows of Volvo Cars. Thus, competitors in Germany seemed to suffer from such inflation. To the extent that inputs were purchased in Germany, costs increased for Volvo when German producer prices increased. Clearly the competitive effect of changes in German prices dominated. The home country price level did not explicitly enter into any regression. It entered through the real effective exchange rate in Table 5.1, however, because a 1% rise in the home price level at a fixed nominal exchange rate amounts to a 1% real appreciation.

The magnitudes of the coefficients in the table are large in some cases. A 1% appreciation of the effective exchange rate with other (included) variables constant caused a 2.0% fall in real sales revenues. Thus, the demand elasticity with respect to price was high but not unrealistic. An appreciation relative to the DEM (now euro) caused a 2.4% decline in real sales revenues according to Table 5.2. The SEK/DEM exchange rate captured the effects of exchange rate changes relative to other countries as well, because the correlations among different exchange rates were substantial. In published statements Volvo claimed that an appreciation of the German mark hurt the firm. The above results indicate the opposite. The declining competitiveness relative to German competitors as a result of a real appreciation of the SEK relative to the DEM (now euro) shows up in the coefficient for the exchange rate, as well as in the coefficient for German producer prices. Real sales revenues increased by 4.7% (6.9% in Table 5.2) when the German producer prices increased by 1%. In comparison with the exchange rate effects, the German inflation effect may be considered large. However, inflation rates in Germany, the United States, and Japan were highly correlated. Therefore, German producer prices stood as a proxy for cost increases in several countries with competing car manufacturers.

Coefficients for interest rates were not consistently significant across different specifications of the cash flows. It makes little difference whether nominal or real values were used, however. The largest negative effect of an increase in interest rates appeared for total cash flows, presumably because interest-rate-sensitive financial flows were included. A 1% increase in the Swedish interest rate from, for example, 10% to 10.1% reduced total cash flows by 0.3% according to Table 5.1. The coefficient in the sales revenue regression indicated that sales revenues fall by 0.1% when the interest rate increased. This result indicates that Volvo should have considered the effects on commercial operations when interest rate exposures were estimated.

Interest rates across countries are naturally highly correlated. Nevertheless, both the home country and the world interest rates contribute to the explanatory value in the regressions for commercial cash flows, but both are statistically insignificant. The estimated coefficients are therefore not certain, but they are nevertheless estimates of interest rate exposures. Using the coefficients as a basis for analysis, the effect of a simultaneous increase in both interest rates is –0.1% in Table 5.1 and zero in Table 5.2. The world interest rate appears with a positive sign in Table 5.1. This result is not as strange as it may seem, because the interest rate captures cash flow effects of a variety of disturbances influencing the interest rate. For example, an increase in the general level of business activity tends to cause an increase in the interest rate and in the volume of sales simultaneously.

### Sensitivity to macroeconomic shocks

Most macroeconomic shocks affect more than one of the price variables in the regressions simultaneously. If the firm's macroeconomic forecasting and risk analysis focuses on sources of changes in interest rates, exchange rates, and so on, rather than on market price variables, then the regression result can be used to calculate the firm's exposure to various macroeconomic scenarios influencing several market price variables simultaneously. To illustrate this in a simple example, assume that there is an increase

**Table 5.3  A scenario: percentage cash flow effects of an increase in world economic activity hypothetically reflected in simultaneous 10% increases in the world and the Swedish interest rates, and a 2% depreciation of the SEK (based on coefficients in Table 5.1).**

|  | Effect on total real cash flows | Effect on real commercial cash flows | Effect on sales revenues |
|---|---|---|---|
| Effective exchange rate | 9.2 | 11.2 | 4.0 |
| Swedish interest rate | – 3.0 | – 1.0 | – 1.0 |
| World interest rate |  | 2.0 |  |
| Total effect | 6.2 | 12.2 | 3.0 |

in the level of economic activity in the world outside Europe, and, as a consequence, the world interest rate increases by one percentage point from 10% to 11%. The home country interest rate rises by the same amount because of assumed financial market linkages. Assume also that world currencies appreciate relative to the SEK by 2%. The cash flow effects of this scenario can be estimated as in Table 5.3 based on coefficients in Table 5.1.

As already noted, the two interest rate effects offset each other for commercial cash flows but not for total cash flows, while exchange rate and interest rate effects offset each other for total cash flows and sales revenues but not for commercial cash flows. Although the coefficients in Table 5.2 are different, the pattern is similar if they are used to estimate the cash flow effects of the composite disturbance.

## Exposure under pegged versus flexible exchange rates

Under flexible rates, macroeconomic shocks are likely to influence all the price variables simultaneously. Under pegged rates, the timing of exchange rate changes is often politically determined.Therefore one can talk about a well-defined exchange rate exposure under pegged rates, at least in the short run.

Another aspect of pegged exchange rates is that an inflation differential relative to trading partners at a pegged exchange rate accumulates over time with an increasingly appreciated real exchange rate. Table 5.4 shows how serious inflation exposure can be for the firm when the exchange rate remains pegged. The figures for commercial cash flow effects are obtained by applying the real exchange rate coefficient in Table 5.1 in each quarter, taking into account that the real appreciation accumulates over time as inflation progresses. In Table 5.4 it is also assumed that the interest rate increases by the same magnitude as the rate of inflation. It is possible that the interest rate could increase further over time, because devaluation expectations become more widespread and stronger when the real appreciation accumulates. In this case the interest rate effect would grow over time, until the central bank is compelled to realign the exchange rate.

**Table 5.4  Domestic inflation with a pegged exchange rate: Negative effects on real commercial cash flows of a 1% increase in the inflation rate relative to the world rate accompanied by a one percentage point (10%) permanent increase in the domestic interest rate.**

|  | First quarter | Second quarter | Third quarter | Fourth quarter | Fifth quarter | Sixth quarter |
|---|---|---|---|---|---|---|
| Real appreciation effect | 12.3[a] | 24.6[b] | 36.9 | 49.3 | 61.5 | 73.7 |
| Swedish interest rate effect | 8.8[c] | 8.8 | 8.8 | 8.8 | 8.8 | 8.8 |
| Total negative | 21.1 | 33.4 | 45.7 | 58.1 | 70.3 | 82.5 |

[a] One-quarter of coefficient (–5.6) in Table 5.1 times average real commercial cash flows (880) divided by 100.
[b] One-half of coefficient (–5.6) in Table 5.1 times average real commercial cash flows (880) divided by 100.
[c] Coefficient for interest rate (–0.1) in Table 5.1 times average real commercial cash flows (880) divided by 100.

## What has financial exposure management achieved?

By comparing sensitivity coefficients for total and commercial cash flows, it is possible to evaluate whether financial positions create a hedge against exposure of commercial flows. Comparing coefficients for the effective exchange rate across different cash flows, it is clear that the financial cash flow effects in the same quarter did not balance out commercial cash flow effects in our case.

Representatives of Volvo Cars emphasized publicly the firm's exposure to the SEK/USD rate. The dollar value of expected sales in one year was regularly sold in the one-year forward market. One reason why this strategy may have failed to reduce exposure is that it did not take into account that the sales volume was influenced by exchange rate changes. Another reason could be that the DEM (now euro) was a more important currency than the dollar. Our results indicate that the SEK/DEM rate was very important, as shown in Table 5.2. The strong effect on cash flows of changes in the German producer price index was a strong indication of a competitive real exchange rate exposure.

An additional observation is that none of our relative prices for oil, raw material, and car prices had a significant impact on cash flows. It seems that fluctuations in cash flows were dominated by macroeconomic and seasonal factors.

## Financial structure as a hedge against macroeconomic exposure

Many firms use their long-term liabilities to hedge exchange rate exposures. It is by no means obvious, however, that simple matching of currency denominations of liabilities with assets committed to sales in different currencies provides a hedge. There are three dimensions to the exposure implications of long-term debt contracts. First, capital gains and losses on foreign currency loans may offset realized cash flow losses and gains owing to exchange rate changes. Second, the firm can choose either fixed or flexible interest rate loans to enhance or dampen interest rate exposure on commercial cash flows. Third, unanticipated inflation causes real capital gains on fixed interest debt contracts.

The annual report of Volvo Cars provided some information about the currency denomination of long-term debt. Disregarding that an unknown share of the loans had been swapped from one currency to another, we calculate the capital loss that occured as a result of a 1% depreciation of the SEK. Table 5.5 contains this information and compares the capital loss with the cash flow gains from the same depreciation using the coefficients in Table 5.1.

Table 5.5 shows that fluctuations in quarterly commercial cash flows as a result of changes in the effective SEK rate were much larger than the capital gains and losses on long-term foreign currency debt. The effects on annual cash flows of exchange rate changes were obviously hedged to an even lesser extent. Similarly, the economic value of the firm was far from hedged because value effects were typically many times larger than quarterly cash flow effects. This exercise demonstrates the importance of deciding on the target variable for exposure management and the importance of capital gains that may be realized in an uncertain future.

**Table 5.5  Capital loss on long-term debt in foreign currency at the end of 1990 from a 1% depreciation of the SEK compared to commercial cash flow gains.**

|  | SEK value of long-term debt in foreign currency (millions)[a] | (Loss) in SEK from a 1% depreciation of SEK | Real commercial cash flow gain from a 1% depreciation of the effective exchange rate |
|---|---|---|---|
| USD | 950 | (9.50) | |
| BEF | 866 | (8.66) | |
| ECU | 201 | (2.01) | |
| ITL | 30 | (0.30) | |
| CHF | 165 | (1.65) | |
| AUD | 22 | (0.22) | |
| FIM | 67 | (0.67) | |
| Others | 380 | (3.80) | |
| Total excl. SEK | 2681 | (26.81) | 49.3[b] |

[a] The firm's annual report includes long-term debt in each currency at the end of the year. We assign half the long-term debt in the annual report to the subsidiary we are dealing with.
[b] This figure is the coefficient for the exchange rate in the real commercial cash flow regression (–5.6) times the mean real commercial cash flows (SEK 880) times minus one divided by 100.

It is also possible to analyze the total exposure to home currency inflation under the assumption that the inflation rate and exchange rate changes are highly correlated. Assume, for example, that the home currency price level increases 1% more than anticipated, and that the SEK is devalued by 1% simultaneously. In this case, there is no real exchange rate change and therefore no commercial cash flow effect if we rely on the regressions in Table 5.1. Nevertheless, inflation exposure is substantial. The following economic effects occur:

- The value of the firm's real assets increases by 1%, reducing the debt-equity ratio of the firm. Therefore, the firm can increase its borrowing without influencing the financial structure of the firm. This effect of inflation can also be thought of as a capital gain in real terms of fixed nominal debt contracts. Assuming that fixed nominal debt includes half of the short-term debt as well as long-term debt, it then amounts to about SEK 25 billion according to the annual report 1990. (We assume that the other half of the short-term debt is so short term that it can be considered indexed to inflation.) Assigning one-half to the car-producing subsidiary, the relevant debt figure is SEK 12.5 billion. Then, an unanticipated inflation of 1% causes a real capital gain of SEK 125 million.
- The home currency also depreciates by 1% causing a capital loss on long-term foreign currency debt, as described in Table 5.5, amounting to SEK 27 million. Exchange rate gains or losses on short-term debt are considered incorporated in cash flow figures. In total, the exposure to home currency inflation as a result of capital gains and losses is SEK (125 minus 27) 98 million per 1% home currency inflation.

## 5.7 USING THE EXPOSURE COEFFICIENTS FOR FUTURE PERIODS

We also obtained sales revenue data from Volvo Cars for the period 1990–1992, enabling us to carry out an analysis of the exposure coefficients and of a financial hedging policy based on the coefficients after the estimation period. Table 5.6 shows in column 1 the percent change in nominal sales revenues from one quarter to another. Columns 2, 3, and 4 show the changes in the SEK/DEM exchange rate, the Swedish short-term interest rate and the German producer prices. The exposure coefficients for these variables were estimated for the period 1981–1989 and presented in Table 5.2.

Column 5 shows the unanticipated exchange rate change measured by the actual change in column 2 minus the (average) interest rate differential during the previous quarter. The struggle to keep the krona pegged to the ECU is shown by the dramatic increase in short-term interest rates in the third quarter of 1992 (column 3).

As noted above, the regression results are derived for total changes in sales revenues and in macroeconomic variables. Some of these changes,

but not all, were unanticipated. It can be assumed that inflation in producer prices is reasonably well anticipated, while exchange rate and interest rate changes are usually unanticipated. However, looking at the
interest rate differentials between Sweden and Germany for the period
1990 through 1992, it is obvious that the period is characterized by a so
called Peso-problem.[3] The three-month Eurocurrency interest rate differential between SEK and DEM (now euro) is consistently positive, indicating that the pegged Swedish currency was expected to be devalued each
quarter, although it remained pegged until November 1992.

The exposure coefficients in Table 5.2, estimated for the period 1981–
1989, have been multiplied by the actual changes in the macro variables
during the years 1990–1992, as shown in Table 5.6.[4] Column 6 in Table 5.6
shows the quarterly sales revenue effect caused by changes in the SEK/
DEM exchange rate, the Swedish interest rate, and the German producer
prices. In column 7 changes in sales revenues net of changes due to macro
variables are presented.

The sales revenue effects of the changes in macro variables are positive
through the third quarter of 1991. These positive effects are explained primarily by German producer price inflation (column 4). The changes in
sales revenues net of changes caused by macro variables in column (7) are,
with the exception of two quarters, negative in 1990 and 1991. In 1992 the
sales revenues increased rapidly. This shift can probably be explained by
the introduction of the new 850 model late in 1991.

The last two periods of 1991 are interesting, because Swedish interest
rates increased dramatically during the third quarter. In order to defend
the krona, the overnight interest rate was raised to 500% for nearly a two
week period. In the fourth quarter, the defense of the krona was given up.
Instead the currency depreciated sharply. Column 6 shows the negative
effect on sales revenues of the interest rate increase in the third quarter
and the positive effect of the depreciation in the fourth quarter. If Volvo
had hedged against effects of these changes, which presumably were
unanticipated, cash flows in column 7 would have been smoothed during
this very turbulent period.

What would have happened to sales had Volvo hedged against unanticipated changes in exchange rates and interest rates using the exposure
coefficients for sales revenues in Table 5.2 to determine the size of the
hedge contracts? We answer this question in columns 8 and 9. Column 8
shows the sales revenue effects of unanticipated changes in exchange rates
(column 5) and interest rates (column 3). Forward foreign exchange and
interest rate contracts could have been used to obtain cash flow gains
(losses) equal to the cash flow losses (gains) in column 8.

Column 8 reveals the Peso-problem once again. Forward hedge contracts based on the exposure coefficients would have been consistently
profitable during the out-of-sample period. The hedge contracts would
have been profitable even during the last two turbulent quarters. During
the third quarter the interest rate forward contract would have offset sales

**Table 5.6 Out-of-sample analysis of nominal sales revenues.**

| | (1) Nominal sales revenues (Change %) | (2) SEK/DEM (Change %) | (3) Swedish interest rate (Change %) | (4) German producer prices (Change %) | (5) Unanticipated change in SEK/DEM (%) | (6) Sales rev. effect of macro variables using Table 5.2 coefficients and columns (2), (3), (4) (change %) | (7) (1) – (6) Sales revenue net of effects of macro variables | (8) Sales rev. effect of unanticipated exchange and interest rate changes using columns (3), (5) | (9) (1) – (8) Cash flow change after hedging exchange rate and interest rate risk |
|---|---|---|---|---|---|---|---|---|---|
| **1990** | | | | | | | | | |
| Q1 | | | | | | | | | |
| Q2 | -3.5 | -0.5 | -7.4 | 1.7 | -5.4 | 14.4 | -17.9 | -13.1 | 9.6 |
| Q3 | -16.5 | -0.8 | -5.5 | 2.0 | -5.3 | 15.7 | -32.2 | -13.2 | 3.3 |
| Q4 | 55.0 | 2.8 | 18.1 | 2.3 | -1.2 | 23.3 | 31.7 | -6.8 | 61.8 |
| **1991** | | | | | | | | | |
| Q1 | -11.0 | 0.8 | -14.4 | 1.7 | -5.3 | 19.3 | -30.3 | -11.4 | 0.4 |
| Q2 | 15.2 | -3.2 | -10.0 | 0.8 | -6.4 | 0.1 | 15.1 | -15.3 | 30.5 |
| Q3 | -23.1 | 1.0 | -10.7 | 1.1 | -2.2 | 14.0 | -37.1 | -3.8 | -19.3 |
| Q4 | -11.0 | 0.7 | 18.0 | 0.1 | -0.8 | -0.9 | -10.1 | -5.8 | -5.2 |
| **1992** | | | | | | | | | |
| Q1 | 55.8 | -0.6 | 1.5 | 0.1 | -3.2 | -1.6 | 57.4 | -9.4 | 65.2 |
| Q2 | 9.4 | -0.5 | -4.4 | 0.7 | -2.8 | 5.4 | 4.0 | -6.7 | 16.1 |
| Q3 | -27.4 | 1.2 | 200.0 | 0.1 | 0.6 | -36.0 | 8.6 | -41.6 | 14.2 |
| Q4 | 49.0 | 9.9 | -62.2 | -0.4 | -18.0 | 36.0 | 13.0 | -36.2 | 85.2 |

revenue losses caused by the increase in the interest rate while the foreign exchange forward contract would have been profitable because it hedged against an unanticipated appreciation or a smaller depreciation than the interest rate differential in the previous quarter. In the fourth quarter, when the depreciation occurred, the hedge contracts were profitable as well, because the extreme interest differential in the third quarter once again overestimated the actual depreciation of the Swedish krona. The large profits from hedging operations are not common under floating rates. The profitability of the hedging contracts for such a long period is due to the strong "leaning against the wind" behavior of the Swedish central bank and the extreme measures it took to defend the currency.

There are two results indicating that cash flow volatility could have been reduced by hedging macroeconomic exposures. First, column 7, in comparison with column 1, shows that the sales revenues, net of effects of macro variables, declined almost quarter by quarter before a new model was introduced. Second, the effects on cash flows of the turbulence during the second half of 1992 are evident in the same column.

It must be noted that evaluating a hedging policy such as the one described here by looking at the variability of cash flows before and after hedging is not always appropriate. If a hedge has a three-month time horizon, then it can reduce uncertainty about the outcome in three months. It cannot be expected to decrease the variance over longer periods because three-month forward rates tend to fluctuate with the spot rate.

Finally, for the outside stakeholder to assess the prospects of Volvo, considerably more information is needed as compared with the standard of the early 2000s (see Chapter 11).

## 5.8 CONCLUDING REMARKS ON THE CASE OF VOLVO CARS

A method for estimating cash flow exposure to macroeconomic variables has been illustrated using actual data from Volvo Cars. We have emphasized the importance of thinking about the objective of exposure management in order to estimate relevant exposure measures before deciding on the currency denomination of long-term debt and before entering hedge contracts in financial markets. It must be remembered that entering financial contracts to hedge exposure that lacks economic relevance amounts to creating economic exposure.

The exposure coefficients for exchange rates, interest rates, and price levels can be used to derive hedge positions using currency denomination, maturity structure, and degree of indexation of long-term debt, as well as short-term financial instruments sensitive to the same variables. The coefficients are also useful for estimating the vulnerability to macroeconomic disturbances that managers consider particularly likely to occur with simultaneous effects on several macroeconomic price variables.

The regression method is most easily implemented when pricing, output, and purchasing strategies remain unchanged. If there is variability in the response of prices, output, or purchases to macroeconomic events, then it could be impossible to obtain a sufficiently long time series for regression analysis. Scenario analysis could be preferable for estimating exposures in such a case. Even so, the regression method provides the conceptual foundation for measurements of exposures.

In contemporary public pronouncements Volvo Cars' exposure to the SEK/USD rate was emphasized, and the USD value of expected sales in one year was regularly sold in the one year forward market. This strategy did not take into account that the sales volume was influenced by exchange rate changes and that the DEM at that time could have been a more important currency. Our results indicate that the SEK/DEM rate was very important for competitive reasons, possibly more important than the SEK/USD rate.

In the case of Volvo Cars, macroeconomic exposures seem to have been more important than exposure to industry- and firm-specific disturbances. In general, exposure coefficients could have been used to separate cash flow effects due to macroeconomic circumstances (beyond managers' control) from cash flow effects caused by managers' efforts to cope with the competitive environment.

To further illustrate the use of exposure coefficients, Volvo Cars' performance with respect to sales revenues for the period 1990–1992 was evaluated using exposure coefficients based on data for the period 1981–1989. With access to the appropriate data, a similar analysis could have been carried out for commercial and total cash flows. It was shown that after netting out macroeconomic effects using the regression coefficients, sales revenues were found to have fallen almost continuously until a new model was introduced. The effects of the dramatic interest rate increases and the depreciation during the last half of 1992 stand out clearly. This analysis of Volvo Cars' exposure using the regression coefficients indicates that Volvo could have increased profits as well as reduced cash flow uncertainty during the turbulent period in 1992 by hedging.

If Volvo had hedged against the effects of unanticipated exchange rate and interest rate changes using the regression coefficients, the hedge contracts would have been consistently profitable for three years. The reason is that the interest rate differential consistently overestimated the actual exchange rate change. Such profitability from hedging cannot be expected in normal times of floating rates, however.

Finally, in order for each stakeholder to form his or her own forecast about the prospects of Volvo, to assess the competitiveness of the firm, or to understand the macroeconomic risks, information about (a) management's forecast, (b) assumptions about relevant macroeconomic variables included in the forecast, and (c) the sensitivity coefficients for these macroeconomic variables is required. We believe that annual reports in the future will meet these requirements better than today (see Chapter 11). The key feature of external reporting will develop from GAAP towards providing answers to "what if" questions.

## NOTES

1 This chapter is an adaptation of Oxelheim and Wihlborg (1995).
2 It is not unusual that cash flows on the average are close to zero. Elasticity coefficients tend toward infinity in such a case. Variables could be expressed as changes rather than percent changes to solve this problem when it arises.
3 The Peso-problem refers to a situation wherein forecast errors in hindsight do not appear random but go in the same direction period after period. This situation often occurs when a central bank is "leaning against the wind," preventing an exchange rate change that is considered likely to happen.
4 A better out-of-sample evaluation would be based on exposure coefficients that were updated quarter by quarter. Since we do not have data for all cash flows for the out-of-sample period we chose the simpler analysis presented here.

# Chapter 6

# Hedging Macroeconomic Exposure

## 6.1 INTRODUCTION

In Chapter 5 it was noted that exposure coefficients are not measured without uncertainty and there is always the possibility that they do not apply exactly in future periods. Traditional transaction and translation measures may seem more exact and less uncertain. This exactness is, however, misleading because the relevance of these traditional measures is questionable. The exposure coefficients discussed above are uncertain but they refer to true economic concerns. Thus, uncertainty about the exact exposure is no reason not to employ an exposure measure of the kind we propose. Here we address only the issue of how hedging can be implemented, while the choice of exposure to hedge, if any, is determined by the risk management strategy. The choice of such a strategy is discussed in Chapter 8.

Standard methods of covering and hedging conventional transaction and translation exchange rate exposures are treated in sections 6.2 and 6.3; conventional interest rate exposures are taken up in Section 6.4. Thereafter, we turn to the hedging of more economically oriented measures of exposure in Section 6.5. We ask how hedge contracts can be obtained from the measures of macroeconomic exposure discussed in previous chapters. The exposure coefficients discussed in chapters 4 and 5 provide the necessary information to determine the size of hedge contracts in combination with information about the objectives of risk management.

In Section 6.6 we discuss how uncertainty about exposure coefficients can be taken into account when methods and magnitudes of hedging are determined. Options and non-standard derivatives are discussed here. Section 6.7 contains a brief discussion of tax considerations when hedging. Concluding remarks follow in Section 6.8.

## 6.2 DERIVATIVE CONTRACTS AND TRANSACTION EXPOSURE: AN OVERVIEW

Hedging and covering can be performed by choosing the currency denomination of long-term debt, as well as of short-term financial positions, such that gains and losses on these positions offset the exposure of the firm's commercial operations. Although there is substantial flexibility in short-term positions, including trade credits, it is possible that the adjustability of these positions is insufficient. If so, the firm can turn to the markets for derivative contracts, which often offer fast, cheap, and liquid positions. Table 6.1 lists "internal" and "external" instruments for adjusting the foreign currency position.

The internal instruments involve some adjustment to business operations or financing plans. Limits to such adjustment force firms to enter contracts with external financial institutions or firms. In what follows we focus on such contracts. For the role of invoice currency, see Box 6.1.

The most common derivative contract is the forward contract (see Box 6.2). Such a contract implies that the price of and the amount for delivery on a specific future date is determined today. Forward contracts are traded in the interbank markets in the same way as spot contracts.[1] When a firm enters a forward contract, a contract is entered with a bank. This contract could be of any maturity but most often contracts are for 30 days, 60 days, 90 days, 180 days or 1 year. Even longer contracts exist, however.

Futures contracts are similar to forward contracts but they are traded on exchanges. One contract refers to a specific amount of one currency to be delivered on one of only a few dates in a year. Futures contracts are therefore less flexible in amount and maturity. Furthermore, the buyer of a futures contract must deposit a certain share of the contract with the exchange and add to the deposit if the value of the contract falls (marking to market).

A more important hedging instrument is the foreign currency option. Markets for options (the right to buy or sell a currency at a specific price on a specific date) in a number of currencies and maturities have developed. With respect to transaction exposure, an option functions as an insurance against unfavorable price movements as opposed to a forward or futures contract where the firm loses the opportunity to take advantage of favorable price movements. For example, if a firm buys a 30-day (call) option to buy pounds at a "striking price" of USD 1.50, then if the pound reaches USD 1.51, the firm exercises its option and sells the pound in the spot market with a one cent profit on the contract. On the other hand, if the price reaches only USD 1.49 the firm does not exercise its option.

An American importer that must buy and deliver one pound in 30 days could make sure that the price of this pound will not exceed USD 1.50. If it reaches USD 1.51 the option is obviously exercised, while if it reaches only USD 1.49 the importer buys the pound in the spot market at this more favorable price. Such an option is naturally not free, but may cost,

## Box 6.1 The choice of invoice currency and exposure

In 2000—following the introduction of the euro in 1999—the dominant role of the dollar in pricing of commodities and goods in world markets became an issue. For example, many of the oil-producing countries threatened to switch from dollars to euros in the pricing of crude oil. Similarly, many European paper and pulp manufacturers talked about switching from pricing in dollars to pricing in euros. Prices on commodities, like oil and pulp, are often set in dollars, but producers can nevertheless invoice in other currencies with the implication that the financial exposures of producers created at invoicing are subject to some choice. The invoice price for a commodity is likely to remain equal to the world price in dollars times the relevant exchange rate.

Many firms having some control over pricing also face a choice of currency in which to set prices and to invoice. There are three aspects to this choice. First, the invoice currency can be part of the pricing strategy of the firm and possibly differentiated across countries and customers. As discussed in Chapter 4, pricing in different markets can affect both prices and sales volumes in these markets and, accordingly, cash flow exposures. Second, the choice of currency in bids and orders for large projects or expensive goods like ships and airplanes affects the contractual exposures of the firms and their customers, sometimes for long periods between bid or order and delivery. Third, the invoice currency determines the denomination of accounts receivables for sellers and accounts payables for buyers.

Let us discuss these issues and start from the end. The third aspect of invoice currency affecting only the financial transaction exposures in accounts receivables and payables would be relatively unimportant for most firms in countries with developed markets for financial instruments. Hedging of exposures are not associated with substantial costs where markets for derivatives and a variety of financial instruments exist. We discussed such hedging of transaction exposures in Chapter 3 and we elaborate on the use of derivatives for hedging macroeconomic exposures in this chapter.

The second aspect of currency denomination for bids and orders for large time-consuming projects can be an important concern for sellers and buyers alike. The willingness of a seller to take on contractual exchange rate risk for long periods and large amounts can provide a competitive edge in countries where financial markets are not well developed. Most often bidding and orders for large items would be denominated in a major currency where financing is also available. Hedging of exposures associated with bids for projects are discussed below in this chapter.

**Box 6.1 continued**

The first aspect of invoice currency as one part of a pricing strategy is most likely important for many firms producing differentiated products. The producers of such products have some pricing power and the ability to differentiate prices across markets with different competitive conditions. If a firm at all times sets the price in each market at the profit maximizing level, the invoice currency should not matter for commercial exposure since the price in this currency should be set equal to the optimal local currency price times the exchange rate. However, there are often costs associated with frequent price changes in many markets. Therefore the optimal pricing strategy would entail some price rigidity in local currency. In this case, the choice of invoice currency would affect both the firm's operating exposure and the price behavior in the local currency. The optimal choice of invoice currency would depend on the ability and costs of changing local currency prices, as well as the operating exposure associated with the chosen pricing strategy in the local market. As noted in Chapter 4, the optimal local pricing strategy would be affected by local macroeconomic conditions including linkages between inflation, interest rates and exchange rate changes. Thus, the invoice currency would be one factor affecting macroeconomic exposures as discussed in Chapters 4 and 5.

Friberg and Wilander (forthcoming) study factors that affect the invoice currency of Swedish exporters. They find that the customer's currency is most commonly used, while the Swedish krona and vehicle currencies (dollars and euros) are used with equal frequency. The invoice currency appears frequently to be negotiated along with the price. The currency of settlement is rarely negotiated, however, since costs of conversion are generally negligable. Another observation is that there is little difference with respect to invoice currency behavior between intra- and inter-firm trade. In a study of contractual rigidities with respect to prices in the invoice currency, Oxelheim et al (1990) find that contracts of large Swedish and Singaporean firms often include clauses that specify payment adjustments conditional on large exchange rate changes. Such clauses imply partial hedging of transaction exposures. They seem to be more common in inter-firm than in intra-firm trade.

say, two cents per pound. Then, the importer has in effect made sure that the pound price will not exceed USD 1.52 (1.50 + 0.02). The option price (premium) will increase with the variability of the pound price. Variability increases the price of the option, because increased variability increases the probability that the striking price will be reached before the striking date.

**Table 6.1  Exposure management instruments.**

**Internal or commercial tools**

1. Change in contract currency
2. Matching of revenues and costs in current operations (structural matching)
3. Matching of net flows in current operations with net flows on the financial side
4. Change in payment rhythm internally (leads/lags parent/subsidiary)
5. Change in payment rhythm externally (leads/lags)
6. Advance payments in other forms
7. Structural changes in debts/claims among currencies
8. Currency reserves (for example, with internal forward hedging)
9. Export financing arrangements in the group
10. Internal pricing routines
11. Inflation and exchange rate indexation
12. Contract clauses specifying division of unexpected losses (gains)
13. Renegotiation and/or price adjustment clauses in contracts
14. Adjustment in level of inventories
15. Change in credit conditions for foreign suppliers or foreign customers
16. Cross-matching based on correlation among currencies
17. Change in prices in export markets
18. Change in prices in local markets
19. Choice of markets

**External tools**

1. Forward market transactions
2. Foreign currency loans
3. Swap arrangements
4. Sell future receivables
5. Currency options
6. Financial futures
7. Export financing arrangements
8. Factoring including currency adjustment
9. Leasing including currency adjustment
10. Fixed versus adjustable interest loans
11. Interest rate options

The opposite of a call option is a put option, which implies the right to sell one unit of a currency for another at a fixed price. An exporter expecting to receive foreign currency could hedge transaction exposure by buying a put option.

**Box 6.2  A forward cover**

The U.S. exporter is expecting to receive GBP 1,000 on March 31. Today, January 3, the firm enters a forward contract to sell GBP 1,000 for US dollars on March 31 at the exchange rate USD 2.00/GBP. On March 31, the GBP 1,000 is received. The firm delivers the pounds and receives USD 2,000 as agreed upon. Note that the same forward contract is to buy USD 2,000 for pounds.

A disadvantage of options is that there is not a continuum of striking prices, maturities, and contract sizes. However, banks to an increasing extent offer option contracts with as much flexibility as forward contracts since they can then match many customers' needs and go to the market for options with the net positions of their customers.

Among financial instruments we should also mention swaps of different kinds. Interest rate swaps are discussed in Section 6.4 below. In foreign exchange markets the term is used for a large number of different contracts, which involves the simultaneous buying and selling of one currency for another. Swaps in forward markets refer to two opposite positions with different maturities. More commonly, foreign exchange swaps are long-term standardized or tailor-made transactions between a bank and a firm, or between two firms with a bank as a possible intermediary, implying that two parties decide to pay each others' loans in different currencies. Such swaps are generally designed to avoid exchange controls, to alleviate political risk, or to overcome information problems in capital markets. Two firms in different countries with access to local credit markets, but without access to the foreign market, could each borrow in the local currency and "swap" obligations for payments on the loans. Thereby, the two firms gain access to foreign currency loans and/or access to credit conditions in foreign markets. A foreign exchange swap becomes, in essence, a series of forward contracts extending into time beyond the reach of forward contracts (see Table 6.5 below).

A particular kind of swap is a parallel loan. For example, a U.S. firm may lend to a U.S. subsidiary of a Brazilian corporation while the Brazilian parent lends to the Brazilian subsidiary of the U.S. corporation. The two firms agree on terms at which the relative value of the two loans can be determined in the future. Indirectly, swaps may help relatively unknown subsidiaries to gain access to the respective local capital markets or, depending on the contract terms, it may be the case that they are indirectly able to borrow in their parents' markets when exchange controls hinder transactions. There is no cross-border transaction in this type of swap; all firms hold assets or liabilities in their local currencies, and the relatively well-known parent companies stand as the borrowers in the capital markets.

## Comparing Instruments

The firm choosing among different ways of covering a transaction exposure, or indeed whether to cover at all, would evaluate the expected domestic currency value and the risk of the exposed positions under different alternatives. If international financial markets work efficiently, then a lot can be said about the relative costs and risks of various alternatives. For example, we discussed International Fisher Parity (IFP) in Chapter 3. If IFP holds, then the expected returns or costs on foreign and local currency positions are the same. Thus risk considerations, and probably transactions costs, determine the preferred currency position.

Another pricing relationship in international financial markets is Interest Rate Parity (IRP). This relationship implies that the return on a covered foreign currency position equals the return on a local currency position. The firm holding, for example, a domestic currency deposit could switch into a foreign currency deposit and sell the future foreign currency value of this deposit in the forward market. At maturity the firm would receive (with certainty) the same amount of domestic currency as if the deposit had been held in domestic currency. IRP can be written in the following way for a three-month time horizon:

$$\begin{bmatrix} \text{Value of domestic currency} \\ \text{(DC) deposit in three months} \end{bmatrix} = \begin{bmatrix} \text{Foreign currency (FC) value of FC} \\ \text{deposit in three months} \end{bmatrix}$$
$$\times \frac{\text{Three-month forward rate (DC/FC)}}{\text{Spot rate (DC/FC)}}$$

IRP implies that the firm expecting a future FC payment would be indifferent about whether to sell the FC value of the payment in the forward market, or borrow foreign currency, switch to local currency at the spot rate, deposit in local currency, and use the future payment to pay back the FC loan. The latter operation is called a money market cover. The choice between the forward cover and the money market cover depends on transactions costs if IRP holds. In the forward market there is a bid-ask spread. In the money market there is a difference between the borrowing rate and the deposit rate. With both IRP and IFP holding, the forward rate equals the expected future spot rate. In this case, the choice whether or not to cover in the forward market depends upon risk considerations.

Similar relations hold in the markets for options. If the option is efficiently priced by risk-neutral market participants, then the expected value of a foreign currency payment without cover equals the expected foreign currency payment if an option is purchased. The firm pays a price for the option in order to get a floor for the amount of future local currency while it retains the possibility of getting more local currency if the exchange rate changes in a favorable direction. In efficient markets, the floor, including the price for the option, must be less than the amount obtained with certainty with a forward contract. A price must be paid for the probability that the firm will receive more local currency than with a forward contract if the exchange moves in a favorable direction. Thus, in efficient markets the choice among the option, the forward cover, and a completely open position depends on the different risk characteristics associated with the alternatives as well as on the bid-ask spreads on different financial market contracts. An example is given in Box 6.3.

## 6.3 PRACTICES IN MANAGING TRANSLATION EXPOSURE

We assume now that the firm's concept of exposure refers to translation exposure. This kind of exposure is not covered but hedged. "Cover" is usually reserved for activities that fix the domestic currency value of known or expected future cash flows, while the firm can "hedge," for example, in order to reduce uncertainty about the value of assets and liabilities. Throughout this book we use the word "hedge" for all activities designed to reduce exposure.

Translation exposure generally refers to uncertainty about a foreign asset's domestic currency value on a consolidation date for which balance sheets are made public. Translation gains or losses between time 0 and time 1 depend on the average translation exposure for the period and the exchange rate change during the period as described in Chapter 3. These gains and losses may potentially be realized at later dates, or they may never be realized but merely offset by future translation losses and gains.

A simple way of hedging the balance sheet is obviously to adjust the currency denomination of exposed assets and liabilities until they are balanced. The required hedge depends on the translation method. For example, under the monetary/non-monetary method, monetary items, including long-term debt, are exposed while plant and equipment are not. Therefore, firms could avoid exposure in foreign subsidiaries in an accounting sense by financing plant and equipment with long-term debt in domestic currency. On the other hand, under the all-current method all assets and liabilities are exposed. Therefore, long-term debt in foreign currency often balances plant and equipment in foreign subsidiaries.

We turn now to a detailed analysis of a hedge of translation exposure. What is accomplished by a forward market hedge of exposure? Assume, for example, that we are in the firm described in Appendix 3.1. At the end of year 1 and on January 1 year 2, the exposure of the foreign subsidiary is FC 500 under the all-current method. The exchange rate is USD 1/FC. The forward rate on contracts maturing at the end of the year is USD 1.05/FC. Since the FC exposure is positive, we try to hedge by selling FC 500 forward for delivery on December 31 of year 2. Table 6.2 illustrates what could happen in this situation. In the left column we have actual outcomes on the consolidation date. The second column shows the translation gain and loss associated with each outcome. Thereafter, we have the cash gain

**Box 6.3   An example of hedging using forward, money, and option markets**

An American importer is scheduled to make a ¥ 150 million payment in three months. Today the spot rate is ¥ 150/USD. The three-month forward rate is ¥ 147/USD, the three-month interest rate in the United States is 10%, and the three-month interest rate in Japan is consistent with IRP: A call option as well as a put option on ¥ 100 with striking price ¥ 150/USD and exercise date in three months costs USD 0.03. The expected future spot rate is ¥ 148/USD.

The financial officer is confronted with the problem of evaluating risk and expected costs associated with the alternatives in order to choose one, given the firm's willingness to accept risk.

(i) Cost of payable with no cover:
   Pay at expected rate ¥ 150,000,000 at ¥ 148/USD ⇒ USD 1,014,000. This figure is uncertain, however, and represents the expected payment.

(ii) Cost of payable with forward cover (buy yen forward):
   ¥ 150,000,000 at ¥ 147/USD ⇒ USD 1,020,000. This figure is certain but higher than the uncertain expected payment in (i).

(iii) Cost of payable with money market cover (borrow dollars, deposit in yen):
   with IRP, costs and risks are identically the same as with forward contracts.

(iv) Cost of payable with options cover (buy call option):
   Pay USD 45,000 option premium today. At the expected exchange rate in three months the option should be exercised, i.e. buy ¥ 150,000,000 at ¥ 150/USD. Cost at expected exchange rate: USD 45,000 (1+0.025) + USD 1,000,000.

Note that the expected cost with options is *not* the cost at the expected rate. The expected cost is lower, as shown in Figure 6.1.

The payment profiles in the figure show that the certainty of the forward contract (and money market contract) is obtained at an expected cost relative to no cover. Thus, IFP does not hold. To evaluate the expected cost of the option, information about the probability distribution for the exchange rate is required. The ceiling cost for the option is higher than the certain cost of the forward cover, but the option offers the possibility of a lower cost when the exchange rate exceeds ¥154/USD. The pattern is consistent with efficient markets in the sense that the option offers "no free lunch." If market prices were dominated by risk-neutral speculators, then the expected cost of all alternatives would be equal.

**Box 6.3 continued**

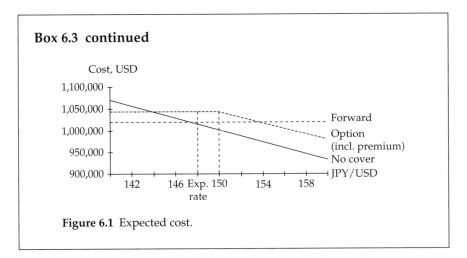

**Figure 6.1** Expected cost.

or loss on the forward contract that must be fulfilled on December 31. For example, if the exchange rate turns out to be USD 1.10/FC, then the contract can be fulfilled only by the purchase of FC 500 at the spot rate USD 1.10/FC while, according to the forward contract, the firm receives USD 1.05/FC when the foreign currency is delivered. Thus, there is a cash loss of 25. The last column in the table demonstrates that the sum of the translation gain (loss) and the cash gain (loss) is constant. This total gain or loss with hedging is equal to the translation gain that would occur if the actual spot rate at the end of the year were equal to the forward rate. Thus, the balance sheet value of the firm is hedged at a USD value corresponding to the forward rate. Remaining uncertainty about the year-end value of the firm depends only on uncertainty about the business operations of the firm. If the forward rate had been below USD 1/FC, then it would not have been possible to hedge an increase in the value of the firm. Instead a loss would have been hedged, insuring the firm against even larger losses.

It is noteworthy that hedging accounting exposure leaves the firm exposed to cash gains and losses on the forward contract against unrealized losses and gains on the translation exposure. This forward contract

**Table 6.2  A hedge—an example. (Based on data from Appendix 3.1)**

| Outcome on December 31 | Translation gain (loss) on FC 500 exposure | Cash gain (loss) on forward contract | Translation gain + cash gain |
|---|---|---|---|
| USD 1.10/FC | USD 50 | USD (25) | USD 25 |
| USD 1.05/FC | USD 25 | – | USD 25 |
| USD 1.00/FC | – | USD 25 | USD 25 |
| USD 0.95/FC | USD (25) | USD 50 | USD 25 |

exposure serves as a hedge. There is, in other words, a mismatch of maturities, though in an accounting sense the firm is not exposed. The hedging could, nevertheless, make economic sense if the unrealized translation gains or losses are expected to be realized in the future when the assets and liabilities produce cash flows. In this case, when the accounting exposure corresponds to economic exposure, a gain (loss) on the forward contract equals the present value of future cash losses (gains). On the other hand, when the accounting exposure does not correspond to economic exposure, the forward contract itself is a source of economic exposure.

## Taxes and hedging

There has been some debate about whether the forward contract should be increased in size relative to exposure in order to hedge translation exposure. The reason for doing so would be that cash gains (losses) are taxable (tax deductible) in some countries while there are no tax effects from translation gains or losses. Tax considerations are discussed in Section 6.7 below, but one specific issue is illustrated with the help of the following hedge example. Assuming a 50% tax rate, we show the accounting and economic results of a double hedge of the translation exposure in Table 6.3. If the firm is concerned only about accounting net worth, then doubling the contract would clearly be necessary to hedge accounting net worth (as shown in the column for translation gain plus after-tax cash gain on the hedging contract). On the other hand, if the translation exposure is viewed as economic exposure, then there is no reason to double the forward contract, as shown in the last column of Table 6.3. In this case, assuming exchange rate changes are expected to be permanent, and translation exposure is the present value of future (taxable) cash flows, a translation gain is the present value of expected future cash flow gains in column 4 of Table 6.3. When actual cash flows occur they will be taxed, or when losses occur they will be deductible. Thus, the present value of expected cash flow gains after tax is half of the translation gain. Then, a regular forward

**Table 6.3  A double hedge.**

| Outcome on December 31 | Translation gain (loss) | After-tax cash gain on double hedge | PV of after-tax cash gains after december 31 | Translation gain + after-tax cash gain on hedge | PV of after-tax cash gain + after-tax cash gain on hedge |
|---|---|---|---|---|---|
| USD 1.10/FC | USD 50 | USD (25) | USD 25 | USD 25 | 0 |
| USD 1.05/FC | USD 25 | – | USD 12.50 | USD 25 | USD 12.50 |
| USD 1.00/FC | – | USD 25 | – | USD 25 | USD 25 |
| USD 0.95/FC | USD (25) | USD 50 | USD (12.50) | USD 25 | USD 37.50 |

contract as in Table 6.2 would be sufficient to hedge the firm's value and fix it at a value corresponding to the forward rate, even when taxes are taken into account.

Assume instead that tax rules allow a translation gain (loss) to be taxable (tax-deductible) when it appears on the books. In that case, the after-tax translation gain (loss) should be compared with the loss (gain) on the forward contract after tax. Doubling of the forward contract does not make sense from either an accounting or an economic point of view, in this case.

As noted in Section 6.7 below, a third possible rule for accounting for exchange rate changes on hedge contracts, as well as for estimating the tax burden, is that the tax treatment for hedge contracts is the same as for the asset or liability being hedged. For example, if a translation gain is not taxed, then the cash flow loss on the corresponding hedge contract would not be tax-deductible. At a later time, when the gains or losses on the asset position are being realized, perhaps long after the expiration of hedge contracts, gains withheld from taxation are being taxed. The corresponding losses on hedge contracts would be deductible.

In the latter case when hedge contracts are taxed like the corresponding asset or liability, there is some room for maneuver for the firm wanting to avoid taxes on cash gains, and wanting to claim the deductibility on losses. The room for maneuver is created by the difficulty of defining what a hedge is versus what a speculative contract is. Clearly, a firm would want losses to appear on taxable speculative contracts and gains to appear as non-taxable hedge contracts. Consider a 10% appreciation of the foreign currency of which half was forecast and reflected in the forward rate at the time a hedge contract was purchased. This situation corresponds to the first line in Table 6.2. Here, the firm would want to classify the hedge contract as a speculative contract to obtain a tax-deductible loss of USD 25.

### False hedging

The term "hedge of exposure" has sometimes been misused to represent protection against expected losses. A forward contract for this purpose creates an expected gain equal to an expected loss. Assume, for example, that the expected (on January 1) exchange rate (for December 31) is one of those listed in the first column in Table 6.4. Assume now that the forward rate on January 1 is USD 0.95/FC. The company has a translation exposure of FC 500. We must then ask what size foreign currency forward contract (C) would create an expected gain equal to the expected translation loss. The following formula can be used to determine this contract:

Expected translation loss = desired cash gain on forward contract

$= C \times (\text{expected spot rate} - \text{forward rate})$

For example, if the expected spot rate is 0.975, then $C = 12.50/(0.975 - 0.95) = 500$. Thus, the firm would buy FC 500 in the forward market. Table 6.4

Table 6.4 "False hedging."

| Expected spot rate | Expected translation loss | Forward contract (C) |
| --- | --- | --- |
| USD 1.000/FC | – | 0 |
| USD 0.975/FC | USD 12.50 | 500 |
| USD 0.950/FC | USD 25 | ∞ |
| USD 0.900/FC | USD 50 | – 1000 |

illustrates that this kind of "false hedging" is highly speculative, if possible at all. Clearly, if the forward rate is equal to the expected future spot rate, then there is no way to offset the expected loss. If the expected rate is 0.975, then the firm must buy FC 500, adding to its exposure, which is already FC 500. Therefore, this kind of activity may actually increase the firm's exposure to unanticipated exchange rate changes. In times of substantial exchange rate uncertainty the activity is obviously dangerous, especially since expected rates often deviate little from forward rates. Large contracts are then necessary to create this "hedge" in an expectational sense. One may, of course, also ask why the forward contract size would be limited to the size of the exposure if the firm has some faith in its forecast. The reason is probably that it is not considered proper to speculate but prudent to hedge. Thus, false hedging allows speculation under the guise of prudence. Tax considerations discussed above can add to the incentives to speculate under this guise.

We have demonstrated two important facts about the role of the forward rate in exposure management. First, the forward rate is the only exchange rate at which the domestic currency value of an exposed position can be locked in. Second, there is no way in which expected losses can be offset if market expectations, as reflected in the forward rate, are equal to the firm's expectations, that is, if IFP is expected to hold. Even if the managers expect to be able to offset an expected translation loss, the required position can be risky and highly speculative.

## 6.4 HEDGING INTEREST RATE AND INFLATION RISKS

Exposure of the firm's financial position to interest rate and inflation risks was discussed in Chapter 3. In this section hedging of such financial risks is discussed. Consider a firm borrowing over two years and assume it has the choice among (a) taking a two-year loan at a fixed interest rate, (b) taking two consecutive one-year loans with an uncertain second-year interest rate, and (c) taking two consecutive one-year loans combined with an interest rate futures contract (to deliver a security with a certain interest rate at the beginning of the second period). If the one-year interest rate increases unexpectedly before the beginning of the second year, the firm in case (b) suffers an increase in borrowing costs, while the firm in case (c) is compensated by an offsetting gain on the futures contract, since it can buy a security at a lower price than the futures price to fulfill the contract. Since the firm obtains the same protection by taking at two-year loan directly with a rate $i_2$, we would expect that the interest rate on the futures contract for the second year would be such that firms are indifferent between cases (a) and (c). This indifference occurs when

$$\left[1+\begin{array}{c}\text{two-period}\\\text{interest rate}\end{array}\right]^2 = \left[1+\begin{array}{c}\text{First}\\\text{one-period}\\\text{interest rate}\end{array}\right] \times \left[1+\begin{array}{c}\text{Second}\\\text{one-period}\\\text{interest rate}\\\text{(futures)}\end{array}\right]$$

(13)

If this condition holds for the expected second-period interest rate, as well as for the rate on the futures contract, then the term structure of interest rates for one and two periods is consistent with the *"expectations hypothesis"* for the term structure. Under these conditions the expected borrowing costs in cases (a), (b), and (c) above are the same. The risk associated with case (b) is different, however.

The expected one-period interest rate for the second period need not be equal to the futures rate. If not, the expectations hypothesis is violated and profit opportunities are expected in the choice between cases (a) and (c) on the one hand, and case (b) on the other.

The incentive to hedge against interest rate uncertainty by means of futures contracts or long-term fixed interest rate contracts depends upon the source of the uncertainty. As noted in Chapter 3, if the uncertainty consists primarily of real sources of interest rate uncertainty, then the contract offers a hedge against real interest rate risk. If, however, interest rate uncertainty reflects inflation uncertainty, then there is less uncertainty about real interest costs when the firm chooses case (b), that is, two consecutive one-period loans.

If a firm for some reason finds itself locked into a two-year fixed interest rate loan and the inflation uncertainty is substantial, then the futures contract can be used as a (partial) hedge against unanticipated inflation. This hedge is more complete, the more the short-term interest rate changes depend on inflation. For example, if after one period there has been a decrease in actual and expected inflation, then real interest cost on the fixed interest loan would have increased. This increased cost would have been offset by a gain on the interest rate futures contract.

Real interest rate risk with its source in either the real factors or in the inflation rate can be diversified away by creating an international portfolio of securities or debt. Under a fixed exchange rate system, inflation rates must be similar across currencies. Therefore, inflation risk cannot be diversified away. Instead, it is primarily real sources of interest rate risk that can be diversified. Under a flexible system, inflation rates can differ and develop independently. Therefore, borrowers and lenders have the opportunity to diversify away inflation risk by holding an international basket of currencies. Especially on long-term fixed interest loan, for which real sources of exchange risk may be less of a concern than inflation risk, the opportunity to hold long-term debt in several currencies can be risk-reducing. Since there are fixed costs associated with bond or debt issues, only very large firms are able to use this opportunity directly. There are currency baskets in which bonds can be denominated. For example, the Special Drawing Right (SDR) gained acceptance during the 1980s as a denomination for corporate bond issues. If inflation rates underlying the different basket-currencies' values are very similar, then there is little value in this diversification.

## Interest rate swaps

A disadvantage of futures markets is that contracts are limited in maturities as well as in size. In the market for interest rate swaps, on the other hand, contracts can be tailor-made to the long-term needs of firms. In analogy with swaps in the foreign exchange market, an interest rate swap implies the simultaneous purchase and sale of liabilities with different payment conditions. A firm borrowing at a fixed rate may "trade" or swap loans with another firm which is borrowing at a floating rate. The reason for "swapping" is that the two firms are unable in their local markets to obtain loans with the desired payment conditions at reasonable costs. One firm may desire a fixed rate loan when its cash inflows are contracted in monetary terms for a long period, while another firm may desire a floating rate loan at a time when its cash inflows are inflation sensitive. If, at the same time, both firms have relatively cheap credit in the undesirable type of loan, then there are grounds for a swap (see Table 6.5). Each firm could obviously change the characteristics of its payments by buying or selling interest rate futures contracts as well, but, in the case of swaps, the two firms can exactly match the account and timing of loans, interest payments, and repayments. Through the swap, both firms may also obtain an interest rate advantage in their desired types of loans, even if each firm lacks access to a market in which the desired loan type is in large supply.

To swap, of course, a firm must find a counterparty that matches it in terms of loan size and maturity. Many large banks today act as counterparties in the market for swaps. The market has developed rapidly and some large banks are market makers in swaps. Banks can match one firm on one side of the swap with a number of firms on the other side with approximately offsetting needs. In the process, the bank may be temporarily or permanently exposed to interest risk for a part of the swap amount.

The increased involvement of banks as intermediaries and market makers has made it possible for a secondary market in swaps to develop. Thus, one party to the swap can reverse the transaction before the loans mature. Options in swaps have also developed. This means that a firm may borrow in, for example, Swiss francs and simultaneously obtain an

**Table 6.5  Different kinds of swaps.**

| Firm 1 borrows at | Firm 2 borrows at | Currency denominations |
|---|---|---|
| Currency swaps | | |
| 1. Fixed (CHF) | Fixed interest (USD) | Different |
| 2. Floating interest (CHF) | Floating interest (USD) | Different |
| Interest rate swaps | | |
| 3. Fixed interest | Floating interest | Same |
| 4. Floating interest | Floating interest | Same |
| Currency and interest rate swaps | | |
| 5. Fixed interest (CHF) | Floating interest (USD) | Different |

Examples

1. Firm 1 (2) obtains USD (CHF) through swapping with Firms 2 (1).

2. Same as 1.

3. Firm 1 (2) obtains a floating (fixed) interest loan in the same currency.

4. Firm 1 (2) borrows at Libor* (US commercial paper) rate and swaps to obtain a loan at US commercial paper (Libor) rate.

5. Firm 1 (2) obtains floating rate dollar (fixed CHF) loan through swapping after borrowing in local market at fixed CHF (floating dollar) interest.

\* Floating rate contracts are often specified relative to the Libor (London Interbank Offered Rate).

option with a bank to swap to a dollar-denominated loan before or at a specific future date.

Table 6.5 shows major types of swap transactions in international financial markets. Types 1 and 2 are pure currency swaps, types 3 and 4 are pure interest swaps, and type 5 is both a currency and an interest swap.

## Hedging the exposure of non-financial assets

The discussion in this section has so far been limited to interest rate and inflation exposure on financial assets and liabilities. However, in previous chapters we have emphasized that a firm's commercial operations are exposed to interest rate risk and inflation risk as much as, or more than, it is exposed to exchange rate risk. In analogy with cash flow exchange rate exposure (see Chapter 3), interest rate and inflation exposure of commercial cash flows are defined as the sensitivities of the commercial cash flows to an increase in interest rates and the inflation rate, respectively:

Interest rate (inflation) exposure of the commercial cash flows

$$= \frac{\text{Change in real commercial cash flow}}{\text{Change in interest rate (inflation rate)}}$$

(14)

The cash flow interest rate exposure can be hedged by buying interest rate futures contracts with an offsetting exposure. If the fluctuation in interest rates depends strongly on changes in the inflation rate rather than on real factors, it is the inflation risk of commercial cash flows that is better hedged using interest rate futures.

We return to hedging commercial cash flow exposures in the next section, taking into account the interdependence between interest and inflation rates.

## 6.5  HEDGING MACROECONOMIC EXPOSURE TO MARKET PRICE VARIABLES

In this section we illustrate how cash flow or value exposures measured as regression coefficients, as described in Chapters 4 and 5, can be hedged. We prefer the term "hedge" to "cover," since there is generally not a one-to-one correspondence between the position in a currency and the offsetting contract. From an accounting point of view this lack of correspondence between the foreign currency position and the offsetting hedge contract may cause a conceptual problem. Once it is recognized that even domestically operating firms are exposed to exchange rate risk, it is obvious that the existence of an FC contract on the books is neither necessary nor sufficient for exposure to exist.

Box 6.4 shows how an exchange rate exposure coefficient provides information about the required size of the offsetting financial position that would constitute a hedge. The exchange rate is here assumed to be the only exposure variable.

We turn now to the hedging of macroeconomic exposure after having estimated exposure coefficients to a number of market price variables. As noted in Chapter 5, exposures can be estimated either for levels of cash flows and explanatory variables or for percentage rates of change. Table 6.6 shows the results of an exposure analysis of real commercial cash flows per quarter. The market price variables that have statistically significant impacts are listed on the left. Exposure coefficients showing the change in DC real commercial cash flows from a one unit change of the price variable from one quarter to the other are listed in the first column for coefficients. On the right are the coefficients for the percentage rate of change of real commercial cash flows from a 1% change in the price variable. Knowledge of exposure coefficients in one column can be translated into coefficients in the other column using knowledge about levels of exchange rates, interest rates, price levels, and cash flows. This information is listed in the table.

The coefficients in the table, obtained from regression analysis, are "hedge coefficients"; they show the size of required hedge contracts using the opposite sign so that a contract can be written on the variable, provided the variables are not correlated.[2]

The exchange rate exposure –7,500,000 shows that if the exchange rate moves from, for example, DC 2/FC to DC 3/FC, then real commercial cash

---

**Box 6.4  Hedging: An example**

Assume that the following relation between cash flows and exchange rates in quarter $t$ has been estimated.

$$X_t^{DC} = 1,000,000 - 1,563S_t + 267S_{t-1}$$

This expression tells management that independent of exchange rates there is a cash flow of DC 1,000,000. If the domestic currency depreciates one unit from, say, DC 4/FC to DC 5/FC from one quarter to another, then the DC value of cash flows falls by 1,563. In the quarter thereafter the DC value of cash flows recovers and increases by 267.

The coefficients tell management that in order to hedge the quarter-to-quarter exposure, the firm should buy FC 1,563 in the forward market for delivery in one quarter. In order to hedge effects over two quarters of a potential quarterly exchange rate change the size of forward contract should be decreased to FC (1,563 – 267) = 1,296.

The 267 coefficient for the lagged exchange rate does not represent exposure for the next quarter, but an anticipated effect of the exchange rate change from the previous quarter. However, with the time horizon of six months, the 267 should be included in exposure. Thus, the firm could buy FC 1,296 in the six-month forward market in each quarter.

One difficulty arises because cash flows are measured over whole quarters. Therefore, the quarterly exchange rates must be viewed as averages. Forward contracts refer to specific days, however. Therefore, the hedge contract could either be purchased in the middle of one quarter, or the contract could be divided into a number of smaller contracts entered into at different times during the quarter.

---

flows fall by the size of the coefficient. A hedge contract of the size of FC 7,500,000 would provide a hedge. In other words, an asset position of this magnitude in FC would offset the commercial cash flow effects of exchange rate changes. This is easy to check. If there is an unanticipated exchange rate change from DC 2/FC to DC 3/FC, then real cash flows fall by DC 7,500,000. If a financial asset worth FC 7,500,000 were held, then a DC gain of the same magnitude would occur. The asset could be any financial asset denominated in FC, or a forward contract for purchase of FC 7,500,000.

The interest rate exposure coefficient –150,000 says that if there is a one percentage point increase in FC interest rate, then cash flows fall by DC 150,000. A hedge contract would be one that creates a gain of DC 150,000 if the FC interest rate rises one percentage point from, for example, 10% to 11%. Since the price of interest rate futures and forward contracts are not

**Table 6.6 Exposure coefficients. Real commercial cash flows per quarter.**

| Variable | Coefficient, level | Coefficients, percentage change (elasticities) |
|---|---|---|
| Exchange rate DC/FC | – 7,500,000 | – 0.5 |
| FC three-month interest rate | – 150,000 | – 0.005 |
| DC price level (CPI) | – 30,000 | – 0.1 |
| Price of output/price index | 180,000 | 0.6 |
| Expected level of cash flows | DC 30,000,000 | |

Note: Exchange rate 2DC/FC; interest rate level 10%; and price index 100.

specified in term of the interest rate, additional information is required to determine the size of the hedge contract. Specifically, knowledge about the gain or loss in DC on a financial contract from a one percentage point increase in the interest rate abroad is required. The number of contracts required to hedge the interest rate exposure of –150,000 can be calculated in the following way (see also Box 6.8):

$$\begin{bmatrix} \text{Number of FC T-bill} \\ \text{futures to hedge FC} \\ \text{interest rate exposure} \end{bmatrix} = 150,000 \bigg/ \begin{bmatrix} \text{Change in DC price of FC} \\ \text{T-bill futures contracts of} \\ \text{one percentage point change} \\ \text{in the foreign interest rate} \end{bmatrix}$$

(15)

A similar calculation can be made to estimate a hedge for the exposure to the domestic price level. First, a financial contract sensitive to changes in the price level must be found. Thereafter, the number of contracts can be calculated in the following way:

$$\begin{bmatrix} \text{Number of contracts} \\ \text{to hedge DC price} \\ \text{level exposure} \end{bmatrix} = 30,000 \bigg/ \begin{bmatrix} \text{Price change on financial} \\ \text{contracts of one unit} \\ \text{increase in price level} \end{bmatrix}$$

(16)

where 30,000 is the negative of the coefficient in Table 6.6 that shows the cash flow effect of a one unit increase in the price level. Notice that if there is no financial contract defined in terms of the price level, but it is defined in terms of, for example, a commodity price index correlated with the price level, then purchasing the contract exposes the firm to commodity price risk.

The coefficients to the right in Table 6.6, showing the exposures as elasticities defined as the percentage rate of change in cash flows of a 1% rate of change in the market price variable, can also be used to calculate the size of hedge contracts. The exposure coefficient defined as an elasticity shows the size of the hedge contract relative to expected level of cash flows. In the exchange rate case, the coefficient is –0.5, and the expected cash flows in FC are 15,000,000. The hedge contract should be 0.5 x FC 15,000,000 = FC 7,500,000. A more general formulation is the following:

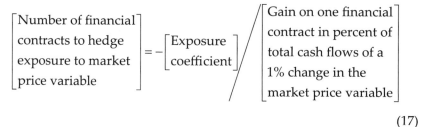

$$
\begin{bmatrix} \text{Number of financial} \\ \text{contracts to hedge} \\ \text{exposure to market} \\ \text{price variable} \end{bmatrix} = - \begin{bmatrix} \text{Exposure} \\ \text{coefficient} \end{bmatrix} \bigg/ \begin{bmatrix} \text{Gain on one financial} \\ \text{contract in percent of} \\ \text{total cash flows of a} \\ \text{1\% change in the} \\ \text{market price variable} \end{bmatrix}
$$

(17)

where the exposure coefficient is the percentage change in total cash flows of a 1% change in the market price variable.

Derivatives that are commonly used for hedging were briefly mentioned above. For foreign exchange exposure, forward contracts and money market contracts were emphasized. Naturally, any FC security that fluctuates in DC value with the exchange rate is a potential hedging device. Only forward and money market contracts are "pure" hedging instruments because their maturities can be adjusted almost perfectly.

Option contracts on the purchase or sale of one currency for another are also useful devices. One approach to using options is to utilize information about an option's "delta." This concept for describing an option reveals the change in the price of the option resulting form a one unit change in the exchange rate. The information in the delta coefficient is precisely the information required to calculate the size of hedge contracts as shown in equations 15–17. Using the exposure coefficients the number of options needed to create an offsetting gain or loss in the options contracts can easily be calculated using the option's delta. Unlike forward contracts, the sensitivity of the price of an option to changes in the exchange rate varies substantially with the time to maturity of the contract, and with the level of the exchange rates. Thus, the use of options for hedging requires a dynamic strategy. The hedge position must be monitored and changed frequently (see Box 6.5).

For interest rate exposure, as for exchange rate exposure, there is, as noted, a menu of financial contracts available for hedging. Interest rate futures, interest rate options, and interest rate swaps exist and are traded in several well-developed financial markets. In countries where such derivatives are not issued, the corresponding derivatives in other countries are close substitutes if interest rates in the different currency denominations

---

**Box 6.5  Options**

In the option literature, the concepts of delta, gamma, theta and lambda are used to analyze how option values depend on underlying stochastic processes for exchange rates, interest rates, and so on.

The option's *delta* is defined as the change in the option value from a (small) change in the price of the underlying asset, that is, the exchange rate for a foreign currency option.

The *gamma* coefficient shows how the option's delta changes with changes in the exchange rate. The gamma reveals how the hedge position must be adjusted when the variable changes.

The *theta* of an option describes the value of the option as a function of time. The value of an option depends on time to maturity. If the firm is concerned about hedging the value of its cash flows, then the value of an option would depend on the time at which cash flows are expected, and the time to maturity of the option. Thus, the hedge contract changes over time when options are used.

Finally, the *lambda* describes how the value of an option depends on the volatility of underlying variables. Option values are highly sensitive to volatility, and it is usually assumed that volatility is constant. Similarly, in the earlier regression analysis for cash flows and other variables, volatilities are assumed to be constant. However, these regression coefficients are less sensitive to volatility than option values.

The delta, gamma, and so on, can also be defined for forward and futures contracts but in general only the delta is interesting for these contracts. Therefore, the hedge position in these derivates does not generally change over the exposure period.

---

are strongly correlated. Even if the derivatives markets are thin or non-existent, the variety of instruments in different maturities and the adjustability of interest rates enable firms to adjust their interest rate exposures within a wide range. Furthermore, it is usually possible to take a short position in one maturity by simultaneous borrowing and lending. Thus, "synthetic" forward contracts can be created. For example, a three-month forward contract to buy a three month T-bill is a promise to deliver such a security in three months. As Equation 13 shows, an identical position can be obtained "synthetically" by taking a three-month loan and investing in a six-month security.

### Inflation risk and the interdependence among market price variables

We have derived the size of a hedge contract under the assumption that exchange rates, interest rates, and inflation rates are independent. In previous chapters, we emphasized that exposure measures should take into account that these macroeconomic variables are likely to be correlated. The correlations should be taken into account in hedging, as well. One way of addressing this problem is to consider a second round of hedging of the first round of hedge contracts. For example, we can ask whether the value of an interest rate futures hedge contract is exposed to exchange rates or inflation rates. To the extent the macroeconomic variables are correlated, complete hedging of exposures requires consideration of the exposures of the hedge contracts in the first round. The second round of hedge contracts will also be exposed, and so on.

There are three ways of approaching the problem caused by lack of independence among the macroeconomic price variables. The first approach is to conduct the first round of hedging and leave it at that. Neglecting the correlations this way is not serious if correlations are not high.

The second approach is to estimate the exposures of the hedge contracts and, thereafter, to solve mathematically for the combination of hedge contracts that simultaneously creates complete hedging of the exposures.[3]

The third approach is to evaluate whether some correlations are particularly high. If so, they cannot be neglected, and a second round of hedging is necessary. One such case is likely to be caused by correlation between interest rates and inflation rates. Box 6.6 provides an example of correlation between a foreign interest rate and domestic inflation.

As the analysis in Box 6.6 indicates, the interest rate futures contract provides a hedge of either real interest rate risk or inflation risk. Hedging one type of risk affects the exposure to the other. Thus, foreign exchange and interest rate derivatives in combination cannot accomplish the task of hedging the three types of exposure encountered in the example in Table 6.6. It is necessary to find a third type of contract or to accomplish hedging of one of the risks by other means.

Commodity or stock-market index derivatives are possible candidates for hedging inflation. Taking positions in these contracts exposes the firm to additional sources of risk, however. A third possibility arises if there are futures contracts in inflation-linked securities of different maturities. In general, longer-term interest rates or the difference between long- and short-term interest rates, are more strongly related to inflation expectation than short-term interest rates alone. Some governments have issued inflation-linked (indexed) bonds but the markets for these securities have developed sluggishly in many countries.

The inflation exposure of a firm can be addressed more directly as well, in contracts with customers, suppliers, and employees. Such contracts can be indexed to inflation. Experience indicates, however, that inflation must go up to double or triple digits before indexation becomes widespread. For moderate inflation rates it is more common that contracts contain clauses with trigger levels of inflation. If these levels are reached, then partial or full compensation for inflation is obtained.[4]

**Box 6.6 Hedging interest rate exposure when the interest rate and inflation are related**

The exposure of real commercial cash flows has been estimated as in Table 6.6. Assume furthermore that one percentage point increase in the FC three-month interest rate causes a DC 2 decline in the value of an FC T-bill futures contract. Using Equation 15, this implies that the number of FC T-bill futures contracts required to hedge the FC interest rate exposure is 75,000 with a negative sign implying that a short position should be taken. Assume that we also have found that the FC interest rate depends on the DC price level (DC-CPI) in the following way:

$$\text{FC interest rate } = 5 + 0.6\,(\text{DC–CPI}) + \text{error term}$$

This equation shows that a one unit increase in CPI causes a 0.6 percentage point increase in the interest rate. As a consequence, the interest rate sensitive position that was entered to hedge interest rate risk is exposed to DC inflation risk.

   If there exists a hedge contract for DC inflation risk, then a hedge requires that both the original DC price-level exposure in Table 6.6 and Equation 16, and the inflation exposure of the interest rate hedge contract must be offset.

   If there is no inflation hedge contract avaliable, but the firm's ambition is only to hedge real interest rate risk, then the above short hedge position of 75,000 contracts should be reduced, because this position represents a hedge against any change in the FC interest rate whether the source is the real interest rate or DC inflation. The amount by which the above hedge position should be reduced in order to hedge only real interest risk depends on the proportion of the variance of the interest rate that is explained by real factors and DC–CPI respectively. The proportion that can be ascribed to the real interest variance is the proportion unexplained variance in the equation above. This information is given as one minus the $R^2$ for the equation.

## 6.6 HEDGING WITH UNCERTAIN EXPOSURE USING DERATIVES

So far we have only analyzed the use of forward contracts and interest rate futures for hedging macroeconomic risk under the assumption that we know the exposure coefficients with certainty. The output when running a regression includes statistics that tell the analyst how uncertain the exposure coefficients are. At times, this uncertainty could be substantial.

Assume, for example, that the coefficient –7,500,000 for the exchange rate in Table 6.6 is lower than –5,000,000 with a probability of 0.2 (20%) and larger (as absolute value) than –10,000,000 with equal probability. Thus, the true coefficient lies between –5,000,000 and –10,000,000 with a probability of 0.6 (60%). With great certainty a forward hedge contract of DC 7,500,000 will turn out to be too large or too small. Should the firm abstain from hedging with this uncertainty? The answer is of course "no" if management wishes to reduce the uncertainty about future cash flows. A forward contract hedging the full estimated exposure of 7,500,000 need not be the most appropriate method, however.

To illustrate the problem, consider the more well-known and intuitive case of cash flow uncertainty. A Swedish-Swiss company is tendering an offer for high voltage power supply equipment to France. The equipment will be built in Switzerland if the company wins the competition and receives the order worth euro 100 million. The decision will be made in three months and the chances of receiving the order are 50-50 in the judgment of management. Clearly, the company's exposure to changes in the CHF/euro exchange rate is substantial.

One way of hedging the exposure for the first three months is to buy an option; in this case we buy a put option on euro 100 million. The option can be allowed to expire if the order is not received.

Even better, it might be possible to buy a call option expiring in three months on a euro 100 million forward contract to sell euro. The option on the forward sale allows the company to obtain a forward contract at the time the order is received, if it is received, and the forward rate will be known today.

The same reasoning can be applied to the general case of uncertain exposure coefficients. The firm in Table 6.6 with an expected exposure of FC –7,500,000 could decide to buy a forward contract on the exposure that it has with, say, a probability of 0.8 (80%). In the example given, the forward contract should be FC –5,000,000 because the probability that the exposure will exceed FC –5,000,000 in absolute terms is 0.8. The probability that it will be as large as FC –10,000,000 is 0.2, however. Thus, the firm could buy a call option on an additional FC 5,000,000 or a call option on a forward contract to buy FC 5,000,000. It is naturally possible to enter contracts for higher amounts as well if managers' risk-aversion motivates such actions.

The risk profile associated with different methods of hedging can be estimated with some knowledge about the probabilities of exposure of varying sizes. In our case the expected exposure is FC –7,500,000. In Box 6.7 the exposure is described if the firm chooses to buy FC 7,500,000 in the forward market. The forward contract itself represents a known exposure of FC 7,500,000. Thus, the actual exposure is the difference between the forward contract exposure and the exposure of the originally exposed position.

In the second case the firm buys FC 5,000,000 in the forward market and a call option on FC 5,000,000. The risk profile after hedging this way is

---

**Box 6.7  Risk profiles for hedging uncertain exposure with a forward contract \***

Hedge contract: Forward contract on FC 7,500,000 offsets expected cash flow exposure

Probability = **0.2** that exposure on original position is less than FC 5,000,000 in absolute terms. With this probability, the exposure including forward contract is FC 7,500,000 – 5,000,000 (or less) = 2,500,000 (or more positive).

Probability = **0.6** that exposure is between 2,500,000 and –2,500,000 including forward contract.

Probability = **0.2** that exposure is –2,500,000 or more negative including forward contract.

\* Probability assumptions for exposure are given in the text.

---

described in Box 6.8. A third possibility is that the firm enters a forward contracts for FC 5,000,000 plus a call option on a forward contract for another FC 5,000,000. This alternative is useful when uncertainty will be resolved before the forward contract matures. The exercise date on the option should occur when the uncertainty about the exposure is resolved to some degree. The closer the exercise date for the option is to the date for the exposure, the more this alternative becomes like the previous one, because the option on the forward contract becomes more like the option on the FC in the spot market.

## Non-standard derivatives

Apart from the standard derivative contracts discussed above, a number of variations and combinations have developed at a rapid pace. "Exotics" are often constructed with a particular risk management function in mind. The firm that first develops a new product for which demand develops is likely to obtain a relatively large share of the market. Often the objective of the innovation is to create an instrument that can be traded in secondary markets. If the innovation is successful, then the transaction costs of using the instrument can be reduced dramatically.

Some of the non-standard contracts developed during the last decade can be useful from the point of view of hedging the type of exposure discussed in Section 6.2. Options on forward contracts were mentioned. Options on options, or compound options, may also be useful for the manager who is uncertain about the magnitude of exposure. The compound option allows the buyer to buy or sell an option at a set price over a period.

---

**Box 6.8  Risk profiles for hedging uncertain exposure with a combination of a forward contract and options \***

Hedge contract: Forward contract on FC 5,000,000. Call option on FC 5,000,000. Expected exposure FC –7,500,000.

Probability = **0.2** that exposure including forward contract is zero or positive and that there is a speculative profit opportunity on the option.

Probability = **0.6** that exposure including forward contract is between zero and FC –2,500,000. A call option provides a hedge against downside risk on the exposure.

Probability = **0.2** that exposure is zero or negative after use of forward and options hedge.

\* Probability assumptions for exposure are given in the text.

---

Another contract is the "range forward," which produces a pay-off like a forward contract over a range for the exchange rate, while allowing the buyer to take advantage of large, favorable exchange rate movements of the exchange rate. The holder of a range forward contract has a put option on the exchange rate at the minimum of the range, and has sold a call at a strike price corresponding to the maximum of the range.

Finally, a "swaption" is an option to enter into a swap contract like the forward option discussed above. Both instruments are used when there is uncertainty about the exposure in the future.

If markets are efficient and conditions for International Fisher Parity prevail, then the expected pay-offs on various contracts are the same. The patterns of pay-off over future exchange rates differ, however (see Box 6.3).

Transaction costs may of course differ among contracts. For these costs to remain low, as for the most common forward contracts in most currencies, the market for a contract must obtain a certain depth and volume. Thus, more exotic contracts are available only for a few major exchange rates. OTC (over the counter) markets offer ample opportunities for firms to tailor contracts to such specific needs.

## 6.7  TAXES AND HEDGE CONTRACTS

As noted in Section 6.3, hedge decisions may be influenced by tax considerations when cash gains and losses on hedge contracts are not treated for tax purposes the same way speculative gains and losses are. A hedge is not easily defined, however. A foreign exchange trader has stated that "a hedge is a deal gone sour that offsets a good deal."

   The problem of defining a hedge can become important when we consider contracts for hedging economic exposure, because the size of the hedge contract does not generally correspond to an asset or a liability on the books of the firm. Identification of a hedge requires that the firm has a written statement about its hedge policy and its concept of exposure, as well as documentation of estimated exposures every period.

   If hedge contracts and speculative gains and losses have different tax consequence and if there is no clear identification of a hedge, then there is one problem from tax authorities' point of view and a different problem from firms' point of view. The tax authorities face the problem that firms might speculate under the guise of hedging. Firms, on the other hand, face the problem that the tax rate applicable on a hedge contract might differ from the rate on the asset, liability, or flow that is being hedged. This possibility was discussed in Section 6.3 in connection with hedging of translation exposure. The general problem is that the timing of taxable (tax-deductible) gains (losses) on the asset or liability being hedged could differ from the timing of taxable (tax-deductible) gains (losses) on the hedge contract.

   A work-group within the IASC (International Accounting Standards Committee) published in November 1995 a report on hedge accounting for tax purposes (Adams and Montesi, 1995). Based on this report, we can conceptually identify four models of accounting for hedge contracts

   1. Mark to market accounting
   2. Mark to market hedge accounting
   3. Deferral hedge accounting
   4. Non-realized gains and losses are accounted for as part of owners'
      equity.

The external accounting method may differ from the tax accounting method. Our concern is about potential tax consequences of hedging.

   "Mark to market accounting" implies that all assets and liabilities are valued at market values. There is no country that applies this principle consistently because it violates traditional accounting principles. If it were applied for accounting and tax purposes, then proportional taxes would be neutral with respect to hedge decisions.

   "Mark to market hedge accounting" means that hedge contracts are valued at market prices. If the firm uses an exposure concept that is also market value based, then this principle works like the principle above, but if the firm uses another principle for calculating exposure, then market valued hedge contracts would be used to offset non-market value exposures. Tax authorities and, therefore, firms face the need to identify hedge contracts in this case and firms might have the incentive to be vague and adjust the classification of contracts with the benefit of hindsight.

   "Deferred hedge accounting" is applied in the United States. This principle implies that the accounting for gains and losses on a hedge contract is linked in time to the accounting for gains and losses in the firm being hedged. Cash gains and losses on a hedge contract could be posted as an asset or a liability for a period under this principle. Thereby, the incentive of firms to, for example, increase the size of a hedge contract to create an after-tax hedge against non-taxable changes in the value of an asset is removed. This possibility was discussed as "double hedging" in Section 6.3. It was also noted that these incentives arise when a clear distinction is not made between economic and accounting valuation principles.

The fourth model implies that "non-realized gains and losses are accounted for under owners' equity." Contracts in financial instruments (derivatives) are divided into two groups: trading and risk management. Mark to market valuation is used in trading, while in risk management only realized gains and losses go to the income statement. For tax purposes the method requires, of course, that the distinction can be made before the results are known, because the firm may have the incentive to reclassify contracts with the results on hand.

The rationale for this method is that if hedge contracts are entered with maturities corresponding to exposures, then changes in the values of derivatives before maturity would not have tax consequences. On the other hand, if the firm is concerned with changes in economic value when hedging, then the distinction between realized and non-realized gains and losses should not matter, however. Under this method, however, the distinction has tax consequences. It is the timing of tax payments as opposed to the economic value of expected tax payments that is affected by the distinction, once again illustrating that many of the problems arising under the different valuation methods are of little significance when economic principles are employed. The principle employed affects the timing of tax payments, however, and firms might be able to profit by classifying hedge and speculative contracts according to what is favorable from a tax point of view.

## 6.8 CONCLUDING REMARKS ON APPROACHES TO HEDGE MACROECONOMIC UNCERTAINTY

Numerous instruments or operations—internal or external—are available to reduce the exposure to the different elements of macroeconomic risk. It was our purpose in this chapter to focus on how to undertake hedging in financial markets after internal adjustments have been made.

The starting point for exposure management is the identification of the exposure of a firm's commercial operations, leaving financial exposures aside. Then internal operation to adjust this exposure can be undertaken. Many internal operations actually involve the adjustment of commercial operation. In Chapter 8 we discuss, in a section on the creation of "real options," such adjustments. In accordance with its strategy the firm then turns to its financial positions and the financial markets to cover or hedge the commercial exposure.

Much of the discussion in this chapter concerned the hedging of short-term positions. We warned about the "false" exactness of traditional exposure measures. Putting emphasis on the traditional measures is tanta-mount to look for solutions somewhere, just because data exist, even if the data are irrelevant. The validity of all accounting-based exposure mea-sures is uncertain even if an accounting figure provides the illusion of exactness. The exposure measures suggested in this book are far more useful; the regression approach provides information about the uncer-tainty of coefficients, and this uncertainty can be dealt with through the use of options, in combination with forwards and futures. However, the primary concern is always to obtain an economically meaningful measure to hedge. The suggested measures in this book meet this objective far more effectively than the traditional ones.

One practical problem arises in the relationship between the company and its auditors. Until the day when the exposure measures suggested here become part of corporate external accounting rules, we can—based on an observed inclination of auditors to stick to easily observable fig-ures—anticipate a debate between the management and the auditors about the true exposure. The burden of proof on the managers is to con-vince the auditors that covering exposures other than those calculated from accounting data is not speculation.

Another inevitable practical complication in exposure management is taxation. Special tax treatment of gains and losses on hedge contracts, as compared with "speculative" contracts, creates incentives for management to be vague about exposure measures, while tax authorities and other stakeholders seek the ability to clearly identify exposures. Since exposures are not easily identifiable by accounting rules, there is an obvious conflict of interest. It is likely that tax authorities in the future will require explicit statements about principles for measuring exposure, when conventional accounting-based measures are abandoned.

If all assets and liabilities were "marked to market," then there would be no reason to distinguish between hedge and speculative transactions. However, as long as gains and losses on exposed positions are realized and taxed according to some accounting rule—and maturities of hedge contracts do not perfectly correlate with the realization of gains and losses on exposed positions—there are incentives to obfuscate the measurement of exposure.

It is possible that a simple "marking to market" rule for accounting and taxation of hedge contracts would inspire management to focus on eco-nomically meaningful exposure measures based on cash flows and pres-ent values of cash flows. This rule is the only one that removes incentives to speculate under the guise of hedging.

## NOTES

1 Any international finance textbook describes the foreign exchange market and the financial instruments in detail.

2 If the variables are not correlated, the regressing cash flows on each variable independently would result in the same coefficient.
3 See also Oxelheim and Wihlborg (1987, Chapter IV) for a discussion of hedging when exposure variables are correlated.
4 See Oxelheim et al. (1990) for empirical evidence from Sweden and Singapore on this issue.

# Chapter 7

# Evaluating Cash Flow at Risk

## 7.1 INTRODUCTION

In this chapter we illustrate a method for estimating the risk to which a firm is exposed and for evaluating the risk-effects of hedging macroeconomic and commodity price exposures. While earlier chapters focused on estimating corporate exposures, this chapter considers how these exposures jointly determine risk from the perspective of the individual corporation. It is assumed that management is concerned with the variance of the cash flows of the corporation over a specific time horizon. Shareholders are able to diversify risk in the markets for securities, and management's concern with risk is consistent with shareholder wealth maximization. As discussed in Chapter 2, the reason for concern with the variance of total cash flows could be that a large unanticipated cash flow loss within a certain time horizon would reduce financial flexibility to take advantage of various opportunities. Although we focus on cash flow risk in this chapter, the analysis would be essentially identical if management had chosen to focus on value risk. The reason for managing value risk would be, for example, the expectations of substantial costs associated with bankruptcy.

In chapters 4 and 5 we discussed how exposures to macroeconomic risk variables can be estimated. While an exposure describes the sensitivity of a firm's value or cash flows to a change in a variable, the risk associated with a particular macroeconomic variable depends not only on the firm's exposure to it, but also on the degree of uncertainty about the variable, as well as its relation to other variables causing exposures. Thus, the incentive to manage the impact on the corporate cash flows of a particular risk-variable depends on four factors: (a) the size of the cash flow exposure to the variable, (b) the degree of uncertainty about the variable, (c) the relationship between the variable and other risk variables, and (d) the distribution of costs and benefits associated with particular cash flow outcomes. The last factor could be, for example, potential costs associated with lack of liquidity.

The desirable extent of hedging a particular exposure would depend on the four factors mentioned in the previous paragraph, as well as costs associated with hedging. In Chapter 6 we were concerned with methods and market costs of hedging. The latter may take the form of transactions costs and, for example, lost interest income of switching from one currency to another. In this chapter, a method for bringing all these factors together in an analysis of risks and hedging will be illustrated.

The method for risk analysis that we use to analyze macroeconomic risk and hedging is Cash Flow at Risk (CFaR). As mentioned in Chapter 2, this method is a variation of Value at Risk (VaR), pioneered by J. P. Morgan & Company in 1993.[1] VaR represents a maximum value loss that a firm can accept with a certain confidence that the loss will not exceed the maximum value. For example, management may state that the loss in value due to unexpected macroeconomic events must not exceed 10 million U.S. dollars with a probability of 0.95, that is, with a 95 percent confidence. CFaR is similarly stated as the maximum cash flow loss the firm can accept relative to expected cash flows with a certain confidence.

Although CFaR conceptually has intuitive appeal, it may not be an easy task to decide on the maximum loss and the corresponding level of confidence. These decisions must be made before the extent of hedging over different time horizons can be determined. The likelihood of outcomes associated with particular costs and benefits, as well as costs associated with hedging, would be important factors behind hedging decisions. Based on these factors, management can set a certain CFaR as a maximum loss and a certain probability that losses will not be larger over a time horizon.

We proceed in Section 7.2 by describing how cash flows and their variation can be decomposed into risk factors based on measures of different exposures. Information requirements for estimation of CFaR are described in Section 7.3. The company used in the illustration, Norsk Hydro, is described in Section 7.4, along with its exposures to macroeconomic and commodity price risk. In Section 7.5, CFaR and its components are estimated. Effects of hedging are analyzed in section 7.6. Concluding remarks follow in Section 7.7.

## 7.2 FROM EXPOSURES TO CASH FLOW AT RISK (CFaR)

The Volvo case in Chapter 5 was used to illustrate how cash flows and cash flow variability can be decomposed using information about macroeconomic and other exposures. The regression analysis for changes in total cash flows in Table 5.2, column (1) showed the following result:

Percent change in Volvo Car's total quarterly cash flows in SEK =

5.2·(percent change in the quarterly exchange rate, SEK/FC)

$$-0.4 \cdot \left( \begin{array}{l} \text{percent change in the quarterly Swedish short} \\ \text{term interest rate} \end{array} \right)$$

$$+28.2 \cdot \left( \begin{array}{l} \text{percent change in the quarterly German} \\ \text{producer price level} \end{array} \right)$$

+ random influence from other factors.

$$(18)$$

As shown in Table 6.6, the exposure coefficients 5.2, –0.4 and 28.2 can be recalculated to show the effects on the level of SEK cash flows of a one unit change in each of the three macroeconomic variables. The only information needed for this transformation is the expected level of cash flows in SEK. There is an advantage to work with percent rate of change, however, since the distribution of changes in price variables typically is closer to the bell-shaped normal distribution. Such distributions can be characterized with information about the expected change and the variance of the change alone.

The expected change in the cash flows can be calculated using Equation 18 with the exposure coefficients and the expected changes in the three macroeconomic variables, assuming that the expected effects of other random influences is zero. The variance of the change in cash flows is more complex, since it depends not only on exposures and the variances of the three factors in the equation above but also on the possible relationship among these factors. It is possible, for example, that an increase in the German producer prices is associated with an appreciation of the Swedish krona, that is, a decline in SEK/FC. In this case, changes in the exchange rate and changes in German producer prices are negatively correlated. Taking into account the variances of the two variables, we say that there is a negative covariance between them.

The variance of the percent change in Volvo's quarterly cash flows can be calculated as follows:

Variance of percent change in total quarterly cash flows in SEK =

$$(5.2)^2 \cdot \left( \begin{array}{l} \text{variance of percent change in the} \\ \text{quarterly exchange rate, SEK/FC} \end{array} \right)$$

$$+(-0.4)^2 \cdot \left( \begin{array}{l} \text{variance of percent change in the} \\ \text{quarterly Swedish short-term interest rate} \end{array} \right)$$

$$+ (28.2)^2 \cdot \left( \begin{array}{l} \text{variance of the percent change in the} \\ \text{quarterly German producer price level} \end{array} \right)$$

$$+ \left( \begin{array}{l} \text{variance of the random term for} \\ \text{influences of other factors} \end{array} \right)$$

$$+ 2 \cdot 5.2 \cdot (-0.4) \cdot \left( \begin{array}{l} \text{covariance between changes in the exchange rate} \\ \text{and changes in the interest rate} \end{array} \right)$$

$$+ 2 \cdot 5.2 \cdot 28.2 \cdot \left( \begin{array}{l} \text{covariance between the changes in the exchange rate} \\ \text{and changes in the producer prices} \end{array} \right)$$

$$+ 2 \cdot (-0.4) \cdot 28.2 \cdot \left( \begin{array}{l} \text{covariance between changes in the interest rate} \\ \text{and changes in the producer prices} \end{array} \right)$$

$$(19)$$

In this equation it is assumed that there is no correlation between the three macroeconomic price variables and the random term capturing influences of other factors. The first three terms capture the variances of the three macroeconomic factors followed by variance of the random term for other influences. The last three terms capture the effects caused by correlation among the three factors to which the firm is exposed. In this particular case there are no industry-specific or firm-specific factors explaining the cash flows except the random term. As the number of factors increase, the number of covariances also increases rapidly. For this reason, variances and covariances are usually described in a matrix when there are more factors, as we will see below, and matrix algebra is applied to calculate the total variance.

The effect of, for example, exchange rate variance on cash flow variance in Equation 19 depends on the exchange rate exposure (5.2), the variance of the exchange rate change in the first term, as well as on the covariances between the exchange rate change and changes in the other variables in the fifth and the sixth terms, weighted with the product of the exposures. Thus, if the firm by means of risk management could eliminate the impact of exchange rate changes, the reduction in the cash flow variance would not depend on the reduced exchange rate variance alone but also on covariance terms. The sum of the covariance terms that include exchange rate changes can be either positive or negative.

Using historical data for changes in the different variables, the above formula can be used to decompose the variance of changes in cash flows to estimate the contribution of each factor to the total variance. CFaR is forward looking, however, and it refers to the concern of management with cash flow risk over the next quarter, the next half year, or a longer period. For this purpose, it is necessary to take into account how the different variables behave over time. Are exchange rate changes following a random walk, implying that the current change is the best predictor of the change over the next quarter, or are changes in the exchange rate mean-reverting, implying that an increase may be expected to be followed by a decrease? In the latter case, expectations for the next quarter depend on what happened during the previous quarter. Information about the current situation is then required to estimate so-called conditional expectations and the conditional cash flow distribution over a certain time horizon. The concept of conditional refers to estimation using available information at a certain time in order to evaluate risk with respect to a certain time horizon.

CFaR can be expressed in terms of a maximum change relative to the expected change in cash flows with a certain confidence for a time period, or it can be expressed in terms of a maximum amount that can be lost relative to expected cash flows over the period. With information about the expected cash flows, changes can easily be recalculated as amounts and vice versa. In the following we define CFaR in terms of amounts.

## 7.3 INFORMATION REQUIREMENTS FOR CFaR ANALYSIS

With information about consequences of cash flow short falls, management can determine its willingness to accept the possibility of short falls of different magnitudes. We assume now that management has made such a determination. Thus, it has determined, as in our previous example, that cash flows over the next quarter must not fall below expected cash flows by an amount exceeding 10 million dollars with a confidence level of 95 percent. Another way to state this objective is that the probability that the 10 million U.S. dollars shortfall will be exceeded must be at most 5 percent (0.05). Next, we turn to the information required to calculate how the variance of cash flows and CFaR depend on the macroeconomic and other risk factors.

1. Using historical data for cash flows and relevant risk factors, exposure coefficients should be estimated as described in Chapter 5. Scenario analysis offers an alternative method for measuring exposures as described in Chapter 4.
2. The expected cash flows can be calculated with information about the expected values for the risk factors identified in the previous stage. The expected cash flows would correspond to cash flows according to a budget for the relevant time period.
3. Next, variances of risk factors and covariances among these factors for the time horizon of concern in risk management should be estimated. Since, the objective is to describe the possible outcomes for a specific time horizon, the current situation and the time pattern of changes in the risk factors are relevant. This step amounts to developing a so-called variance-covariance matrix as shown below. Historical data for the different variables would normally be used in this step.
4. Identify hedge instruments, cash flow effects of hedging, and transactions costs for the instruments.

Using the information described in these steps, a distribution of cash flows over a period can be estimated without and with hedges in place by means of, for example, simulation methods as discussed below. Steps 2–4 should be repeated each period based on new information about cash flows and risk factors.

## 7.4 NORSK HYDRO AND ITS EXPOSURES

Norsk Hydro[2] is a Norwegian industrial conglomerate headquartered in Oslo. Formerly a widely diversified conglomerate, Hydro in the 1990s initiated a strategy of focusing on three main business areas: oil, aluminum, and fertilizers. By acquiring the German aluminum maker VAW in 2002, Hydro established itself as one of the world's three largest integrated players in the aluminum market. In 2003 the board decided to divest the fertilizer division. The divestment took place in early 2004, following the period we are analyzing. Of operating revenues of NOK 172 bn in 2003 for the entire Hydro Group (HG), the oil and gas division accounted for 35 percent, aluminum for 40 percent, and agriculture for 22 percent. Other activities made up the remaining 3 percent. In this chapter we limit our analysis to the entire group, HG.[3]

Data for EBITDA (Earnings Before Interest, Tax and Depreciation Allowance) from the first quarter of 1996 through the last quarter of 2003 have been obtained as the measure of cash flows of concern for management. EBITDA captures commercial cash flows and excludes all financial cash flows. Cash flow effects of financial hedge instruments will be included as well in the analysis below, but interest costs and capital gains or losses on financial positions are not included. Capital expenditures and new financing during the period are excluded in the analysis. These cash flow items would be relevant only if they would depend on the outcome of the risk factors.

We include four groups of macroeconomic and market prices of possible relevance to Hydro in the analysis of exposure. These groups are commodity prices, exchange rates, inflation rates, and interest rates. All the business areas are clearly sensitive to commodity prices. The oil and gas division is primarily exposed to changes in the price of oil, the aluminium division is exposed to changes in world aluminium prices as well as energy prices, and the fertilizer division is sensitive to the price of Urea and Can on the output side and ammonia and energy on the input side.

We need not go into details about the sources of exposure to macroeconomic variables and commodity prices, but a few facts can be noted. The price of Urea is set in dollars in the world market, while the price of Can is set in Euros. Thus, it is possible that changes in the USD/EUR rate can affect the relative attractiveness of Urea and Can. These two fertilizer products are close substitutes. As for currency exposures on the cost side, there are major production centers in Norway and Belgium. Sales occur worldwide and there are a number of competitors in North America, Europe and Asia.

The macroeconomic price variables that constitute potential exposures are listed in Table 7.1. Different specifications were tested to obtain a "best" model with a limited number of exposure coefficients. The final specification presented in the table was based on the statistical significance of variables, as well as their economic rationale from the point of view of HG. Since there is substantial correlation among some variables, several alternative specifications yield similar results qualitatively. The table shows that only commodity prices and seasonal factors remain in the final specification for the Hydro Group. The other listed macroeconomic variables had explanatory value for one of the subsidiaries.

Since exposures properly refer to unanticipated changes in the different risk factors, assumptions must be made about expected changes in both cash flows and risk factors. Considering our frequency of observations (quarterly data), we make the simplifying assumption that all variables follow random walks in levels. Accordingly, all changes are unanticipated. As discussed elsewhere, this assumption may not be entirely appropriate but to the extent that exchange rates, interest rates and other price variables are determined in well-functioning liquid markets, a very high proportion of the variation in these variables tends to be due to unanticipated changes.

Exposure can be estimated using data in levels, first differences, or percentage changes. Statistical properties of the time series should guide the decision. In particular, the time series should be stationary. In this case, the dependent variable is the change in EBITDA for HG in NOK on a quarterly basis. The independent variables listed in Table 7.1 are specified in first differences.[4] In Table 7.1, Brent crude is the USD reference price for oil produced in the North Sea. The aluminum price is the USD spot price as quoted on the London Metal Exchange, converted to euros. Urea and Can are fertilizer prices in USD and EUR and $NH_3$ is the USD price of ammonia. The long-term interest rates are the yields to maturity on 10-year German, Norwegian, and U.S. government bonds. Inflation rates are based on CPIs Quarterly dummies are included to control for seasonal cash-flow patterns.

The data period for the regression analysis is 1996:I to 2003:IV. It is important that the analysis is performed on structurally stable data for cash flows. Although one significant acquisition occurred during the period, HG's overall business model was stable through 2003 before the fertilizer business was sold.

The exposure coefficients obtained from the regression analysis for HG are also presented in Table 7.1. The p-values in parentheses indicates the probability that the coefficient is different from zero.

Although the divisions of HG are exposed to macroeconomic risk factors, HG as a whole is exposed only to commodity prices in the final model.

**Table 7.1 Estimated exposure models for the Norsk Hydro Group (HG) 1996:I to 2003:IV. Coefficients show average cash flow changes in Mn NOK from a one-unit increase in each variable. (p-values in parentheses)**

|  | HG |
| --- | --- |
| Intercept | 488 (0.17) |
| Brent crude | 161 (0.03) |
| Aluminum | 4 (0.07) |
| $NH_3$ |  |
| Urea | 22 (0.10) |
| Can |  |
| NOK/USD |  |
| NOK/EUR |  |
| NOK/CAD |  |
| Gvt 10y US |  |
| Gvt 10y Norway |  |
| Gvt 10 Germany |  |
| Inflation US |  |
| Inflation NO |  |
| Inflation EMU |  |
| Inflation CA |  |
| Q1 | 788 (0.15) |
| Q2 | −784 (0.12) |
| Q3 | −938 (0.07) |
| $R^2$ | 0.62 |
| SE of regression | 967 |
| BG statistic | 1.49 |
| JB statistic | 0.64 |

The coefficients show that the group gains from increases in the prices of oil, aluminum, and Urea. For example, a one dollar increase in the price of Brent crude leads to a NOK 135 mn increase in EBITDA for the group. Although there is no independent exchange rate exposure for the group, the commodity price variables are correlated with the exchange rates. The NOK/USD and the NOK/EUR rates have correlation coefficients of 0.47 and -0.39 with Aluminium and Brent Crude, respectively. As shown in Table 7.2, this means that an analyst of exchange rate exposure, without taking commodity prices into consideration, would find exchange rate exposure, while in our analysis the exposures are identified as commodity price exposures.

## 7.5 ESTIMATING CFaR

In this section the exposure coefficients will be combined with information about the distributions for the risk factors identified in the previous section in order to estimate a distribution for the commercial cash flows of Norsk Hydro, and thereafter, to assess the CFaR at a specific level of confidence.

To derive a conditional distribution of cash flows in one quarter, starting with information about current cash flows and current values of the risk factors, the exposure coefficients in Table 7.1 are used, along with information about variances for the risk factors and the covariances between the risk factors. The exposure coefficients show how cash flows respond to a one unit change in each variable. Variances and covariances show how unanticipated changes in the risk factors may occcur over the next quarter. The information about standard deviations and correlations shown in Table 7.2 constitute the elements needed to obtain a variance/covariance matrix for the risk variables. Variances of the three commodity prices are the squares of the standard deviations and the covariances can be calculated using the correlation coefficients in the table as well. In addition, the variance of the error term in the cash flow equation must be taken into account, since other factors influencing cash flows are captured by this term. If the error term is well behaved, it has by definition no correlation with any of the explanatory variables and its own past values.

The final step in the estimation of the distribution of cash flows is to simulate cash flows for random values of the commodity prices in the exposure model, taking into account the relations implied by the variance/covariance matrix. Using this matrix, a simulation software program called @Risk is programmed to run 10,000 scenarios of the variables in the forecasting system. HG's cash flows are the sum of each of the simulated macroeconomic and market variables, multiplied by the relevant exposure coefficient, plus a constant and a simulated value of the error term. The standard deviation of this term is given by the standard error of regression in Table 7.1. For each of the 10,000 simulations, the @Risk program calculates the value of Hydro's cash flows; 10,000 scenarios for the commodity prices provide us with 10,000 simulated values of cash flows. Figure 7.1 describes the simulated distribution.

Table 7.2  Standard deviations and correlations between risk factors for Norsk Hydro (quarterly changes 1996:I-2003:IV).

|            | Standard deviation | Aluminum | Urea |
|------------|--------------------|----------|------|
| Brent crude | 2.9               | 0.37     | 0.21 |
| Aluminum   | 86                 |          | 0.01 |
| Urea       | 14.6               |          |      |

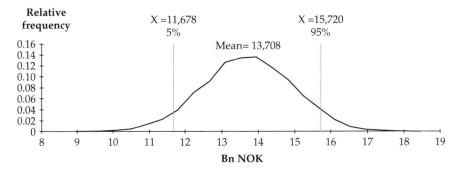

Figure 7.1 Simulated distribution for HG's cash flow, 2004:1

The probability of different outcomes for cash flows are shown vertically, while levels of cash flows are shown horizontally. The cash flow level
corresponding to the 95 percent confidence level is shown at the vertical
line denoted 5% and the CFaR at the 95 percent confidence level is the difference between the mean and this level (2030). Figure 7.1 and table 7.3
summarizes the information about CFaR for the firm for the next quarter,
using a 95 percent confidence level. The figures in the table imply that cash
flows will not fall below 11,678 with a probability of .95. Equivalently, the
probability that cash flows will fall below this level is 0.05. If the cash flows
decline to the level implied by the chosen confidence level, they will fall
14.8 percent. If management considers a 5 percent likelihood of such a loss
unacceptable, then risk management instruments must be considered.

## 7.6  HEDGING EXPOSURE TO REDUCE CFaR

A benefit of exposure-based CFaR analysis is that the evaluation of hedging
decisions is greatly facilitated. Management can evaluate the impact on CFaR
of different hedging strategies. The maximum risk reduction that can be
obtained if all commodity price risk can be hedged depends on the contribution of these risk factors to the total variance of cash flows. Table 7.1 shows
that the R-squared for the regression is .69, meaning that 69 percent of the
cash flow variance is explained by commodity prices and seasonal factors.
Using this information, the CFaR with 95 percent confidence can be calculated

Table 7.3  Exposure-based CFaR estimates for 2004:I (Mn NOK).

|  | Expected Cash Flow (A) | 95% percentile Cash Flow (B) | CFaR (C = A−B) | CFaR in percent (D = C / A) |
|---|---|---|---|---|
| HG | 13,708 | 11,678 | 2,030 | 14.8% |

**Table 7.4 Hydro Group's CFaR estimates under different hedging strategies**

|  | Base case CFaR (no hedge) | Hedged CFaR (100% hedge of each risk factor) | Risk reduction in % |
| --- | --- | --- | --- |
| Brent crude | 2,030 | 1,762 | 13.2% |
| Aluminum | 2,030 | 1,886 | 7.1% |
| Urea | 2,030 | 1,881 | 7.3% |

for the case when all commodity price risk has been perfectly hedged. This CFaR figure is 1,509. In other words, the CFaR can be reduced from 2,030 to 1,509 if all influences on cash flows from changes in commodity prices for the next quarter can be removed.

The impact on CFaR of hedging a particular commodity price risk depends on (a) the size of the exposure, (b) the volatility of the risk factor being hedged, and (c) the correlation between the risk factor being hedged and other risk factors in the model. In Table 7.4, the results of hedging each individual commodity price risk, while leaving the others unhedged are reported. The base case CFaR is 2,030 as shown in Table 7.3 and Figure 7.1. The middle column shows CFaR at the same confidence level in each hedge case. If only one exposure is to be hedged, the greatest risk reduction is obtained by hedging the exposure to Brent crude oil. Urea has a higher volatility than Brent but the exposure to Brent prices is larger, as shown in Table 7.1. The exposure to the aluminum price also seems relatively large in Table 7.1, but the risk reduction from hedging the aluminum price is relatively small as a result of the greater stability of this commodity price.

## 7.7 CONCLUDING REMARKS ON CASH FLOW AT RISK

In this chapter the exposure coefficients described in previous chapters were put to use in risk management using a particular method for measuring risk. We have illustrated how CFaR can be made an important aspect of MUST analysis. CFaR represents one way to set clear objectives for macroeconomic risk management, and it helps to conceptualize the risk management process. The quantitative implementation of this approach requires a large amount of historical data as well as the use of advanced statistical methods. In the next chapter, we discuss alternative ways of formulating risk management objectives and strategies. We argue that the need for complexity and expertise can be reduced substantially under reasonable conditions.

## NOTES

1 Jorion (2006) describes and applies VaR on a number of finance problems, and he discusses strengths and weaknesses of using VaR as a tool in risk management.

2 This section is based on Andrén, Jankensgård, and Oxelheim (2005)
3 Andren, Jankensgård, and Oxelheim (2005) analyze the exposures of the different product areas as well.
4 Error terms have been subjected to the Breusch-Godfrey test for serial correlation and the Jarque-Bera test for normality.

# Chapter 8

# Strategies for Risk and Exposure Management

## 8.1 INTRODUCTION

In Chapter 2 the potential for value enhancement of having an explicit risk management program in place was discussed. An important part of such a program is an explicit strategy for risk management. The strategy provides the general rule based on which operational decisions can be made. Few firms seem to have a clear concept of the relationship between a strategy for risk management, and the firm's overall objectives. Rather, it seems as if the relatively easy access to some kinds of accounting-based data determines the exposure concept, while operational decisions with respect to hedging and cover are based on managers' personal risk attitudes. These attitudes depend strongly on how managers are evaluated when there are gains and losses due to exchange rate changes, inflation, interest rate changes, and so on.[1]

Given the firm's objective with respect to shareholders and other stakeholders, it is naturally desirable that a risk management program is consistent with the objective. This consideration generally implies that a risk management strategy should refer to some concept of economic exposure rather than being accounting-based. Furthermore, once a strategy is determined, it is important that managers themselves are evaluated in such a way that their incentives are consistent with the firm's objective. To develop criteria for such an evaluation, an explicitly formulated strategy is needed. In this chapter we discuss the necessary elements for an "economic" management strategy. Performance evaluation and risk management incentives are discussed in Chapters 9 and 10.

A firm's objective can be defined in several dimensions. Although the most fundamental objective may be shareholder wealth maximization, operational objectives are often stated in terms of a target variable, time horizon, and risk attitude. The target variable could be earnings, cash flows or stock market value. The time horizon would to some extent be determined by the choice of target variable, but if earnings or cash flows are viewed as target variables a time horizon must be considered explicitly. Risk attitude is often defined as risk averse or risk neutral with respect to the target variable. The risk-averse firm is willing to accept a cost in order to reduce uncertainty about the target variable over some time horizon, while the risk-neutral firm is not willing to incur costs.

We discuss four types of strategies: laissez-faire or do nothing, aggressive, minimize variance, and selective hedging. These strategies can be chosen for any target variable and any time horizon. They are distinguished by management's risk attitude and management's view of profit opportunities in financial markets.

Choosing a strategy is, to a large extent, an information problem. Information about the firm's overall objective, and expectations about goods and financial market price relationships and price behavior, are needed to determine a desired strategy. Information requirements for a desired strategy may be so overwhelming that the range of feasible strategies does not encompass the desired one. In this situation management is faced with the need to determine what risk management objectives can be achieved with the available information. If economic exposure is considered important, but information includes only accounting data, then it is necessary to consider whether the available data are a good enough approximation of economic data for hedging purposes.

Among the mentioned factors that determine the impact of risk on a firm, exposure is the one subject to most control and influence by the management facing macroeconomic uncertainty. Other risk factors, such as uncertainty about exchange rates are not within management control. For this reason, macroeconomic risk management becomes largely management of exposure, and we will use the terms *risk management* and *exposure management* interchangeably.

A corporate management that wants to be consistent in its management of exposure must make its views on the following points quite clear in its policy:

- target variable and time horizon
- attitude to risk
- efficiency of price adjustment in different markets
- information requirements
- flexibility of operations (real options) versus financial risk management.

These determinants of strategy are discussed in sections 8.2–8.6.

## 8.2 CHOICE OF TARGET VARIABLE AND TIME HORIZON

The interests of various stakeholders were discussed in Chapter 3. It was concluded that shareholder wealth maximization is consistent with a concern about the probability of bankruptcy. This probability depends on uncertainty about the value, the sensitivity to macroeconomic disturbances and the current value of the firm. Thus, a degree of risk-aversion—in the sense of a willingness to sacrifice profits to reduce the variability of value and cash flow—can be rationalized when the probability of bankruptcy is not negligible. Since the probability of bankruptcy can vary over time, exposure management strategy may vary as well.

In Chapter 7 it was noted in connection with the discussion of Cash Flow at Risk that the incentive to manage the impact on the corporate cash flows of a particular risk-variable depends on four factors:

(a) the size of the cash flow exposure to the variable
(b) the degree of uncertainty about the variable
(c) the relationship between the variable and other risk variables
(d) the distribution of costs and benefits associated with particular cash flow outcomes.

The last factor could be, for example, potential costs associated with lack of liquidity.

The choice between cash flows or profits in the near term, as opposed to economic value, is to a large extent a question of time perspective since the economic value is the discounted value of expected future cash flows.

Accounting measures of the value of the firm are generally very poor measures of economic value. Nevertheless, if financial markets and institutions make credit assessments based on accounting figures, then a concern with accounting measures of exposure can be rationalized.

As noted in Chapter 2, the management seeking to maximize share-holder value is indirectly concerned about other stakeholders because their behavior influences the costs and revenues of the firm. Price uncertainty may affect sales and output, while employment variability would affect labor costs. Thus, the management of macroeconomic exposure may have to include considerations of factors that affect the variability of prices, output, and employment. We discuss below some measures that management can adopt to reduce the costs of operation caused by macroeconomic fluctuation. These measures are discussed below under the heading "Real options."

The time perspective in risk management would depend on potential costs associated with particular outcomes for risk factors in, for example, the macroeconomic environment. Over the long term, there is most likely a lot of flexibility in a firm's structure and operations (real options). As a result, exposure over several years may not be a serious concern. Furthermore, the long-term exposure can be low because prices, interest rates, and exchange rates adjust relative to each other toward long-term relationships as described in appendices 3.2 and 3.3. These factors and their role in macroeconomic risk management are discussed in more detail.

In Chapter 5 it was pointed out that the time horizon of the firm in exposure management should determine the specification of exposure coefficients that are being estimated. The exposure coefficients for Volvo Cars in Chapter 5 were specified as the sensitivity of changes in cash flows from one quarter to another in response to changes in macro price variables between the same quarters. Hedging based on these coefficients each quarter reduces the variance of the cash flows in the next quarter. This variance reduction, however, does not necessarily reduce the variance of cash flows over a longer time horizon or the variance of the firm's value proportionately.

Consider the following alternative objectives of a firm:

- Firm I is concerned with the variance of cash flows one quarter ahead.
- Firm II is concerned with the variance or variability of cash flows over the next two years.
- Firm III is concerned with the variance or variability of the present value of its future flows.
- Firm IV is concerned with the variance of its value in three months.

Firm I can obviously reduce the variance of the flow in three months by hedging in the three-month forward market. Firm I is the one we have discussed above. The argument for this risk management objective would be that a substantial cash flow loss could geopardize plans for investments in three months or reduce the ability to take advantage of profit opportunities. Froot, Scharfstein and Stein (1994) discuss this type of risk management objective.

Firm II worries about the variability of quarterly cash flows over a longer period. Quarter by quarter hedging has the consequence that the variance over the next two years depends on the variance of the forward rates at which hedging will be performed.

If hedging is not done, then the variance of cash flows depends on the spot rates in each quarter. In general the variance of forward rates (as opposed to forward premia) is not substantially smaller than the variance of spot rates (as opposed to a percentage change in exchange rates); see, for example, Fama (1984) and Oxelheim (1985). The variance reduction of hedging depends entirely on the three-month difference between the observation of the forward rate and the spot rate. To substantially reduce the variance of cash flows over the time horizon, the firms should each quarter hedge expected cash flows in the following eight quarters.

Reasoning in the same way for firm III, it follows that the variance of the present value of cash flows is not reduced substantially by the expected consecutive hedging of quarterly exposures because, except for the first quarter, the forward rates at which hedging occurs are not known and they can be expected to fluctuate with the future spot rates.

It is possible, however, to hedge the value for firm IV in, say, three months, if the sensitivity of the value to changes in the exchange rate over the next three months is estimated the way Volvo Cars' cash flow sensitivities were estimated in Chapter 5.

What would be the point of hedging the value in three months if such hedging did not reduce the variability of the value over time? Recall that, in Chapter 2, it was argued that the risk-aversion of management might increase with an increase in the probability of bankruptcy. The firm approaching distress can decrease the probability of bankruptcy within the next three months by hedging the value exposure in three months against effects of unanticipated changes in the exchange rate over the same period.

Concern about the stock-market value or the economic value in the future is really equivalent to concern about today's value, since the values at different times are linked by the firm's cost of capital. Uncertainty about this value depends on uncertainty about all future cash flows as well as on the expected pattern of these flows over time. The variability of cash flows needs not translate into variability of the value if relatively high cash flows one quarter are expected to be offset by lower flows another quarter. On the other hand, if relatively high cash flows are expected to be followed by high flows for some time, then the variance of flows could translate into variability of the value.

In summary, when deciding on, and when evaluating a strategy for hedging, it is important to know what the hedging is supposed to achieve in terms of reduced costs and variability. The objectives of different stakeholders were discussed in Chapter 2. Reducing cash flow exposure in three months' time is generally not going to achieve much in terms of uncertainty about the firm's value, but it may alleviate potential near-term liquidity problems. Note also that the observation in hindsight that variability of cash flows was not reduced by hedging does not necessarily imply that hedging failed for firms I and IV. We return to evaluation of risk management in Chapter 10.

## 8.3 MANAGEMENT'S RISK ATTITUDE

The major distinction to be made here is between risk-neutrality and risk aversion. If there are incentives to limit the variance of a target variable or to reduce the possibility that bad outcomes occur, a firm is risk averse in our terminology. On the other hand, a risk-neutral firm is not concerned with the variance of the target variable, presumably because substantial costs of particular outcomes are not within range, or because the distribution of costs and benefits associated with different outcomes for a variable is symmetric.

In the case of risk aversion a decision must be made about the target variable that risk aversion refers to. Without a conscious decision of this kind on a top management level, it is easy for subordinate managers' own risk attitudes to shape the exposure management strategy.

We have argued that risk aversion with respect to value and cash flows can be motivated by a concern for the probability of bankruptcy and liquidity. Value at Risk or Cash Flow at Risk can be appropriate objectives in these cases.

Risk-neutrality with respect to value and total cash flows does not exclude the possibility that the variance of commercial cash flows is of concern as a result of employees' attitudes toward job security, costs of shifting employees among different activities, and the cost of holding inventories. The greater the sensitivity of the optimal output level to changes in demand and cost conditions, the more important are these concerns.

The task for management is to determine the value of reducing the variance of cash flows. In other words, those responsible for exposure management and, specifically, the size of exposed positions or the sensitivity of cash flows or value after hedging, should explicitly or implicitly be able to evaluate the acceptable cost of a reduction in variance. Only if shareholders value a reduction in the variance in market value or cash flows positively, does hedging possibly translate into a gain in value. If management determines that risk-neutrality is an appropriate attitude for value and total cash flows, then it is still possible that there are gains in terms of, for example, the wage costs of reducing the variance of sales and employment. In this case the "pricing" of reduced variance can be translated directly into cost savings.

## 8.4  PRICE ADJUSTMENT IN GOODS AND FINANCIAL MARKETS

Real exchange rate changes influencing, for example, the attractiveness of countries as production sites correspond to deviations from Purchasing Power Parity (PPP). If PPP holds, financial positions in different currencies are not subject to exchange rate risk. However, inflation uncertainty remains a concern as long as nominal returns on securities are not perfectly linked to inflation in the currency of denomination (see, for example, Wihlborg, 1978).

From the firm's point of view, deviations from the "Law of One Price" (LOP) for outputs and inputs is of greater concern for the determination of a firm-specific real exchange rate. LOP implies that exchange rate changes are passed through to prices with the consequence that prices in different currencies are the same when translated into one currency. If prices adjust to LOP without effects on sales volumes, then the exchange rate exposure of the firm's commercial operations is eliminated. Inflation uncertainty is eliminated as well if prices on outputs, inputs, and wages are adjusted to changes in the price level without effects on the volume of sales.

While price adjustments in goods markets affect the nature of exposure, price adjustment in financial markets influences the desirable approach to the management of this exposure. In financial markets it is primarily International Fisher Parity (IFP) that must be considered. As discussed in

Chapter 3, IFP implies that the expected returns on equivalent securities denominated in different currencies are the same and that the costs of loans denominated in different currencies are the same. Thus, under IFP, financial positions can be shifted from one currency to another without affecting the firm's expected cash flows and value. This possibility has strong implications for exposure management, because there is no trade-off between risk and return when choosing the currency denomination of financial positions. These positions influence the exchange rate exposure of the firm, however. The risk-neutral firm would be indifferent between positions in different currencies under IFP. The risk-averse firm, on the other hand, would choose the position that minimizes the variance of the target variable. Thus, the financial position can be chosen to simply offset the exposure of commercial operations without influencing the firm's expected profitability.

In domestic financial markets there are no expected gains from borrowing long-term at a given interest rate versus obtaining a series of short-term loans, if the long-term interest rate is a weighted average of a series of consecutive expected short-term interest rates. This condition implies that there are no risk premia associated with interest rates for different maturities. When this relationship holds for the term structure of interest rates, we say that the "expectations hypothesis" for interest rates on different maturities holds. This hypothesis for domestic markets is comparable to IFP in international markets.

The risk-neutral manager who believes in the expectations hypothesis is indifferent between loans of different maturities and indifferent between fixed rate and adjustable rate loans when comparing general market rates. Thus, the choice of maturity structure and adjustability would be determined by firm-specific spreads offered by different financial institutions for different maturities and degrees of adjustability.

A third market relation of interest for exposure management is Fisher Parity (FP). This relation implies that the nominal interest rate for a certain maturity fluctuates with expected inflation given the expected real interest rate. In other words, the expected real interest rate is independent of expected inflation, and the nominal interest rate is the sum of the two independent components. From an exposure management point of view FP implies that the maturity structure and the adjustability of interest rates can be determined either with the objective of hedging commercial real interest rate risk—if inflation-linked securities exist—or with the objective of hedging commercial inflation risk—if there are other securities available for hedging real interest rate risk. On the other hand, if FP does not hold, then the correlation between the real interest rate and the inflation rate must be considered. Any position taken with the objective of hedging real interest rate exposure has implications for inflation exposure and vice versa.

## 8.5 CHOICE OF EXPOSURE MANAGEMENT STRATEGIES

The choice of exposure management strategy is summarized in Table 8.1. We assume that the firm has estimated a certain commercial exposure for

Table 8.1 Financial market relations, risk attitude, and exposure management strategy for total exposure using financial positions.

| Market | Manager's view of the market | | Manager's risk attitude | |
|---|---|---|---|---|
| | | | Risk-neutral | Risk-averse |
| International financial market | IFP | | Laissez-faire[a] w.r.t. currency denomination | Minimize exposure to exchange rate uncertainty |
| | Non-IFP | | Aggressive strategy w.r.t. currency denomination | Selective hedging trading off risk-return |
| Domestic bond market | Expectations Hypothesis | FP | Laissez-faire[a] w.r.t. maturity structure and interest rate adjustability | Minimize exposure to real interest exposure |
| | | Non-FP | | Minimize exposure considering real interest rate linkage with inflation |
| | Non-Expectations Hypothesis | FP | Aggressive strategy w.r.t. maturity structure and interest rate adjustability | Selective hedging of real interest rate exposure |
| | | Non-FP | | Selective hedging considering real interest rate linkage with inflation |

[a] Laissez-faire implies that currency denomination and maturity structure are determined entirely by the most favorable transaction fees and spreads offered to the specific firm in the market.

its desired time horizon and management must determine how to use financial positions to achieve a desired total exposure for value or cash flows. The strategy for hedging depends in this situation on the risk attitude and management's view of IFP, the expectations hypothesis, and FP.

In Table 8.1, risk attitudes are either risk-neutral or risk-averse, indicating a willingness to sacrifice return on an exposed position to reduce the variance of the target variable. Vertically, a distinction is made between international and domestic markets. Management's belief in financial market pricing relations and risk attitude are indicated horizontally.

We distinguish between strategies with respect to exchange rate and interest rate exposures, because lack of speculative opportunities in, for example, international financial markets need not imply lack of opportunities in domestic financial markets. The latter markets determine the strategy with respect to interest rate risks. For simplicity it is assumed that inflation exposure is managed by securities in other markets, or by indexation of contracts.

The four different strategies with respect to exchange rate exposure can be found in the two first rows. "Laissez-faire" about the currency exposure that arises in normal business operations is the strategy chosen by the risk-neutral manager, who believes that there are no profit opportunities in financial markets (IFP). This manager finds that nothing is to be gained by adjusting the currency position other than to achieve outright cost savings in normal commercial operations.

The manager with the same belief about markets, who is willing to incur a cost to reduce exposure, chooses the "minimize exposure" strategy. Only risk matters for this manager's choice of currency denomination under IFP. Thus, financial positions are adjusted to offset the exposure of commercial operations.

While the strategies under IFP are very simple, they become more complex if forecasting is believed to be profitable when IFP is not expected to hold. The risk-neutral manager will simply try to maximize speculative profits with an "aggressive strategy" using own or purchased forecasts of the exchange rate. The risk-averse manager faces the problem of trading off risk and return, choosing to hedge partially or "selectively" in order to benefit from forecasting. One approach is to determine an acceptable Value at Risk or Cash Flow at Risk (see Chapter 7) depending on the ability to forecast and on costs associated with unanticipated losses.

The lower part of Table 8.1 refers to domestic bond markets and the manager's hedging strategy with respect to interest rate risk, assuming again that a commercial interest rate exposure has been estimated.[3]

As noted, the expectations hypothesis implies that there are no profit opportunities available by forecasting future short-term interest rates. The difference between long- and short-term rates contains information about the "best available" forecast. Similarly, there are no expected gains to be made from borrowing in fixed (adjustable) rate loans instead of adjustable (fixed) rate loans. "Laissez-faire"—choosing the maturity that is associated with the best offered business conditions—becomes the strategy of the risk-neutral firm under the expectations hypothesis. If the firm is instead risk-averse, then the maturity structure is chosen so as to offset the commercial interest rate exposure.

As in the international markets, an "aggressive strategy" or a "selective hedging" strategy is chosen by the manager who believes that "the market can be beat" by forecasting.

In the domestic bond markets we also distinguish between the case when FP is perceived to hold and when it is not. FP implies simply that real interest rate fluctuations are independent of fluctuations in the expected inflation rate. In other words, changes in both real interest rates and expected inflation are fully reflected in changes in the nominal interest rates. If FP does not hold, then real interest rate fluctuations in bond markets depend on changes in expected inflation as well. Under these conditions the real interest rates on inflation-indexed bonds of different maturities depend on the expected inflation rates over different time horizons. Thus, hedging the pure real interest rate risk of commercial operations by means of positions in inflation-linked securities will have the consequence that the financial position becomes exposed to inflation uncertainty. The correlation between the inflation rate and the interest rate must therefore be considered even when inflation-indexed bonds exist.

Table 8.1 can be used to determine a strategy under given specific assumptions, and also to identify management's working assumptions given a strategy. Box 8.1 provides an example of this way of thinking that could help top management understand what exposure managers at operating levels are doing relative to the firm's objective.

## 8.6 INFORMATION REQUIREMENTS

The choice of a risk management strategy depends not only on market price relationships and risk attitudes, but the feasibility of obtaining the information required to implement a strategy must be considered as well. In Table 8.2, we summarize the information needs associated with the strategies in Table 8.1.

The belief in the market price relationship reflecting expectations both in international and domestic financial markets simplifies the exposure management strategy whether management is risk-neutral or risk-averse. Under risk-neutrality, currency denomination and maturity choice are irrelevant. Only transaction costs, bid-ask spreads, fees and the like matter. Thus, the information requirements for implementing the "do nothing" strategies are simply relative transaction costs associated with financing from different institutions offering different currencies, maturities, and degrees of interest rate adjustability.

The information requirements for the "minimize variance" strategies are first of all exposure coefficients for commercial cash flows or the values of assets devoted to commercial operations. Knowledge of exposure coefficients for financial positions enables management to use financial positions to offset commercial exposure, as described in Chapter 6.

---

**Box 8.1  How management's attitudes can be inferred from the management of exposure: An illustration**

The finance division of a multinational firm chooses currency denomination of long-term debt by taking loans that offer the lowest spreads between the loan rate and government bond rates for the same currency. Financial positions up to two years' maturity are determined with the following operational objective in mind:

- Total financial positions including forward contracts should hedge commercial cash flow exposure for horizons up to two years.

What can be said about the objectives and attitudes of the management in this firm?

First, the objective is stated in economic terms, because it is concerned about cash flows over various time horizons, rather than book profits. Second, it is risk-averse, because it hedges commercial cash flow exposures for up to two years. Third, management seems to believe in IFP, because it wishes to hedge the commercial cash flow exposure up to two years completely. This is a "minimize variance" strategy. Fourth, management seems to believe that PPP is a reasonable assumption for time horizons over two years, because it hedges exposures only for shorter horizons than two years. Finally, management believes in IFP for the long term as well, because it does not attempt to forecast exchange rates but considers government bond rate differentials the best avaliable forecasts. Therefore, the "cheapest" loan is the one that offers the lowest rate relative to the risk-free rate.

---

Once management holds the belief that it is able to forecast profit opportunities, the information requirements obviously include exchange rate, inflation, and real interest rate forecasts. If management, furthermore, is risk-averse, then this information should be combined with information about exposure coefficients, variances, and covariance among returns in currencies and maturities. Furthermore, those making actual decisions on the financial positions must know how to trade off risk and return. The implementation of for example, a Cash Flow at Risk approach as a "selective" strategy in accordance with the firm's economic objectives is extremely demanding in terms of information requirements. The possibility that the strategy will be mismanaged must be weighed against the possible gains that can be obtained by getting involved in forecasting.

When asked, most firms would state that they are risk-averse and that they can forecast deviations from IFP and the other parity conditions. Thus, most firms face the greatest possible information needs in Table 8.2. One must ask how much would be lost by assuming that parity relations hold, or if managers should really aim for implementing the most demanding strategy.

**Table 8.2  Financial market relaions, risk attitude, and information needs.**[a]

| Market | Manager's view of the market | | Manager's risk attitude | |
|---|---|---|---|---|
| | | | **Risk-neutral** | **Risk-averse** |
| International financial market | IFP | | — | Commercial exposure to exchange rate changes<br>Exposure of financial positions |
| | Non-IFP | | Exchange rate forecasts (relative to interest rate differentials) | Exposure coefficients as above<br>Exchange rate forecasts<br>Variances and correlations among currency positions |
| | Expectations Hypothesis | FP | — | Commercial and financial interest rate exposure coefficients |
| | | Non-FP | — | Interest rate exposure coefficients<br>Inflation exposure coefficients<br>Interest rate–inflation correlations |
| Domestic bond market | | FP | Interest rate forecasts over the maturity spectrum | Interest rate exposure coefficients as above<br>Interest rate forecasts<br>Interest rate variances and correlations across markets |
| | Non-Expectations Hypothesis | Non-FP | Interest rate forecasts over the maturity spectrum | Interest rate exposure coefficients as above<br>Inflation exposure coefficients<br>Inflation forecasts<br>Inflation variances and correlations across maturities<br>Inflation–interest rate correlations |

[a] All strategies require information about transaction-fees and bid-ask spreads in addition to the information listed here.

## 8.7  ADJUSTABILITY OF COMMERCIAL OPERATIONS: REAL OPTIONS

The exposure management strategies discussed so far have been based on the assumption that the exposure of commercial operations is given and that financial positions are taken to reduce the total exposure if so desired. There is an obvious substitutability between hedging with financial contracts and adjustment of commercial operations, however. Over time horizons when there is adjustability of commercial operations in different dimensions, risk management by means of financial positions may not be the best strategy for dealing with exposure. Some exposure management instruments listed in Table 6.1 in Chapter 6 referred to adjustment of commercial operations. We elaborate on such instruments here. An important aspect of these instruments is that they often can be thought of as "real" options that enable a firm to both reduce exposure and increase expected profits. Thus, they are not only substitutes for financial instruments but complements as well, and they should be considered by all firms regardless of risk attitude.[4]

Deviations from PPP can be long lasting and affect the profitability of a firm's operations to such an extent that the viability of the operations is threatened by such factors as low domestic currency prices on exported outputs, high costs of imported inputs, or lack of competitiveness in the market relative to foreign producers. Over longer time horizons when PPP holds, there is no exchange rate risk but there may be exposure of commercial operations owing to uncertainty about relative prices among outputs and inputs. In general, exposure to price differences between outputs and inputs can be managed by adjustment of commercial operations in different dimensions. Such adjustment is generally costly, however. Principles for managing such exposure have been developed theoretically by applying the theory of option pricing. The ability to move a production site from one country to another, to shift from a supplier in one country to a supplier in another country, to abandon a market where losses mount, and to enter a new market where profits are expected are all "options" that can be exercised at a cost. By creating flexibility of operations in different dimensions, these costs can be reduced, enabling the firm to better take advantage of profit opportunities. Thus, exposure management by means of commercial operations affects the firm's profitability as well as its exposure to real exchange rate changes and relative price shifts.[5]

The multinational firm with production units in more than one country can shift production from one country to another (if spare capacity exists), when relative labor costs change as a result of exchange rate changes (see Kogut and Kulatilaka, 1994). In many industries, the hindrances to such shifts are substantial either because of non-standardization of products or because of labor relations in producing units. A more valuable option for many firms would be to expand purchases of inputs from suppliers in countries with favorable real exchange rates and reduce purchases from others.

Abandoning markets where losses are made is also associated with costs, if the firm hopes to reenter in the future. Customer relations may be hurt and there are costs associated with reentry and regaining market share. The costs of entering a market the first time are likely to be even higher. Thus, to either abandon or enter a new market is generally not worthwhile for small relative price changes even if a conventional project evaluation would indicate that the changes are profitable. The reason why conventional project evaluation techniques fail to give the correct signals is that they do not take into account that, under uncertainty, reversals of decisions may become necessary and there are costs specifically related to these reversals. Thus, when there is uncertainty about real exchange rates and relative prices there is "a band of inaction"; within this band current operations continue unchanged even if losses occur.

The "options" associated with adjustability of commercial operations are more valuable as the uncertainty about real exchange rates and relative prices increases. They are also more valuable if the irreversible costs of changes can be reduced. Thus, high uncertainty makes flexibility or adjustability more valuable because it enables the firm to take advantage of profit opportunities in commercial operations. For example, spreading input purchases among suppliers in different countries reduces the costs of expanding these purchases in the country with the most favorable exchange rates.

The firm's rule for responses to changes in exchange rates, interest rates, and other sources of cost changes constitute the firm's pricing strategy. Commercial exposure is strongly influenced by this strategy, as noted in Chapter 4. Increased uncertainty in exchange rates and the macroeconomic environment can make it worthwhile to change the pricing strategy in order to allow greater flexibility and greater pass-through. The benefits of adjusting prices to levels that lead to higher short-run profits under different circumstances must be weighed against the costs of not being able to offer customers a stable price. To some extent the price adjustment to changes in, for example, exchange rates can be predetermined in contracts. Trade credit terms can also include payment adjustment in response to inflation and exchange rate changes. The use of such adjustment clauses is not unusual (see Oxelheim et al., 1990).

The general implication of this discussion is that flexibility and adjustability of operations and pricing are exposure management tools which, to be worthwhile, require a minimum degree of uncertainty about future prices. If uncertainty is high, however, there are reasons to invest in the ability to adjust operations even in the short run, thereby reducing the need for exposure management by financial positioning and increasing expected profits. Over the longer term the costs of adjustability can be diminished, because options are "built in" by the need to replace assets and individuals. Over such horizons, exposure management by adjustment of financial positions is superfluous.[6]

## 8.8  CONCLUDING REMARKS ON THE CHOICE OF STRATEGY

The choice of risk and exposure management strategy can be divided into two components. One component is the ability to adjust commercial operations and pricing to take advantage of profit opportunities. We call this exploiting real options. The benefits of such adjustability, that is, of having real options, require a threshold degree of uncertainty about macroeconomic conditions; investments in adjustability could be worthwhile if uncertainty is high. Over shorter time horizons, when adjustability of operations and prices is low, the second component of exposure management comes into play. This component involves adjustment in the financial structure of the firm in terms of currency denomination, maturity, and adjustability of interest rates. The firm's liability position in these dimensions can be adjusted in order to offset the exposure of commercial operations. To the extent that there is not sufficient flexibility in the financial structure, financial derivatives are available for exposure management.

The strategy for using financial positions to reduce or offset the commercial exposure should be determined at top management level if economic exposure is taken seriously. The factors that determine a desirable strategy are the target variable, such as cash flows or stock-market value, the time horizon, the risk attitude, and management's belief about the efficiency of pricing in financial markets.

Most firms would specify their objectives in such a way that "selective" strategies are desirable, implying a trade-off between risk and expected return. Such strategies require so much information, however, that they often are not feasible. By working under the assumption that there are no profit opportunities in financial markets, information requirements are reduced drastically. The possible costs of this simplifying assumption must be weighed against the costs of managing the exposure with misleading or missing information.

### NOTES

1  See Wharton/CIBC Wood Gundy (1995) for an overview of exposure management practices in the United States.
2  The case when cash flow predictions are uncertain was discussed in Chapter 6.
3  Using the regression methods in Chapter 4 the interest rate exposure can be considered a real interest rate exposure when inflation is an explanatory variable in the regression.
4  Miller (1992) discusses the various commercial and financial exposures under the concept "integrated risk management.
5  Capel (1997) elaborates on this issue and demonstrates how exchange rate changes can be "exploited" to increase expected profits. See also Capel (1992).
6  Trigeorgis (1996), Amran and Kulatilaka (1999), and Copeland and Antikarov (2001).

# Chapter 9

# Recognizing Macroeconomic Fluctuations in Value-Based Management

## 9.1 INTRODUCTION

Value-Based Management (VBM)[1] has become a key instrument for evaluating corporate strategies, projects, and overall performance. Although VBM can be used together with standard discounted cash flow (DCF) in the planning stages, its principal use has been in developing performance measures like Economic Value Added (EVA) and Cash Flow Return on Investment (CFROI). These can be used to evaluate ongoing corporate projects and company-wide performance—that is to say, after the corporate investment decisions have been made and the capital committed.[2] Perhaps even more importantly, VBM performance measures often provide the basis for bonus systems that aim to align managerial incentives with those of shareholders.

The primary advantage of VBM frameworks is their ability to overcome the deficiencies of accounting-based performance measures like Earnings Per Share (EPS), in part by focusing on corporate cash flow. One limitation of most VBM frameworks is their failure to distinguish between changes in cash flows that reflect changes in a firm's competitive position, and cash flow changes that derive mainly from fluctuations in the macroeconomic environment that show up in variables like exchange rates and interest rates. We return in this chapter to issues of evaluation of managers for the purpose of deciding on executive compensation in the presence of macroeconomic fluctuations. In Chapter 10, we discuss evaluation of risk management efforts on different levels in the firm. Our aim in this chapter is to develop a framework that enables management to isolate the effect of such variables on performance, while taking into account the interdependence and correlation between the variables in responding to broader changes in the macro environment.[3] Within the MUST analysis, as described in Figure 1.3, we are now looking back in time in order to disentangle different sources of changes in performance.

Changes in macroeconomic variables are, of course, beyond management's control. Even if they can be forecast, management may not be able to adjust operations to take advantage of expected changes. To the extent that changes in interest rates and exchange rates affect corporate cash flows and value, these effects can weaken the link between managerial pay and performance.[4] As shown in Oxelheim et al. (2008), the macro effects may constitute a quite substantial part of a bonus. For this reason, "cleansing" performance measures of macro effects may strengthen managers' incentives to add value by doing what they do best—allocating capital effectively and increasing operating efficiencies.

Besides strengthening managerial incentives, another argument for filtering out macro influences on corporate performance measures is that it may replicate a process that, at least to some extent, is actually performed by investors when setting stock prices. For example, a company with abnormally high profits that result from a depreciating currency is likely to trade at a lower P/E ratio than if the same profits were generated without such a change. By compensating managers for a currency-adjusted contribution to value added in this case, managers' bonuses may be a more accurate reflection of the market value added (or MVA) built into a company's stock price.[5]

In previous chapters, we have argued that corporate managers can measure the exposure of their firm's cash flows to macro conditions by estimating their exposure to a set of macro price variables such as inflation, exchange rates, and interest rates. In this chapter we use *exposure coefficients* (measured within a multivariate regression framework) to quantify the effect of either unexpected or actual changes in macro price variables on corporate cash flows (or, alternatively, on the value of the assets generating the cash flows). The exposure coefficients are used in a VBM context to remove the effects of macro variables on a firm's cash flows (or value) during a specific time period and so arrive at a measure of a company's "intrinsic" cash flows and value.

The chapter is organized as follows. The basic framework for "decomposing" changes in cash flows using exposure coefficients is laid out in Section 9.2. In Section 9.3, we use the case of Electrolux to illustrate the decomposition procedure and the potential size of the macro influences we are seeking to remove. We discuss when and how the procedure should be applied for purposes of management compensation in Section 9.4. The effect of flexibility (real options) on the magnitude of macroeconomic effects and performance assessment is discussed in Section 9.5. Concluding remarks on the use of the MUST analysis in VBM are presented in Section 9.6.

## 9.2  VBM AND MACROECONOMIC FLUCTUATIONS

The framework of Value-Based Management rests on the premise that the value of the firm is equal to the discounted net present value of its expected cash flows, or its DCF value. Introducing real options as well,

$$V_{A,t} = \sum_{j=0}^{\infty} \beta^j E\left[X_{t+j}\right] + PVRO_t \qquad (20)$$

where $V_A$ is the value of corporate assets, $X$ is the cash flow in a given period (j), $\beta^j$ is the discount factor for each of the j periods, and PVRO represents the present value of real options that cannot be captured in conventional present value analysis. In most of the chapter that follows, we ignore real options and focus just on current cash flows as the basis for performance evaluation, since bonus systems are based on current cash flows adjusted for a capital charge in most VBM frameworks.

Changes in cash flows in any period can be decomposed into two components. One component represents changes under unchanged macroeconomic conditions. To the extent that these conditions persist during a given period, changes in the cash flow for any individual firm are assumed to be attributable entirely to changes in the firm's competitiveness in the market place and the growth in demand for the firm's output. Moreover, given a firm's technology, employee and managerial competence, and product demand, there is at any time a level of cash flows that can be identified as the intrinsic level of cash flows for the period. We denote changes in this intrinsic level $x_L$.[6]

The other component of cash flow changes during a period depends on changes in macroeconomic conditions, as reflected in changes in variables such as exchange rates, interest rates, and price levels. We denote these changes $x_M$. This in turn means that total changes in cash flow can be expressed as the sum of the two components:

$$x_{t+j} = x_{L,t+j} + x_{M,t+j} \qquad (21)$$

Under most circumstances, a regression equation of the following general form can be used to estimate the effects of changing macro variables on firm performance.

$$x_t = a_e e + a_i i + a_p p + a_r r \qquad (22)$$

where $e$, $i$, and $p$ represent percentage changes in sets of exchange rates, interest rates, price levels in period $t$.[7] The variable $r$, on the other hand, is used to capture changes in firm- and industry-specific conditions that may be signficantly correlated with macro events. The partial derivatives with repect to $e$, $i$ and $p$ ($a_e$, $a_i$, and $a_p$) represent sensitivity coefficients (in multivariate regression analysis) that are meant to reflect the exposure of a firm's cash flows to changes in macroeconomic price variables.[8]

The coefficients in Equation (22) reflect more than just the direct impact of each variable on cash flows. Each coefficient also captures the effect of correlations among the variables in question, and among other macro variables that do not show up in the equation. Moreover, for every firm there is likely to be a specific set of variables that best captures cash flow effects from macro events. For example, as we show in the next section, our regression analysis suggests that the effect of changes in macro conditions on the cash flows of one well-known Swedish company is best reflected by changes in four variables.

Performance evaluations can also be based on changes in the value of corporate assets rather than on changes in cash flows. In this case, Equation 22 can be applied directly using the actual (or estimated) changes in value as the independent variable. But if the firm's equity is not traded, or it is the performance of a corporate division that is being evaluated, then Equation 20 can be used to derive value effects that are based on the estimated cash flow effects of macro variables.[9]

## 9.3  CASH FLOW DECOMPOSITION AND VALUATION: THE CASE OF ELECTROLUX

Electrolux AB is one of the world's largest manufacturers of white goods equipment. Through acquisitions the company has become a truly global player. Its headquarters is located in Sweden and, in spite of widespread Swedish and international ownership, the company is controlled by the so-called Wallenberg group through its holding company Investor.

Using statements of quarterly real operating cash flows for the Electrolux group from 1986 through 1994 that we obtained from the firm, we decomposed changes in these flows into the components described in the previous section. As in the Volvo Cars case presented in Chapter 5, we identified a number of key variables with potential economic explanatory power after getting answers to the following questions: Where does Electrolux produce; where does it buy its inputs; where are these inputs produced; what are the major markets for its products; and what are the major currencies and interest rates that affect the value of Electrolux's financial liabilities? After this initial part of the analysis, the company's major competitors were identified and the same questions were asked for them. This analysis generated a set of 11 macro price variables, with potentially significant effects on Electrolux's cash flows during the period in question. The changes in real operating cash flows[10] were then regressed on changes in the variables from the fundamental analysis consisting of exchange rates between the Swedish krona and a few major currencies, interest rates, and rates of inflation.[11]

Table 9.1 summarizes the results of our analysis.[12] The macro price variables listed in the table explain about 50% of the fluctuations in (seasonally adjusted) changes in quarterly real operating cash flows. Moreover, our analysis suggests that a one percent depreciation of the Swedish krona vis-à-vis the British pound, holding the other variables constant, is expected to lead to a .55% increase in Electrolux's operating cash flow. Because the Swedish krona is the company's home currency and the firm

**Table 9.1 Sensitivity coefficients of seasonally adjusted real operating cash flows to macroeconomic variables, Electrolux Group.**

|  | 1986–92 | 1986–93 |
|---|---|---|
| SEK/GBP | .55* | .92* |
| Long DEM interest rate | .47* | .43* |
| Short GBP interest rate | .24* | .33* |
| Short Swedish interest rate | −.28* | −.29* |
| R² (adjusted) | .46 | .51 |
| D.W. | 2.1 | 2.3 |

*Significant at a 5% level. All variables are measured in percent rate of change.

derives significant net revenues from operations based outside Sweden, the company's stockholders benefit from any transaction in which a net positive foreign position is converted into that currency. The company also benefits from the stronger competitive position in Sweden that results from a weaker krona.

By contrast, an increase in Swedish short-term interest rates has a significant adverse impact on Electrolux's real operating cash flows, to a large extent because the demand for capital goods falls with an increase in interest rates. The other two interest rate components, British short rates and German long rates, are both positively correlated with the company's cash flows. The most plausible explanations of these correlations is the association of higher rates in both these countries with improving macroeconomic conditions and increases in aggregate demand.

Table 9.2 illustrates the decomposition of changes in total cash flows into intrinsic and macroeconomic components for the (out-of-sample) periods 1993 and 1994.[13] Column (1) shows actual quarterly cash flow changes in 1993 and 1994. Columns (2), (5), (6), and (7) list the changes in the price variables, which are multiplied by the coefficients in Table 9.1 to obtain the changes in cash flows caused by changes in all the macro variables $(x_M)$ in column (8). Changes in intrinsic cash flows $(x_L)$ are registered in column (9).

Although we have not yet addressed this issue, some changes in macro variables like exchange rates and interest rates can be anticipated using futures rates (or, in the case of exchange rates, differences between two countries' interest or inflation rates). In some cases (to be discussed in the next section), it may make sense to distinguish between anticipated and unanticipated changes, and to insulate managers' performance only from the changes they cannot anticipate and protect against.

To that end, Table 9.2 shows also how changes in cash flows caused by unanticipated macroeconomic events can be estimated under the assumption that the coefficients in Table 9.1 apply to both expected and unanticipated macro fluctuations. The difference between Swedish and UK interest

Table 9.2 Decomposing Electrolux' cash flows out of sample into "intrinsic" cash flows and cash flows caused by anticipated and unanticipated macroeconomic events.

| Year/Q | | (1) Real Group operating cash flows % Change from previous quarter $x_t$ | (2) Actual SEK/GBP % Change | (3) Anticipated SEK/GBP % Change (interest rate differential) | (4) Unanticipated SEK/GBP % Change | (5) 10-Year German Interest rate % Change | (6) Three-month Great Britain Interest Rate % Change | (7) Three-month Swedish interest % Change | (8) Operating cash flow effect of all macro variables % Change $x_M$ | (9) Operating cash flows net of all macro variable effects (Intrinsic cash flows) % Change $x_L$ | (10) Operating cash flow effect of unanticipated changes in macro variables % Change $x_M^U$ | (11) Cash flow change after hedging unanticipated changes in macro variables % Change $x_L + x_M^A$ |
|---|---|---|---|---|---|---|---|---|---|---|---|---|
| 1993 | 1 | 27.18 | 11.47 | 0.79 | 10.68 | -7.78 | -14.02 | -22.94 | 13.04 | 14.14 | 12.61 | 14.57 |
| | 2 | 5.39 | 1.96 | 0.71 | 1.25 | -2.09 | -6.59 | -7.82 | 2.68 | 2.71 | 2.30 | 3.09 |
| | 3 | 9.36 | 5.92 | 0.56 | 5.37 | -5.07 | -1.01 | -7.84 | 7.58 | 1.78 | 7.27 | 2.09 |
| | 4 | 9.74 | 1.89 | 0.40 | 1.49 | -8.55 | -6.33 | -12.55 | 7.08 | 2.66 | 6.87 | 2.87 |
| 1994 | 1 | 0.03 | -4.27 | 0.42 | -4.69 | 5.72 | -4.83 | -2.62 | -5.43 | 5.46 | -5.66 | 5.69 |
| | 2 | 2.78 | -0.48 | 0.47 | -0.96 | 13.54 | -2.73 | 1.10 | -7.60 | 10.37 | -7.85 | 10.63 |
| | 3 | 1.42 | 1.06 | 0.50 | 0.56 | 5.64 | -8.80 | 8.40 | -2.35 | 3.78 | -2.63 | 4.05 |
| | 4 | 18.74 | 0.88 | 0.47 | -1.35 | 3.92 | 11.56 | 6.61 | -1.43 | 20.18 | -1.69 | 20.43 |
| Mean | | 9.33 | | | | | | | | 7.63 | | 7.93 |
| Std.dev | | 9.37 | | | | | | | | 6.66 | | 6.66 |
| 100 × (Mean/std.dev) | | 99.56 | | | | | | | | 114.72 | | 118.97 |

rates in the previous quarter is used as a proxy for the anticipated exchange rate changes in column (3). Unanticipated exchange rate changes follow in column (4). It is assumed that all changes in interest rates are unanticipated in columns (5), (6), and (7). After multiplying unanticipated changes with the coefficients in Table 9.1, unanticipated cash flow changes caused by macro events ($x^U_M$) are registered in column (10). Finally, column (11) shows intrinsic cash flow changes plus cash flow changes caused by anticipated macro events ($x_L + x_M^A$).

Assuming that our task is to evaluate managers' performance in the out-of-sample period (again, 1993 and 1994), we came up with three different measures of changes in cash flows. As reported in column (1), the average quarterly change in total operating cash flows was 9.33%, while the average quarterly change in intrinsic cash flows net of all macro effects in column (9) was 7.63%. Adding cash flows caused by expected macro developments in column (11), the average change is 7.93%. It can also be seen that cash flows attributable to macro fluctuations add significantly to the standard deviation of changes on a quarterly basis. Columns (8) and (10), which measure changes caused by all macro changes and unanticipated macro changes, respectively, show large variations in quarterly changes in 1993 and 1994. Indeed, in the fourth quarter of 1993, macro effects dominated the changes in quarterly cash flows.

In sum, the data presented in Table 9.2 for Electrolux suggest that a very large proportion of the variability of operating cash flows is caused by macroeconomic fluctuations. Furthermore, most of the variability attributable to macro changes is caused by *unanticipated* events (as can be seen by comparing columns 8 and 10). Thus, if Electrolux linked its managerial bonus payments to the intrinsic cash flows, the variability of bonus payments would be significantly reduced relative to the case in which bonus payments are linked to total cash flows. But, as we discuss next, the choice of which cash flow variable to use for performance evaluation depends on the extent of management's flexibility to respond to changes in macro variables.

## 9.4 DECOMPOSITION IN PERFORMANCE ASSESSMENT

An important—arguably, the most important—task of VBM is to link managerial bonuses to changes in shareholder value. In what follows, we assume that a company's operating cash flows, adjusted for a capital charge for a given period, provide a reasonable basis for determining managerial remuneration for that period. The key issue here is whether components of operating cash flows that can be confidently attributed to fluctuations in macro conditions should be filtered out from the cash flows generating bonuses because these flows are beyond management's control.

Table 9.2 effectively provides three choices of the cash flows to be used as the basis for managerial rewards. They are the total (unadjusted) operating cash flows in column (1), the intrinsic cash flows in column (9), and the cash flows net of those caused by unanticipated macroeconomic events in column (11).

If management has little or no control over cash flows caused by macro events, an efficient compensation scheme should be linked mainly if not entirely to intrinsic cash flows. In this case, compensation based on the intrinsic cash flows in column (9) creates the strongest incentives for management to devote effort to enhancing the firm's long-run competitiveness. To the extent that a bonus system is linked to cash flows over which management has no control, managers are effectively rewarded (or penalized) for events beyond their control. This means that managers face greater risk (for which they must be compensated with a higher salary or more equity-based pay) and a weaker link between pay and performance.[14]

Some compensation experts argue that holding management accountable for cash flows caused by macro events not only puts them in the same shoes as their shareholders, but gives them incentives to respond more effectively to changes in the macro environment. But this argument assumes that operations can be adjusted in various ways to changes in expectations about macro events. If that is so, then management should have incentives to make such adjustments, and the adjustment to total cash flows for purposes of management compensation should be limited to cash flows caused by *unanticipated* changes. In other words, the cash flows in column (11) of Table 9.2 would provide the relevant input for performance measurement under these circumstances.

The choice between adjusting cash flows for changes in all macro effects and adjusting for only unanticipated effects depends mainly on three considerations: how far in advance changes in macro conditions and variables can be forecast; how long the changes in the variables in question are expected to last; and how quickly operations can be adjusted to respond to such changes. For example, if it takes longer to adjust production volumes than an unanticipated exchange rate change is likely to remain in effect, then it clearly makes sense to base performance measures on intrinsic cash flows. But, to use another example, if managers can quickly respond to an anticipated change in the exchange rate by shifting production among countries, then they should be held accountable, at least to some extent, for the effects of such currency changes on their operating results.

## 9.5  TAKING FLEXIBILITY INTO ACCOUNT

In Equation 20 the present value of real options is one component of the value of a firm. Real options are sometimes inherent in businesses (such as an oil company's effective call options on oil prices) or can be created by investments that increase a firm's ability to take advantage of positive changes in cost and demand conditions, and to reduce the impact of negative changes.[15]

Such investments in real options can be motivated by uncertainty about factors that directly affect intrinsic cash flows, as well as about macroeconomic conditions. Our concern in this chapter is with the effects of investments in "flexibility" in response to uncertainty about macroeconomic conditions. For example, investments that reduce the expected costs of changing suppliers or production sites enable a firm to reduce the cash flow impact of negative changes in real exchange rates, and increase the cash flow impact of positive changes.[16] Multinational firms like Electrolux should have relatively high flexibility in these respects. Investments in customer relations may also be viewed as creating a real option insofar as they enable a firm to pass through large exchange rate or interest rate changes into prices.[17] An exporting firm may be able to write contracts including a clause that shifts exchange rate risk to the buyer if the exchange rate changes more than $x$ percent. Similarly, inflation above a certain level may trigger wage and price adjustment by contractual agreement. The fact that such contractual price changes usually do not happen unless the exchange rate or the inflation rate reaches a certain "trigger level" indicates that contractual flexibility is costly.

The important characteristics of real options for the analysis here are (a) that the costs typically take the form of investments in one period designed to reduce adjustment costs in future periods, and (b) that such investments typically reduce the size of macro shocks that would trigger the exercise of the option—for example, the shift of suppliers, the change of production locations, or the change in contractual terms.

The performance evaluation and remuneration scheme should preserve management's incentive to invest in real options that create flexibility in responding to macro shocks. Thus, after investing in real options, cash flow benefits in future periods should affect management's remuneration positively.

The linear decomposition of cash flows developed above for Electrolux filters out cash flows beyond management control in a certain period. However, the issue now is whether the decomposition also filters out cash flows created by investments in real options in earlier periods. We argue that the linear decomposition does not filter out such cash flows, and that it is also appropriate for performance measurement when the firm has real options to manage exposure.

To develop the argument further, consider Figure 9.1 showing the magnitude of macro shocks on the x-axis and cash flow effects of the shocks on the vertical axis. Think of the shock as the unanticipated real percentage depreciation of the krona relative to the pound (SEK/GBP). The straight line shows the cash flow effects of the disturbance if there are no real options—that is, no flexibility in pricing, sourcing, location of production, and so on—no matter how large the shock. In the absence of real options, a linear relation can be assumed. The broken line shows the cash flow effects of the same shock, when an increasing number of real options are triggered as the magnitude of the shock increases beyond trigger levels.

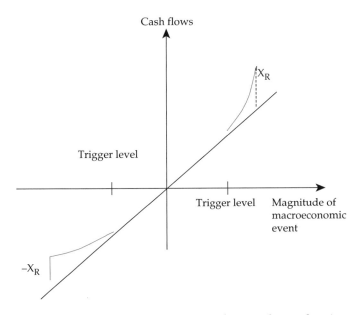

**Figure 9.1** Cash flows caused by macroeconomic factors when real options are present ($X_R$ represents cash flow effects caused by the exercising of real options in a period).

When the option is exercised, the cash flows denoted $X_R$ are generated. These cash flows rise with the magnitude of a positive event. When the event is increasingly negative, the cash flows generated by the option reduce a negative effect on cash flows. Clearly, we do not want to filter out these positive contributions to total cash flows when evaluating managerial performance. Therefore, when we want to evaluate the cash flows that cannot be influenced by management, the cash flows shown by the straight line are the appropriate ones to filter out. Thereby the cash flows generated by real options (denoted $X_R$) remain part of the performance measure.

If $X_{R,\,t}$ is positive to the right in Figure 9.1, the cash adjustment has underestimated the total cash flow effect of the unanticipated positive macroeconomic event, but correctly filtered out cash flows beyond management control. If $X_{R,\,t}$ is negative to the left in Figure 9.1, the linear adjustment has overestimated the total cash flow effect of the negative, unanticipated macroeconomic event, but correctly filtered out cash flows beyond management control.

The conclusion of this discussion for the Electrolux case is that the calculated cash flow changes from macroeconomic events based on a linear regression analysis remain the appropriate ones to use for performance evaluation. An econometric problem may arise, however, when estimating the desired linear regression coefficients, if the relation between macroeconomic shocks and cash flows are non-linear as in Figure 9.1.[18] Thus, the analyst estimating the linear sensitivity coefficients for macroeconomic effects on cash flows may have to limit the regression to observations of macroeconomic changes within the range bounded by the trigger levels for which the relation can be assumed to be linear. The regressions resulting in the coefficients presented in Tables 9.1 and 9.2 did not reveal errors that could be interpreted as non-linearities of the type discussed here.

## 9.6  CONCLUDING REMARKS ABOUT MUST ANALYSIS IN PERFORMANCE ASSESSMENT

Value-Based Management (VBM) is a tool for designing performance evaluation and incentive compensation systems that aim to maximize shareholder value. In this chapter we argue that macroeconomic fluctuations cause cash flow and value changes that to a large extent cannot be controlled or influenced by management. Such changes should be filtered out of performance measures so that, to the greatest extent possible, the measures reflect only management's ability and effort. For example, a multinational firm's operating results in a given year may have as much to do with unexpected exchange rate and interest rate fluctuations as with managerial skill and decision-making; and managerial rewards, particularly at the operating level, should reflect mainly the latter.

In this chapter, we have argued that VBM performance measures should be fully (or partly) cleansed of macro influences such as unanticipated changes in exchange rates or interest rates in cases where management has limited ability to respond to the resulting exposures. A framework for filtering out macro influences on operating cash flows is developed using multivariate regressions to identify the impact of specific macro variables on changes in cash flows. Using the case of Electrolux, a Swedish multinational, the framework reveals that changes in the krona/pound exchange rate and various interest rates contribute significantly to the variability of the firm's cash flows; and that, for operating managers with little ability to anticipate or respond to such changes, the effects of changes in such performance measures should be removed from performance measures.

We have discussed under what circumstances only unanticipated effects of macroeconomic events should be filtered out from the performance measure, and we have argued that the filtering method used provides incentives for management to invest in real options that enhance flexibility (and thereby value) in response to macroeconomic events. In the next chapter, our focus shifts to incentive effects of evaluation of managers involved in risk management on operational and tactical levels.

## NOTES

1  This chapter is adapted from Oxelheim and Wihlborg (2003).
2  There are a number of VBM frameworks. The two best known are Shareholder Value Analysis (SVA) (see Rappaport, 1986) and Economic Value Analysis

(EVA) (see Stewart, 1990). However, there are a number of challengers, including Cash Value Added (CVA) (see Ottoson and Weissenrieder, 1996) and Cash Flow Return on Investment (CFROI) (see Madden, 1999).

3 There are methods of adjusting performance for macroeconomic variables, including exchange rates' deviations from Purchasing Power Parity (see Stewart, 1983) and oil price changes (see McCormick and Gow, 2001). However, no VBM framework takes into account the fact that macroeconomic variables often respond simultaneously to changes in macroeconomic conditions.

4 It is well established in the incentive contract literature that if risk-averse managers' remuneration is linked to noise factors beyond their control without strong linkage to shareholder value, then their incentive to exert effort on behalf of shareholders may be weakened. See, for example, Milgrom and Roberts (1992), Chapter 7.

5 It thus also represents a possible explanation for large observed differences between market values and economic values as measured by EVA. See O'Byrne (1997).

6 The intrinsic level cannot usually be observed, and it is not constant. It is independent of influences of macroeconomic events, however, and reflects the ability of management to employ resources productively. The fact that the intrinsic level is not directly observable does not mean that it lacks practical significance. On the contrary, we argue that management should estimate it and use it as a key input in major business decisions.

7 In most macroeconomic models different shocks affect these particular price variables in different combinations. The price variables are essentially signals of macroeconomic conditions. Economic models differ about the magnitude and duration of change in the price variables in response to different macroeconomic shocks but most open economy models have in common the mentioned price variables.

8 This formulation assumes a linear relationship for percentage changes, which is appropriate if the impact on cash flows of a macro event is expected to vary proportionally with the change in the particular variable. To the extent that managers can take measures to protect a firm's cash flow in response to large percentage changes in macro variables—for example, by exercising real options—then this assumption can be modified, as discussed near the end of this article.

9 It should be kept in mind that there are three limitations with this application. First, the coefficients in Equation 22 refer to *single-period* cash flow effects, while changes in value reflect changes in expected *future* cash flows as well as current performance. Second, the discount factor in Equation 20 incorporates all risk factors and may therefore not be applicable to two separate components of cash flows. In other words, the appropriate discount factor for "intrinsic cash flows" may differ from the appropriate discount factor for cash flows caused by macroeconomic events. Third, changes in the value of real options (PVRO in Equation 20) from macroeconomic events must be estimated separately.

10 Deflated by producer prices in manufacturing, and measured as the revenues from goods sold minus costs of goods sold.

11 Total European housing starts were included to control for changes in the industry's conditions. Dummy variables were used to adjust cash flows for seasonality. Regressions were run for the whole period 1986–94, as well as for the periods 1986–92 and 1986–93. The latter regressions are reported below because they make it possible to use coefficients for out-of-sample analysis.

12  The set of significant coefficients shown in Table 1 were obtained from a backward stepwise regression using contemporaneous dependent and independent variables. Lagged variables were introduced but without substantial changes in results.

13  The coefficients in Table 9.2 were employed out-of-sample in such a way that the 1986–92 coefficients were used to estimate the impact of macroeconomic events in 1993, and the 1986–93 coefficients were used to estimate the impact in 1994.

14  Incentive effects of the choice of exchange rate in budgeting decisions are discussed in Lessard and Lorange (1977). In their analysis the choice of exchange rate influences measures of performance and therefore incentives.

15  By investing in flexibility, the firm can narrow the range of conditions within which it cannot adjust its operations to changes in the environment. This range is defined by "trigger levels" for demand and cost conditions beyond which adjustment of operations is profitable. See, for example, Dixit and Pindyck (1994).

16  See, for instance, Capel (1997).

17  Corporate strategies to create flexibility to counter exchange rate fluctuations are discussed and empirically documented in Oxelheim, Wihlborg and Lim (1990).

18  If the number of periods used in the estimation is large and flexibility is symmetric as in Figure 9.1, the slope coefficients are not affected by the existence of real options but the errors will depend on the magnitude of the macroeconomic variables.

# Chapter 10

# Evaluation, Feedback, and Organization

## 10.1 INTRODUCTION

In previous chapters arguments for risk management have been discussed from a shareholder perspective. Risk management strategies are, or should be, set by top management, but important risk management decisions are made on tactical and operational levels. Objectives and incentives of managers on all levels need to be consistent with shareholder wealth maximization. Problems of aligning top management's objectives with shareholders by means of executive compensation programs based on performance measures were discussed in Chapter 9. On tactical and operational levels it may not be possible to use pecuniary rewards to provide incentives for managers. Nevertheless, the performance measures and the reward structure should induce managers to act with the appropriate degree of risk aversion with respect to the appropriate target variable over the appropriate time horizon to use the terminology of risk management strategies from Chapter 8.

This chapter discusses the development of evaluation systems for managers involved in risk management on different levels with the purpose of developing reward structures that induce managers to act in accordance with risk management objectives. These objectives should be consistent with the over-arching corporate objective. We do not discuss whether reward systems should be pecuniary. There are "carrots and sticks" of many kinds available in a corporate hierarchy. Implicitly or explicitly they must all be based on some kind of performance evaluation. For risk management objectives to be achieved, those involved in risk management must be evaluated with these objectives in mind. The area of performance evaluation in risk management remains largely unexplored in the literature and we do not claim to develop a complete analysis of the problems. Rather we point out some issues that require special consideration. Much of the attention is devoted to problems of obtaining the relevant information that would allow risk management activities to be evaluated properly.

In Chapter 8 we emphasized that information availability must be considered when a risk management strategy is determined. The specific information required to evaluate performance need not be exactly the same as the information that determines the strategy, since the "benefit of hindsight" is available when performance is being evaluated. This benefit is also a potential source of pitfalls, however.

Risk management cannot be made consistent with corporate objectives unless systems for budgeting, evaluation, and feedback are developed independently of, or complementary to, the regular accounting systems. One reason is that accounting rules may be misleading relative to economic objectives as we noted in Chapter 3. Another reason is that risk is a concept that is not easily measured in an objective fashion. It is forward looking, like expectations about corporate sales and profits, and observations with the benefit of hindsight are not always useful for evaluation of decisions made with less and different information.

We proceed in Section 10.2 with the problems of achieving consistency between managers' incentives and corporate objectives. The issue is very much the extent to which hindsight information can be used to assess performance. Managers on top, tactical, and operational levels are considered. In Section 10.3 we focus on information problems related to the distinctions between realized and non-realized gains/losses and between anticipated and unanticipated gains/losses. The general problem is that the consequences of decisions are not necessarily observed within the evaluation periods. An additional evaluation problem is caused by the fact that most accounting and reporting is expressed in nominal terms, while shareholders' concern is with the purchasing power of their dividend income and wealth. This issue is discussed in Section 10.4.

In Section 10.5 we turn to evaluation of specific risk management strategies as they were specified in Chapter 8. For example, one could ask how to evaluate whether a minimize variance strategy actually reduces variance below the level that would have been obtained with a laissez-faire strategy. Finally, in Section 10.6, implications for centralization versus decentralization of macroeconomic risk management of the information and incentive problems are discussed.

## 10.2 MANAGERS' INCENTIVES AND THE FIRM'S OBJECTIVES

The evaluation of a managers' performance on any level influences their behavior and motivation. Three levels of risk management and the types of decisions made on each level are described in Table 10.1.

Top management consists of the board of directors and the managing director. On this level the overall risk management strategy needs to be determined in accordance with the fundamental corporate objective. We have mostly assumed the latter to be shareholder wealth maximization but the objective may also be maximization with respect to a broader spectrum of stakeholders. Top management would also evaluate the performance of managers on the tactical level. The head of finance and the head of sales represent this level, for example. These individuals would determine how to implement, for example, a minimum variance strategy by means of enhanced flexibility of operations, or a pricing strategy that specifies price responses to macroeconomic events. Since the commercial exposures tend to become financial exposures at delivery, as described in Chapter 3, a division of labor in risk management between, for example, the sales and finance functions must be determined at the top management level. A risk management group reporting to the top level could be assigned the task of coordinating risk management tasks of different functions, and in particular, of determining the scope for investments in operating flexibility (real options) as opposed to reliance on financial risk management.

Firms differ naturally in terms of the length of contract periods and the degree to which they have a choice of invoice currency and payment conditions. In some firms with flexibility in pricing and payment terms, exposures are non-contractual to a greater extent. Then, tactical decisions for the head of sales refer to pricing and sales in different currencies and countries, the choice of invoice currency, and payment terms, while the finance area is limited to entering financial contracts of different types in

**Table 10.1 Levels of decision making in risk management.**

| | Title/individuals | Example of decision choice | Evaluation |
|---|---|---|---|
| Top level management | Managing Director (CEO) and Board of Directors | Risk management strategy (laissez-faire, minimum variance, etc.) | Self-evaluation and market monitoring |
| Tactical level | Head of Finance (CFO), Head of Sales, and other divisional heads | Making strategies operational by deciding on risk levels Approach to exposure management Type of exposure management tool | Level and variance of cash flows<br><br>Costs of financing |
| Operational level | Treasurer | Timing of forward contracts and options, Minimize transactions costs | |

order to reduce the residual exposure. Tactical decisions for the head of finance include determining whether the risk-return objective imposed from above is best met by internal or external hedging transactions, and whether options or forward markets should be employed.

The operating level chooses, for example, the exact timing of contracts, bank connections, and the type of security to issue or to invest excess cash in. This level is in principle easy to evaluate since its objective can be stated in terms of transactions cost and market returns. No risk-return trade-off is determined at this level. The tactical level, on the other hand, may face an objective that includes variance reduction as well as cost and profit aspects. Evaluation criteria should incorporate the same aspects. We focus here on the evaluation of the tactical level where there is more leeway for individual interpretations of tasks than on the operational level. Evaluation of top-level decisions with respect to the choice of risk management strategy was discussed in Section 8.5.

Any evaluation must have a reference point. Though the budget may have many purposes, we consider for the sake of discussion the situation when the firm creates a budget as some kind of forecast and, thereafter, evaluates managers relative to this budget. The evaluation of subsidiaries' and divisions' performance can take many different forms. Cash flows or accounting profits may be used. The evaluation may be based on outcomes in foreign currency or in the parent company's currency using different exchange rates. Translation gains and losses may or may not be considered.

Lessard and Lorange (1977) discussed what exchange rate to use for budget and evaluation, respectively, in order to induce local managers at the subsidiary level (heads of sales and heads of finance) in a firm to (a) behave in accordance with the firm's objective and (b) to restrict themselves to decisions for which they have the expertise. Lessard and Lorange limited their discussion to the case in which the firm wants to maximize profits, and distinguished between the following exchange rates for potential use in budgeting and evaluation.

1. The actual rate at the time of the budget
2. An internal exchange rate representing a forecast such as the forward rate
3. The end of period exchange rate, which for the budget is a continuously updated actual rate.

If different rates are used for budget and evaluation, respectively, such as the rate at the time of the budget for budgeting and the end-of-period exchange rate for evaluation, managers are induced to form their own forecast of exchange rate changes, and to act based on these forecasts. If the expertise lies elsewhere, according to the top management, this situation may lead to inferior decisions about sales efforts in different countries. Furthermore, the managers will be induced to try to make exchange rate gains by means of changes in currency of invoice and other means by which positions in different currencies could be influenced.

A further drawback of using the rate at the time of the budget is that production and planned sales levels in different countries would not take anticipated exchange rate changes into account. Using an internal rate based on a best available forecast resolves this problem. Alternatively, the budget can be updated continuously to incorporate new information for firms in which production levels and sales efforts can be adjusted on short notice.

How can managers be induced to take risk into account appropriately in case top management sets an objective that includes variance aspects? If the budget as well as the evaluation is based on an internal forecasting, managers would wish to maximize performance at the internal rates and they would not be held responsible for performance changes caused by exchange rate changes. Presumably, they would not take exchange rate uncertainty into account in their decision-making. Thus, using the same rate for budgeting and performance evaluation seems best suited for the risk-neutral firm.

Consider instead the case in which the budget is based on internal forecasting while the performance is based on actual end of period rates. Thus, managers are held responsible for unanticipated changes in performance. In principle, it would be possible to adjust the internal rates for risk but the criteria for making such an adjustment can easily become arbitrary. We know of no firms employing such methods to induce a particular behavior toward risk. Instead, risk aversion might be induced by the managers' own risk aversion with respect to remuneration or by their desire to avoid large losses that could jeopardize their reputation and possibly get them fired. It is quite possible that excessive risk aversion would be induced in this case. There is, of course, no obvious mechanism that aligns the risk aversion of managers with top management's desired risk attitude. Thus, if top management would want to induce a particular risk-averse behavior with respect to exchange rates or any other risk factor, it may have to use specific constraints on particular types of actions at the tactical level.

To be more specific regarding risk management objectives, a division could be given an objective with respect to profit maximization subject to a cash flow at risk (CFaR) constraint. It is obviously problematic to evaluate in hindsight what CFaR-objective managers have used in commercial as well as in financial decisions. Performance on a period-by-period basis can be evaluated based on profitability, but the CFaR constraint would have to be induced by means of specific repercussions associated with particular pre-specified "bad" outcomes that tactical managers can be held responsible for. We return to this issue below.

## 10.3 REALIZED VERSUS NON-REALIZED AND ANTICIPATED VERSUS UNANTICIPATED GAINS AND LOSSES

To begin with an extreme example, we go back to the late 1960s and early 1970s when long-term interest rates in Great Britain hovered around or over 15 percent while in Switzerland they were as low as 5 or 6 percent. Many British firms chose to borrow long-term in Swiss francs. Then, over a five-year period, the price of the Swiss franc in pounds doubled. Thus, even on a before-tax basis, the Swiss franc loans became extremely expensive relative to pound loans. To make matters worse, British tax authorities did not allow deductions for exchange rate losses, while outright interest costs were tax-deductible. On these grounds, the Swiss franc loans became the direct cause of ruin for a number of firms, and the downfall of an even larger number of managers who were held responsible for the Swiss franc loans.

Even more extreme exchange rate losses were part of the Asian crisis in 1997–98. Many Asian firms had borrowed at relatively low dollar interest rates while domestic interest rates were a couple of percentage points higher; central banks and governments were sticking to fixed exchange rate policies. Obviously, disaster struck many firms when the Asian currencies depreciated rapidly. An additional wave of speculative activity based on differences in nominal interest is the so called carry trade. This trade was triggered by the zero interest policy in Japan in 2000s and took primarily place between the Japanese yen and the Australian and New Zealand dollars.

Were the persons responsible for taking loans denominated in the foreign currencies appropriately fired in these cases? The answer would depend on what these individuals could have been expected to foresee and what risk level was acceptable. The non-deductibility of exchange losses in the Swiss franc case can be a heavy burden, even if interest rate differentials exactly offset anticipated exchange rate differentials. This fact does not speak in favor of those taking Swiss-franc loans.

In cases in which exchange rate gains (losses) are taxed (deducted) at the same rate as interest costs, the situation is different. In the Asian case, for example, it could be argued that the depreciation of the Asian currencies in excess of the interest rate differentials was completely unanticipated. The *ex ante* likelihood that the dollar loans would be better than the domestic currency loans was large, and the higher domestic interest rates indicated a low likelihood that the dollar would appreciate. Under these circumstances, managers should be evaluated in hindsight only on what could reasonably have been anticipated (and possibly on the risk they were taking).

What if those seeking foreign currency loans in the above cases considered only interest costs, neglecting even expected exchange rate changes? That would have been a serious error, but given many firms' reporting systems, it may perhaps have been reasonable from the point of view of the financial managers. Interest costs show up as an outright expense each period but exchange rate losses are generally not realized until the loan is repaid. Therefore, the managers that chose the domestic currency loans at higher interest rates were burdened with higher outright costs of financing for a long period and they may have been fired before their wisdom was revealed. Figure 3.6 shows that it can take many years before relative interest costs and exchange rate gains and losses offset each other, even in countries with well-functioning financial markets.

Appropriate "fair value" or market value accounting methods for foreign currency loans would take actual exchange rate changes into account, and the "fair" values would reflect non-realized gains and losses in domestic currency.

There is still disagreement about the appropriate timing of accounting for non-realized exchange rate gains and losses, and there is not one "correct" solution to the problem. Under fixed or pegged but adjustable exchange rates, one can reasonably expect exchange rate changes to cause realized gains or losses in the future. Thus, such exchange rate changes should be taken into consideration when evaluating the cost of a loan. Under floating exchange rates, however, there could be wide fluctuations from month to month or week to week. Thus, exchange rate changes are often temporary, and translation gains (losses) are often reversed before cash flows are realized. It is naturally hard or even impossible to determine whether an exchange rate change is permanent or temporary. We noted in Chapter 3 that a Purchasing Power Parity (PPP) rate may serve as a measure of long term exchange rates but, given the long periods over which there are deviations from PPP, a moving average of rates over some time or a forward rate at the beginning of the year may be superior translation rates.

The problems of evaluating in hindsight the choice between long term and short term borrowing are similar to the problems of evaluating the choice of currency denomination. To what extent could interest rate changes have been anticipated? Are changes in bond values due to changes in interest rates permanent or temporary?

The distinction between anticipated and unanticipated changes is important for evaluating specific cover and hedge transactions as well. The cost of cover should reflect the anticipated opportunity cost of covering. Accordingly, the relevant cost at the time that hedging decisions are made is observed in the difference between the forward rate and the anticipated future spot rate. If International Fisher Parity (IFP) holds, then the expected cost of covering is zero, as noted above. Looking at costs of cover with hindsight period by period, it is likely that large losses as well as large gains occur with high frequency. Thus, we are back to the problem of evaluating hedging operations and risk management activities more generally.

If *ex post* spot rates are used in evaluation of covers, then in the words of Dufey and Giddy (1978) it is important to obtain a sufficient number of observations in order "to determine whether the manager systematically makes costly cover and hedge decisions. Otherwise, the poor predictive power of the forward rate could imply occasional large *ex post* opportunity costs of covering. In order to avoid such losses a manager could be induced to be risk-averse even when this is not called for."

## 10.4 NOMINAL VERSUS REAL MAGNITUDES

External and internal accounting and information systems do not generally correct for inflation. In periods and countries with low inflation it does not make much difference whether inflation adjustments are made. During some hyperinflationary periods, such as the 1970s in Brazil, balance sheets and income statements were corrected for inflation. In other countries with more modest inflation rates, the effects of inflation on firms' net worth must be noted in annual reports.

Maximizing nominal cash flows in a currency is equivalent to maximizing real cash flows, but risk in nominal terms is not necessarily the same as risk in real terms. In Chapter 3 it was noted that fluctuations in nominal interest rates might correspond to fluctuations in expected inflation. Large fluctuations in nominal interest costs may simply correspond to fluctuations in inflation rates under these circumstances. A flexible rate long-term loan or a series of short-term loans could be the result of a sensible policy to hedge inflation risk. Similarly, over the longer term, exchange rate changes may correspond to differences in inflationary developments and a foreign currency loan could be used to hedge against domestic inflation risk, while exposing the borrower to foreign inflation risk.

In the analysis of cash flow exposure to macroeconomic fluctuations in Chapter 5, it was noted that the exposure coefficients were not strongly affected by the choice of nominal cash flows as the dependent variable instead of real cash flows. At the time of the analysis, the Swedish inflation rate was in the order of magnitude between 5 and 10 percent. The results would have been seriously affected by not including inflation rates among the independent risk factors, however, since the German inflation rate had a very strong impact on cash flows. The exchange rate and interest rate exposures would also have appeared different had the inflation rate not been included.

## 10.5 EVALUATION OF RISK MANAGEMENT STRATEGIES

In Chapter 8 we argued that the choice of exposure management strategy among laissez-faire, minimum variance, maximum expected return, and risk-return trade-off would be based on top management's view of the world with respect to the validity of market equilibrium relationship in goods and financial markets, and its perception of what risk-attitude and time perspective best serve shareholders' interest. The evaluation of an implemented strategy could take the form of indirectly testing for assumptions implied by the strategy about PPP in goods markets, IFP in international financial markets, and the relation between short- and long-term interest rates. In addition, the relationship between cash flow variance and value variance can be analyzed with cash flow and stock market data.

In this section we are concerned with the question of whether the success of a risk management strategy can be directly evaluated *ex post* by comparing the level of risk to which a firm has been exposed to the level of risk exposure under a different strategy. Such an evaluation would enable management to determine whether the gains from the choice of a strategy exceed the costs of its implementation in terms of, for example, employee time. Information requirements associated with a risk-return trade-off strategy are much larger than information requirements associated with a minimum variance strategy, as discussed in Chapter 8. Since information requirements are associated with costs, the gains from the trade-off strategy in terms of risk management objectives might be more than offset by costs of implementation.

There are serious pitfalls when evaluating risk management strategies ex post. These pitfalls can be the result of confusion between the risk concept that should be used from the perspective of fundamental corporate objectives and the concept of risk that can be measured. In particular, the time horizon of risk management is important for measuring risk *ex post*. In cases in which risk aversion refers to the actual variance in cash flows or value, historical data can be used to observe variances *ex post*. But if the risk of concern refers to a specific horizon at a specific time, *ex post* measurements of cash flow variance can be misleading because the relevant variance is conditional on the current situation of the firm and current market conditions.

Consider the case of Electrolux in Chapter 9. In Table 9.2, the mean change in cash flows and the standard deviation of cash flows during a six-year period are calculated in one case when no exposures were hedged and, in another case, when exchange rate and interest rate exposures of commercial cash flows were hedged. In the latter case, it was assumed that anticipated exchange rates were reflected in interest rate differentials and that the expected interest rate equaled the current rate. Under these assumptions, the consequence of hedging for mean cash flows and the variance of cash flows could be calculated easily. The table shows that hedging all exposures would have reduced the mean change in cash flows from 9.33 percent per quarter to 7.93 percent, while the standard deviation would have been reduced from 9.37 to 6.66. The ratio between the mean and the standard deviation would have increased from approximately 1 to 1.18. Can these figures be interpreted to mean that hedging would have been beneficial and would have reduced the cash flow risk of Electrolux?

First of all, it can be noted that the decline in the mean cash flow changes is inconsistent with IFP, since hedging on the average should be costless under IFP. However, the time period used in the evaluation could have been characterized by special market conditions and may have been too short for exchange rate gains and losses to equal the interest rate differential on the average. If so, the decline in the mean need not be representative. If we disregard the change in the mean and focus on the change in the standard deviation, the decline implies that hedging would have reduced the variance of quarterly changes in cash flows during the period. Assume that we accept this observation as representative for consequences of hedging.

If the risk management objective were to reduce this (unconditional) variance, then the hedging strategy would have been effective. If the hedging strategy instead would have aimed at reducing the (conditional) variance three months into the future, conditional on specific conditions each quarter, then we cannot say with certainty whether hedging achieved the objective. It is possible that the variance reduction was relatively large in periods when the firm's concern with variance was low, and that the variance was high in periods when concern was high as a result of, for example, liquidity needs and credit market conditions.

Using Cash Flow at Risk (CFaR) as an objective in risk management is one way of evaluating in each period the risk that the firm faces over a specific time horizon. The data for cash flow variance in the Electrolux case can accordingly not be used directly to evaluate in hindsight whether CFaR in particular periods of special concern would have been reduced by means of hedging. The decline in the variance of cash flow changes in the Electrolux case only implies that, on the average over the period, CFaR would have been lower if the firm had hedged exchange rate and interest rate exposures. The CFaR objective may vary from period to period, however, depending on liquidity needs, credit market conditions, the firm's solvency, and current macroeconomic conditions relative to average conditions.

The difficulty of evaluating a risk management strategy referring to period-specific risk, as in the case of CFaR, depends on the impossibility of observing forward-looking variance at a particular time *ex post*. The specific outcome in each period can be observed, but the avoidance of a big loss does not mean that such a loss could not have occurred. Analogously, the fact that a big loss occurred during the period does not mean that another strategy should have been chosen. Any evaluation in hindsight must consider what information was available at the time that risk management decisions were made.

The difficulties of evaluating risk management strategies in hindsight implies that the focus in risk management should lie on creating the correct incentives for those involved in risk management, and on the continuous updating of information about exposure and measures of the variances and covariances for macroeconomic risk variables. For example, exposure coefficients as measured in Chapter 5 and their implication for corporate risk management need to be updated quarter by quarter.

## 10.6  CENTRALIZATION VERSUS DECENTRALIZATION OF RISK MANAGEMENT

In this section we draw implications of the previous discussion for the organization of risk management on a centralized or decentralized level. An increased tendency toward centralization of risk management has been observed for at least two decades. This tendency may be explained by scale advantages when buying and selling currencies, opportunities for netting within a multidivisional firm, the scarcity on local levels of expertise, and advantages in global tax planning and exchange control avoidance at a centralized level. Centralization may help the firm take advantage of differences in transaction costs among markets.

By centralization we mean that decisions are made in entity units with independent bankruptcy risk and independent access to credit markets. Subsidiaries are in many firms so closely integrated that they cannot be considered independent units, even though they formally are different legal entities. In this case centralization implies that decisions are made on a consolidated level.

An evaluation program for macroeconomic exposure management should naturally include an evaluation of its organization, and how objectives are best met with different degrees of centralization of risk management decision on the tactical level in particular. Decreased motivation when responsibilities are removed from local and functional decision makers may offset advantages of centralization from the point of view of the firm's objective.

On the face of it, centralization would seem advantageous for a risk-averse firm, since cash flows or market-value variance should be reduced for the firm as a whole and a local unit's contribution to the variance can only be evaluated at a central level. As discussed in Section 10.2, internal pricing schemes for macroeconomic variables and the appropriate choice of prices in budgets and performance evaluations can be used to induce local and functional managers to make their decisions based entirely on centrally determined forecasts of exchange rates, interest rates, and so on, without concern about uncertainty about these variables. Thereby, risk management would have to be centralized while other operational decisions would be decentralized.

Risk-taking responsibilities are not easily decentralized, because performance evaluation with respect to risk-taking is problematic and, as a result, appropriate incentives based on performance evaluation would generally not include risk considerations. As argued in Section 10.2, top management would have to rely on the personal risk attitudes of managers or constrain their behavior in relevant dimensions.

There are also advantages of decentralization. For example, it may be advantageous to decentralize decisions to a unit at which relevant soft information is quickly available. By soft information we mean that it is not easily quantified and transferred within a firm. Furthermore, motivation and morale of subsidiary managers and functional managers may be reduced when important profitability-related tools are beyond their control. There are ways around the second problem in financial risk management in particular. Local managers can be given responsibility to hedge exposures using financial instruments with the central finance function as a counter party. In this case, exposures are transferred to the central level, where decisions with respect to total exposures can be made.

One issue of concern from an organizational point of view is that an exposure to macroeconomic uncertainty is not purely a financial issue. We have made a point of emphasizing the operational aspects of exposure and the possibility of managing exposure by means of investments in operational flexibility. If the issue were limited to inclusion of the exposure of operations through sales, price, and cost effects, it would still be possible to leave responsibility for risk management to the finance area of a firm. Since the finance area tends to be evaluated based on its performance with respect to financial flows and positions, there could be some reluctance to take responsibility for managing exposure of commercial cash flows. Hedge positions would often differ substantially from observable financial positions, since they would depend on, for example, sales elasticities concerning exchange rates and interest rates. Gains and losses from hedge positions would not offset losses and gains on financial positions. Therefore, auditors and external analysts may interpret hedge positions as speculative.

Operational functional areas may deal on their own with commercial cash flow exposures to exchange rates, interest rates, and other macroeconomic variables, while the finance area takes the responsibility for exposure of financial positions. Since exposures of commercial cash flows become financial exposures as soon as goods have been delivered, the responsibility of the finance area would have to be strictly limited to explicit financial positions. It may be more practical and cost effective to manage all exposures over specific time horizons without distinguishing between non-contractual exposures of, for example, sales and contractual exposures of, for example, accounts receivables.

The division of risk management responsibility becomes more complex when considering the opportunity of operational areas to invest in flexibility of, for example, input suppliers and to adjust prices to exchange rate changes. The flexibility would affect the exposures of commercial cash flows and actually make the exposures in foreign currency unknown as long as options exist. We discussed this issue in Chapter 6. The implication for organization of risk management would be to strengthen the argument for limiting the responsibility of the finance area to explicit financial positions, while other functional areas take responsibility for their operational exposures.

As noted above in connection with the discussion of evaluation of risk management, a centralized risk management group can be given the responsibility to keep track of exposures and to clarify the responsibilities of the operational and the finance areas. This risk management group would also have to specify procedures for sharing of relevant exposure information in accordance with the division of responsibilities.

## 10.7 CONCLUDING REMARKS ON EVALUATION, FEEDBACK, AND ORGANIZATION

Evaluation of managers provides the basis for rewards and penalties for their actions, and these rewards and penalties affect the incentives of the managers. In this chapter we have focused on evaluation of managers on a tactical level, since these managers typically have substantial leeway on risk management. If the top management has determined that shareholder wealth maximization does not require macroeconomic risk management, the tactical level managers can be evaluated in a relatively simple way by considering them heads of profit centers. As soon as risk of cash flows or value becomes part of the operational objectives, the question arises how to evaluate managers' performance with respect to risk.

Any evaluation in hindsight must consider what information was available at the time that risk management decisions were made. To obtain relevant information it is important to distinguish between anticipated and unanticipated changes in risk factors, and between realized and non-realized gains and losses.

Risk is always forward looking and cannot easily be measured in hindsight. In particular, if the willingness to take risk varies over time, as one would expect in a shareholder wealth-maximizing firm, decisions cannot be evaluated properly in hindsight using observations of fluctuations in cash flows and value. These difficulties of measuring risk *ex post* have implications for performance evaluation that affect incentives of tactical managers, as well as evaluation of alternative risk management strategies.

We argued that appropriate risk-taking incentives for managers on the tactical level might have to rely on the individual risk preferences of the managers, complemented by specific constraints on their behavior. The difficulties of evaluating some risk management strategies in hindsight implies that the focus in risk management should lie on creating the correct incentives for those involved in risk management, and on the continuous updating of information about exposure and measures of the variances and covariances for macroeconomic risk variables. These aspects of risk management have been discussed in different parts of this book.

The creation of appropriate incentives and the appropriate organization from the point of view of risk management are closely linked. In this book we have argued throughout that macroeconomic risk is not a purely financial issue. Therefore, the division of risk management responsibility between the finance area and operational areas must be carefully considered. Considering the opportunity of operational areas to invest in real options—such as flexibility of input suppliers—and to adjust prices to exchange rate changes, exposures may not be known as long as flexibility remains. The implication for organization of risk management would be to strengthen the argument for limiting the risk management responsibility of the finance area to explicit financial positions. In order not to neglect the operational exposures and the relation between these exposures and financial exposures, a risk management group on the central level may perform a useful function of coordinating risk management efforts by assigning responsibilities across corporate divisions and functional areas.

# Chapter 11

# What Shareholders Ought to Know

## 11.1 INTRODUCTION

Transparency has become a catchphrase in the 2000s[1]. Transparency is a multifaceted word with information asymmetry as a common denominator. The lack of it has been used in retrospect as an explanation of spectacular corporate scandals like the case of Enron, Parmalat, Tyco and Worldcom. The turmoil in the credit markets in association with the so-called subprime loan crisis in 2007 and 2008 was aggravated by lack of transparency of new financial instruments and of the vulnerability of firms and financial institutions to macroeconomic shocks. Transparency has also been used in a forward-looking way as a miracle medicine, as in the Lisbon Strategy for the European Union (EU) to catch up with the United States as a successful, knowledge-intensive economy. Be it a lack of corporate or institutional transparency, it will materialize in a lower economic growth than would otherwise be the case (Oxelheim, 2006a).

Skyrocketing CEO compensation in the mid-2000s have made outsider shareholders ask for more transparency about the achievements motivating the unprecedented amounts paid out to CEOs. What information can and should the company release in response to this demand? What is the "optimal transparency" in this particular case (Bushman et al, 2004; Oxelheim 2006b)?

As the world's equity markets have become increasingly integrated, while countries have retained different accounting and reporting practices developed independently over a long period, there is now a pressing need to bridge the international information gap. The search for a common, cross-border body of reporting rules and the coordination of practices have both become issues of international concern.

Over the last three decades there has been an intensive debate about the kind of information that companies should be obliged to release. Without becoming too involved in this sensitive debate in accounting research we need only note two essential types of information. First, internal and external stakeholders need information of predictive value for assessing a firm's prospects and risks. Second, there is a need for information allowing for control, taxation and evaluation *ex post*. The information should make intertemporal comparisons for an individual company possible, as well as comparisons across companies (benchmarking) and national borders. This chapter emphasizes a particular kind of information about the effects on the firm of a turbulent macroeconomic environment. The macroeconomic environment of the firm is here viewed along the lines suggested in the previous parts of this book, as represented by three sets of relative prices: exchange rates, interest rates, and inflation rates.

Given the increased financial and economic integration that prevails today, no firm can claim any longer to be unaffected by what is happening on the global economic arena. Even so, today's external reporting is not geared to indicating the extent to which profits are generated by fluctuations in the company's macroeconomic environment during the reporting period. Without that information the outside shareholders have no chance of figuring out what has happened to the intrinsic profits and thus to the firm's competitiveness. Consequently, as regards the effects of a volatile macroeconomic environment, current accounting practice is failing to achieve one of the fundamental goals of external reporting satisfactorily; that is to provide information for control purposes to shareholders and other stakeholders. Moreover, although the international-standard setting bodies support the notion of "decision-relevance" for shareholders, no real progress has been made when it comes to achieving the other fundamental goal of external reporting, namely to provide outside shareholders with information about the future prospects of a company. However, the contents of the IAS 1 issued by the International Accounting Standards[2] Committee (IASC)—revised in 1997 and effective for reporting periods from July 1 1998—suggested that a shift in this direction was on the way.[3]

As part of the International Financial Reporting Standards (IFRS), a revised IAS 1 was launched and valid for all public European companies as of January 2005. Considering the fairly small changes, compared to the previous version, and the longer period available for analysis, we will in this chapter start with a discussion and evaluation of the impact of IAS 1 (rev. 1997). At the end of the chapter we then turn to what can be expected of IAS 1 as part of the IFRS.

Extensive efforts over time to create accounting standards or improved practice for the reporting of macroeconomic influences have fallen short for many reasons. A common denominator in the criticism of these efforts is their lack of focus on corporate performance and competitiveness. Accounting for the effect of a changing macroeconomic environment is static and partial. It is partial since it ignores the interrelation between the macroeconomic variables in question. It is also partial since it only recognizes the effects of items denominated in foreign currencies. Moreover, volume effects due to changing exchange and interests rates are ignored, fueling the criticism that it is both partial and static. A comprehensive approach calls for the simultaneous consideration of effects caused by changes in all these variables at home and abroad. Having said this, the relevant questions boil down to the availability today of relevant tools for management to produce this kind of information.

As has been fully clear from the previous parts of this book, in exposure management, but not in accounting, it is recognized that exchange rates are correlated with other macroeconomic variables, and that this should be taken into account when measuring and dealing with exchange rate exposure. The MUST analysis is developed as a management tool and builds on representing full recognition of the interdependence between macroeconomic variables constituting the macroeconomic environment of the firm. This approach generates an output that, if passed on to the outside shareholder, should mean an improvement on all the issues of the criticism raised above. Hence, the existence of a comprehensive management model for how to deal with effects stemming from the macroeconomic environment should make it possible for companies to improve their information release.

The purpose of this chapter is to discuss the reasons why the corporate supply of relevant information on the impact of macroeconomic fluctuation does not meet the demand by outside shareholders and financial analysts for such information. On the "supply-side," technical barriers associated with such things as the extent to which the output of the MUST analysis lends itself to publication, will be discussed below along with political barriers. Will IAS 1 (rev. 1997 and 2005 as part of IFRS), given the "right" interpretation and implementation, enhance the outside shareholders' understanding of the impact of macroeconomic fluctuations on the company's performance, and their recognition of the magnitude of macroeconomic risks in essential respects? Finally, in order to assess the magnitude of the political barriers fully, the corporate response to the "recommendation" within this standard will be analysed.

The chapter is organized as follows. Section 11.2 addresses efforts to create a global accounting standard for the impact of a volatile macroeconomic environment on corporate performance and why these have fallen short of achievement. Alternative interpretations of IAS 1 (rev. 1997) are also suggested in this section. Then follows in Section 11.3 a brief presentation of the MUST analysis as a vehicle for achieving high-quality information in corporate reporting. In Section 11.4 the current reporting practices in two global industries are compared with the recommendations of IAS 1 (rev. 1997). The way the result of the multivariate exposure framework should be reported to outside shareholders is illustrated in Section 11.5, along the lines suggested by IAS 1 (rev. 1997). Finally, the IAS as part of IFRS, together with technical and political implementation aspects, are discussed in Section 11.6.

## 11.2 EFFORTS TO CREATE STANDARDS

Since 1973 and the breakdown of the Bretton Woods agreement a good deal of effort has been spent on thinking about ways of reporting effects assumed to have been caused by the different variables that constitute the macroeconomic environment of the firm. The relative weights allotted to the different variables in the research literature have changed over time. Below is a brief review of how the four categories of variables previously mentioned have been discussed in contemporary research.

In the mid-1970s the increasing volatility in exchange rates triggered an intensive debate about how to report the effects of changing exchange rates. The debate focused on two issues: methods for evaluating foreign assets and liabilities in individual companies, and methods to use when a foreign entity was to be consolidated with the group account. A key document in that debate was Standard No. 8 issued by the Financial Accounting Standards Board (FASB 8, 1975), which was followed by FASB 52 (1981). Dukes (1978); Evans, Folks, and Jilling (1978); Jilling (1979), and Shank, Dillard, and Murdoch (1979) enriched the debate with empirical evidence about the economic and behavioral impact of FASB 8. Concurrent recommendations were issued by the Accounting Standard Committee (ASC); Exposure Drafts 18 (1976), 21 (1977) and 27 (1980). Of vital importance at that time were also the recommendations published by the Canadian Institute of Chartered Accountants (CICA) in 1978, 1982, and 1983 and by the International Accounting Standards Committee (IASC) in 1982 and 1983. Different aspects of the two topics have been dealt with by Aliber and Stickney (1975); Beaver and Wolfson (1982); Huefner, Ketz, and Largay (1989); McNown and Wallace (1989); Mahdavi and Zhou (1994); Makar, Stanko, and Zeller (1996), and Ziebart and Choi (1998), among others. Which methods are to be preferred is still in dispute. In the 1990s a third topic has attracted much attention, namely the reporting concerning financial instruments. Recommendations concerning this issue are formulated in for example FASB 133, IAS 32 and IAS 39.

The accounting for exchange rate fluctuation has over time focused on the conversion of assets, liabilities and cash flows outside the home jurisdiction. Hence, this implicitly means that the focus has been on the effects of nominal exchange rate changes. The unresolved issues concern the inclusion of effects of real exchange rate changes and an increased recognition of competitive exposure (Oxelheim and Wihlborg, 1991b). In the early 2000s, the typical way of reporting the effects of exchange rate fluctuations on performance still is to report the difference between the actual and a benchmark performance derived under the assumption of unchanged exchange rates.

The impact of other macroeconomic price variables (interest rate, inflation rate and political risk) is covered in the literature in a similar way. The inflationary aspect in accounting research is dealt with primarily by two different approaches. One strand of literature that was particularly influential during the 1970s emphasized the inflationary effects generated within a country. The focus was then on general price-level statements (see, e.g., Ijiri, 1976; Staubus, 1976; and Vickrey, 1976). One particular issue here concerned the appropriateness of using the general price level rather than a specific price level (see, e.g., Rosenfeld, 1972, and Sterling, 1975). Another group of researchers emphasized the choice of an appropriate price index (see, e.g., Bromwich, 1975, and Staubus, 1975). A third issue that recaptured attention in the 1970s (its origins can be traced back to the late 1920s and to names like Sweeney, 1927, and Schmidt, 1930) was current cost accounting (see, e.g., Bromwich, 1977; Kennedy, 1978; Prakash and Sunder, 1979; Samuelson, 1980; and Westwick, 1980).

The other strand of the literature on inflation accounting is closely linked to the problem of foreign investments and is concerned with the differences in inflation between the countries in question. It focuses on the Purchasing Power Parity relationship and whether the methods used in accounting give a satisfactory picture of that relationship (see, e.g., Aliber and Stickney, 1975; Beaver and Wolfson, 1982; Makar, Stanko, and Zeller, 1996; and Ziebart and Choi, 1998). The body of literature in this area, as in the case of the exchange rate area, still lacks consensus as regards the methods to be preferred.

In accounting for interest rate fluctuations there are two main traditions. The first is concerned with debt, and its main focus is on the translation of foreign debt. Any deviations that occur are seen as related to differences in the exchange rate and/or in the interest rates in the countries concerned. These questions are interrelated and are often dealt with simultaneously, albeit implicitly rather than explicitly (see, e.g., Oxelheim, 1983). The other tradition is concerned with accounting for financial instruments as defined in FASB 133 and IAS 39, although the question of risk may not be relevant in the case of all the instruments covered by these recommendations (see, e.g., Francis, 1990; Bierman, Johnson, and Peterson, 1991; and Miltz and Sercu, 1993). At the beginning of the 2000s, the typical way of reporting the effects of interest rate fluctuations on performance is to report effects on the financial side only. The effects of these changes on commercial exposure and overall performance are entirely ignored.

The subject of political risk is not covered very adequately in accounting literature as a whole. Some studies investigate firms' exposure to sudden increases in product price and the accounting actions that ensue (see, e.g., Watts and Zimmerman, 1986, and Han and Wang, 1998). The effect generated by the realization of a political risk is often treated in accounting as an extraordinary item. Several studies have shown the problem in using "extraordinary items" in this context as an instrument for the smoothing out of income (see, e.g., Barnea, Ronen, and Sadan, 1975; Craig and Walsh, 1989; Walsh, Craig, and Clark, 1991; and Dempsey, Hunt, and Schroeder, 1993). However, these studies have not dealt appropriately with the effects of political risk on a firm's performance. Rather, they have shown how the accounting system is used in a creative way when it comes to absorbing the effects caused by a political risk that has materialized.

Overall, then, attempts to create a standard, or standards, to account for the macroeconomic influence on the firm justify the criticism raised in the introduction of this article. However, IAS 1, *Presentation of Financial Statements* (rev. 1997) does represent a step forward in this respect. It applies to all types of companies with a profit goal, including banks and insurance companies (for which further requirements are specified in IAS 30, Disclosure in the *Financial Statements of Banks and Similar Financial Institutions*). IAS 1 contains the following formulation as paragraph 8 under the heading "Components of Financial Statements":

> *Enterprises are encouraged to present, outside of the financial statements, a financial review by management which describes and explains the main features of the enterprise's financial performance and financial position and the principal uncertainties it faces. Such a report may include a review of:*
>
> (a) *the main factors and influences determining performance, including changes in the environment in which the enterprise operates, the enterprise's response to those changes and their main effect, and the enterprise's policy for investment to maintain and enhance performance, including its dividend policy;*
> (b) *the enterprise's sources of funding, the policy on gearing and its risk management policies; and*
> (c) *the strength and resources of the enterprise whose value is not reflected in the balance sheet under International Accounting Standards.*

This paragraph marks a move toward information-channeling as appropriate for scenario analysis and risk assessment, including profit-filtering for historical performance analysis and control. The standard as a whole recommends the minimal requirements regarding the content of reporting. Financial information of an interim character is not included.

The standard may be seen as a compromise, and in this capacity it has a very loose framework. *Environment* can be given different interpretations. Here it is interpreted as macroeconomic environment. *Factors and influences* are interpreted as macroeconomic variables with an impact on the corporate profit capacity (performance) in product, service and financial markets, that is, currencies, interest rates and consumer/producer prices. *The enterprise's response to those changes and their main effect* can be expressed in many ways. To be useful for control purposes and to be applicable in a forward-looking manner, it should be aimed here at measurement in the form of sensitivity coefficients, that is, a measurement of the change in a company's profit as a consequence of a change in each and every one of the most important macroeconomic variables. *Risk management* policies under 8(b) should, in line with earlier interpretations, pertain to strategies for how the company is handled with respect to the above-mentioned variables and the possibility of changes in this respect during the next reporting period. Here the company is expected to provide information about the type and extent of different hedging operations as response to macroeconomic uncertainty.

IAS 1 (rev. 1997) provides no explicit requirement for a uniform analysis and quantification, which opens up for a variety of responses to its paragraph 8(a–b). One alternative here is to separate two categories: non-quantitative responses (1–2, below) and quantitative responses (3–4, below). Although they open up for some discretion, the following four categories or levels of information are used in order to extract additional insight into the current status of corporate reporting:

(1) No specification of the variables, no measurement or strategies as named above, that is, paragraph 8(a–b) is not considered.

(2) The publication of variables, measurements and strategies *in general terms* but without much detailed specification, that is, the reporting continues in the way that is most common today. "The results for the period have been influenced negatively by currency fluctuations" or "the lower interest levels have had a positive influence on the result" are typical examples of wording under this alternative.

(3) The publication of *some but not all information* about the most significant variables, the magnitude of the influence and the appropriate strategies for handling these variables. This alternative, involving a certain amount of information, undeniably comprises a step in the right direction, insofar as the information provided is correct. However, if only one coefficient is given, for example, to live up to the standard of being correct it should have been estimated by considering its relationship to the other relevant variables. And even if the information is correct, this alternative still means that the information is insufficient as a basis for weeding out noise of historic profits and assessing the prospects of the company.

(4) The publication of a *complete specification* of the most significant macroeconomic variables, of the sensitivity coefficients for these variables estimated within a multivariate framework, and of the company's strategy for handling fluctuations in these variables over the past period and in the future. An information release that is congruent with the information content of the output of the MUST analysis is briefly described in the next section.

As stressed in the introduction, we concentrate here on IAS 1 (rev. 1997) and turn later to IAS 1 as part of IFRS, while remaining well aware of the forces at work in the interplay between IASC and other key actors in the standard-setting arena—forces that should be considered once causality as regards the development in accounting is discussed.

## 11.3  A COMPREHENSIVE APPROACH TO ASSESSING THE IMPACT OF MACROECONOMIC FLUCTUATIONS ON THE FIRM

If there is to be anything informative to report about the impact of macro-economic variables on corporate performance it is necessary that the company has made and continues to make systematic analyses of this impact. Powerful outside forces—of which the one exerted by financial analysts may be the strongest—should be at work to increase management's interest in answers to the important question of how far the profits of the company are to be seen as intrinsic and due to the quality of the product or service and how far they stem from changes in the macroeconomic environment[5]. The need to sort these things out is evident in the choice of strategy, in discussing bonuses or in the evaluation of subsidiary managers. By filtering out the (temporary) macroeconomic "noise" from corporate profits as a first step, a picture is obtained of the "intrinsic" profits, that is, a measure of the company's competitiveness. After this filtering, an apparently favorable result may thus be transformed into a strong signal about reduced competitiveness, that is, to a "leading indicator" regarding the need to develop the product/service and/or production process, or, vice versa, that is, in the case of an unfavorable result. Step two is the formulation of a risk management strategy, that is, whether the company should handle the risks generated by future macroeconomic fluctuations, and, if so, how. For companies that handle steps one and two intelligently, step three means that there is something valuable to communicate to the outside shareholders of the firm.

The central concept in this book is that the vulnerability of a company to changes in its macroeconomic environment can be expressed by measures of sensitivity to changes in the relative prices of three categories—exchange rates, interest rates, and inflation rates. The choice of these categories of macroeconomic variable is—as previously noted—not *ad hoc* but is derived from international equilibrium relationships. The relative prices contained in these relationships are reflections of macroeconomic shocks or disturbances involving changes in GDP, aggregate demand, monetary policy and other macroeconomic variables. One option is to study in a direct way the vulnerability of corporate performance to macroeconomic shocks. However, as opposed to the fundamental shocks, the relative prices have the great advantage of being easily observable at all times. In addition, the relationship between a fundamental shock and the relative prices may be unstable due to policy regime shifts whereas the relationship between the relative prices and the performance of the firm is fairly stable and directly reflects the competitive situation.

One of the equilibrium relationships is Purchasing Power Parity (PPP), which is based on variables from two of the categories: the nominal exchange rate and relative inflation. Deviations from PPP generate excess profits or losses on the commercial side of the individual firm. In case of a deviation of the home country currency in the form of an overvaluation (undervaluation) we can—as previously noted—compare the effect of this with a tax (subsidy) of comparable magnitude on home country production vis-à-vis production abroad.[6] The other equilibrium relationship is the International Fisher Parity (IFP), which in addition to the nominal exchange rate[7] contains the third category of macroeconomic price variable, i.e. interest rates. Deviations from IFP cause excess profits or losses on the financial side of the individual firm. However, as stressed previously, interest rate changes may also impact the commercial side of the firm, for example through their influence on the demand for capital goods. In addition, political risk expresses itself as the need for a reestimation of the sensitivity coefficients for the three categories. It then remains for the individual firm to determine which variables are the most influential within each category.

The need for "filtering" calls for a set of sensitivity coefficients determined within a *multivariate* framework. The MUST analysis in this book represents such a framework for the company to estimate sensitivity coefficients and to carry out steps one and two (see Figure 1.3). It offers a basis for: (a) identifying the macroeconomic variables that are most important to the particular company, (b) determining the effect on performance generated by fluctuations in these variables, and (c) formulating a suitable strategy for handling these variables. Moreover, it can be routinized since it demands only standard regression programs offered as standard equipment to most computers.

## 11.4  CONTEMPORARY PRACTICE RELATIVE TO IAS 1 ON REPORTING OF MACROECONOMIC INFLUENCES

Data for this chapter has been collected and analyzed on an annual basis (1985–2000). The data concerns the way companies in different industries and countries report and deal with the impact on their performance of changes in their macroeconomic environment. The annual analysis starts with an examination of the way companies report relevant variables, measures of vulnerability and strategies. A follow-up is also conducted, albeit not reported in detail here, charting the way the companies handle these issues *de facto*. In this way a picture is obtained of the size of the difference between the information given in the external reports and the actual way these issues are currently viewed in the company. The picture that emerges, which will not be further discussed in this chapter, is that companies in general are no more sophisticated in their analysis of the macroeconomic impact than the annual reports reveal. However, the fairly low ambition currently prevailing relative to the more comprehensive approach discussed in the previous section will naturally affect the companies' interpretation of IAS 1 (rev. 1997). Implementation in line with alternative (4) above would, thus, call for considerable adjustments on the part of most companies.

The accounting part of the study is presented in tables 11.1 and 11.2, where the column numbers concide with the numbering of categories in Section 2 of this chapter. It contains an analysis of the annual reports of companies in the automotive industry for the fiscal years 1996/97 and 1998/1999, that is, the years immediately before and after the IAS 1 (rev. 1997) recommendation came into force. Only explicit statements are taken into account in the study, generally consisting of the notes to the financial statements, the CEO's letter to shareholders or statements elsewhere in the annual report. Table 11.1 provides us with a firm conclusion: as late as 1999 no company in the automotive industry (the study was carried out on a group basis) published information in its external reporting which would enable shareholders to understand the extent of macroeconomic influence on corporate performance. The same conclusions can be drawn from Table 11.2 as regards the global paper and pulp industry.

To qualify for a listing in column 4 the company should have provided information in line with the outcome of a multivariate approach of the kind discussed in the previous section. With the help of a multivariate regression technique three to four variables can normally be identified as channels for the bulk of the influence on the firm stemming from its macroeconomic environment. Table 11.1 shows that only one company—Rolls Royce—provided a satisfactory specification regarding the macroeconomic variables that have the most impact on corporate performance. Six out of twenty-four companies made an effort to identify at least some variables, albeit not a complete set according to a multivariate identification procedure. The majority of companies provided sweeping formulations about various categories of macroeconomic variables without pinpointing any specific ones. Hence, apart from arousing a feeling that something could be blamed or thanked, the information they provided had no further value for the shareholder.

When it comes to the magnitude of the impact on corporate performance deriving from the variables that have been identified as relevant, only Scania followed up their partial information with such figures. All the other companies refrained from making a quantitative specification of the impact. They either provided no information at all or referred vaguely to the impact in terms such as big, small or similar.

In 1999 quite a few companies tried to specify their hedging strategies, but the lack of information about the relevant variables and sensitivity coefficients for these greatly reduces the value of any such information. However, also in this respect Scania is an exception. This company comes closest to a useful—albeit not complete—specification of the macroeconomic impact on the firm.

None of the companies, with the possible exception of Scania, provided their shareholders with the chance of seeing what had happened regarding the intrinsic profits, that is, the profits after the macroeconomic noise had been eliminated. There was no possibility for the investors to make any kind of analysis of what would happen to the company given a development like the Asian crisis, for example.

Annual reports before and after the IAS 1 (rev. 1997) came into force have also been compared. The result shows fairly small changes as regards the pinpointing of relevant macroeconomic variables. Five companies improved their information content and one company went the other way. Only Rolls Royce, however, improved its release in a substantial way that made a difference to the shareholders. In terms of release of exposure measures there was no change at all, whereas the propensity to release information on strategies for handling macroeconomic influence on the firm improved substantially. Seven companies improved their information content in this respect. Thus, we have witnessed a significant improve-

Table 11.1 Accounting for macroeconomic influences in the global automotive industry. Annual reports 1998–99.

| (A) Information on macro price variables influencing performance | | | |
|---|---|---|---|
| (1) No information | (2) General information about being affected, no specification of individual variables | (3) Partial specification of individual macro-price variables | (4) Complete specification of macro-price variables influencing performance |
| | Audi (D) | Ford (US) | Rolls Royce (UK) |
| | BMW (D) | Honda (JP) | |
| | Daihatsu (JP) | PACCAR (US) | |
| | DaimlerChrysler (D) | Renault (F) | |
| | Fleetwood (US) | Scania (SE) | |
| | GM (US) | Volvo (SE) | |
| | Isuzu (JP) | | |
| | Man (D) | | |
| | Mazda (JP) | | |
| | Mitsubishi (JP) | | |
| | Navistar (US) | | |
| | Nissan (JP) | | |
| | Oshkosh (US) | | |
| | Peugeot (F) | | |
| | Toyota (JP) | | |
| | Winnebago (US) | | |
| | Volkswagen (D) | | |

*continued*

**Table 11.1 continued**

| (B) Exposure measures in annual reports | | | |
| --- | --- | --- | --- |
| (1) No information | (2) General information | (3) Partial specification of exposure measures | (4) Complete specification of exposure measures |
| Audi (D) | BMW (D) | Scania (SE) | |
| Daihatsu (JP) | Fleetwood (US) | | |
| DaimlerChrysler (D) | Ford (US) | | |
| GM (US) | Man (D) | | |
| Honda (JP) | Mazda (JP) | | |
| Isuzu (JP) | Oshkosh (US) | | |
| Mitsubishi (JP) | PACCAR (US) | | |
| Navistar (US) | Peugeot (F) | | |
| Nissan (JP) | Rolls Royce (UK) | | |
| Renault (F) | Volvo (SE) | | |
| Toyota (JP) | | | |
| Winnebago (US) | | | |
| Volkswagen (D) | | | |

| (C) Publication of information about exposure management strategy | | | |
| --- | --- | --- | --- |
| (1) No information | (2) General information | (3) Partial specification of management strategy | (4) Complete specification of management strategy |
| Daihatsu (JP) | GM (US) | Audi (D) | |
| Fleetwood (US) | Man (D) | BMW (D) | |
| Isuzu (JP) | Nissan (JP) | DaimlerChrysler (D) | |
| Winnebago (US) | Peugeot (F) | Ford (US) | |
| | Toyota (JP) | Honda (JP) | |
| | Volkswagen (D) | Mazda (JP) | |
| | | Mitsubishi (JP) | |
| | | Navistar (US) | |
| | | Oshkosh (US) | |
| | | PACCAR (US) | |
| | | Renault (F) | |
| | | Rolls Royce (UK) | |
| | | Scania (SE) | |
| | | Volvo (SE) | |

**Table 11.2 Accounting for macroeconomic influences in the global paper and pulp industry. Annual reports 1998–99.**

| (A) Information on macro price variables influencing performance | | | |
|---|---|---|---|
| (1) No information | (2) General information about being affected, no specification of individual variables | (3) Partial specification of individual macro-price variables | (4) Complete specification of macro-price variables influencing performance |
| | Amcor (AU) | Bunzl (UK) | |
| | AssiDomän (SE) | Fort James Corp (US) | |
| | Bemis (US) | Holmen (SE) | |
| | Boise Cascade (US) | International Paper (US) | |
| | Buhrmann (NL) | Norske Skog (N) | |
| | Cartiere Burgo (I) | Rock-Tenn (US) | |
| | Champion International (US) | Sappi (ZA) | |
| | Chesapeake (US) | SCA (SE) | |
| | David S Smith (UK) | Tembec (CA) | |
| | Domtar (CA) | UPM-Kymmene (SF) | |
| | Fletcher Challenge (NZ) | | |
| | Georgia Pacific (US) | | |
| | Haindl (D) | | |
| | Industrieholding Cham (CH) | | |
| | Inveresk (IE) | | |
| | Kimberly Clark (US) | | |
| | La Rochette (F) | | |
| | Louisiana Pacific (US) | | |
| | Mayr-Meinhof (AT) | | |
| | Mead (US) | | |
| | Potlatch (US) | | |
| | Rottneros (SE) | | |
| | Sonoco Products (US) | | |
| | St Laurent | | |

*continued*

**Table 11.2  continued**

| (1) No information | (2) General information about being affected, no specification of individual variables | (3) Partial specification of individual macro-price variables | (4) Complete specification of macro-price variables influencing performance |
|---|---|---|---|
|  | Paperboard (CA) |  |  |
|  | Temple-Inland (US) |  |  |
|  | Westvaco (US) |  |  |
|  | Weyerhaeuser (US) |  |  |
|  | Willamette Industries (US) |  |  |

(B) Exposure measures in annual reports

| (1) No information | (2) General information | (3) Partial specification of exposure measures | (4) Complete specification of exposure measurers |
|---|---|---|---|
| Bemis (US) | Amcor (AU) | AssiDomän (SE) |  |
| Fletcher Challenge (NZ) | Boise Cascade (US) | Fort James Corp (US) |  |
| Haindl (D) | Buhrmann (NL) | International Paper (US) |  |
| Holmen (SE) | Bunzl (UK) | Inveresk (IE) |  |
| Industrieholding | Cartiere Burgo (I) | Kimberly Clark (US) |  |
| Cham (CH) | Champion | Mead (US) |  |
| La Rochette (F) | International (US) | Norske Skog (N) |  |
| Louisiana Pacific (US) | Chesapeake (US) | SCA (SE) |  |
| Mayr-Meinhof (AT) | David S Smith (UK) | Tembec (US) |  |
| Potlatch (US) | Domtar (CA) | UPM Kymmene (SF) |  |
| Rock-Tenn (US) | Georgia Pacific (US) |  |  |
| Sappi (ZA) | Rottneros (SE) |  |  |
| St Laurent | Sonoco Products (US) |  |  |
| Paperboard (CA) | Temple-Inland (US) |  |  |
| Westvaco (US) | Weyerhaeuser (US) |  |  |
| Willamette Industries (US) |  |  |  |

*continued*

**Table 11.2  continued**

| (C) Publication of information about exposure management strategy | | | |
| --- | --- | --- | --- |
| (1) No information | (2) General information | (3) Partial specification of management strategy | (4) Complete specification of management strategy |
| Haindl (D) | Amcor (AU) | AssiDomän (SE) | |
| La Rochette (F) | Bemis (US) | Bunzl (UK) | |
| Louisiana Pacific (US) | Boise Cascade (US) | Cartiere Burgo (I) | |
| Potlatch (US) | Buhrmann (NL) | Chesapeake (US) | |
| Willamette Industries (US) | Champion International (US) | Holmen (SE) | |
| | David S Smith (UK) | International Paper (US) | |
| | Domtar (CA) | Kimberly Clark (US) | |
| | Fletcher Challenge (NZ) | Mead (US) | |
| | Fort James Corp (US) | Norske Skog (N) | |
| | Georgia Pacific (US) | Rock-Tenn (US) | |
| | Industrieholding Cham (CH) | Sappi (ZA) | |
| | Inveresk (IE) | SCA (S) | |
| | Mayr-Meinhof (AT) | Tembec (US) | |
| | Rottneros (SE) | UPM Kymmene (SF) | |
| | Sonoco Products (US) | | |
| | St Laurent Paperboard (CA) | | |
| | Temple-Inland (US) | | |
| | Westvaco (US) | | |
| | Weyerhaeuser (US) | | |

ment (at the 5% level) for the automotive industry[8] between 1996/97 and 1998/99.[9]

Even if we can see some improvement after the IAS 1 (rev. 1997) came into force, it would be going too far, on the basis of this study, to claim that the improvement was due to IAS. The significant improvements regarding the choice of strategies for handling changes in the macroeconomic environment may rather reflect FASB 119 and IAS 32 or an early adjustment to FASB 133 and IAS 39, which regulates accounting for derivatives/

instruments and hedging activities in the annual reports. Several of the American companies have mentioned FASB 133, which was issued in June 1998 and expected to come into force in June 1999 (later deferred one year by FASB 137). Hence, FASB 133 may explain some of the moves towards more extensive reporting about choice of strategy that was found in the annual reports for 1998/1999. Another explanation may be found in the response to a stronger demand for information on the part of shareholders, as a result of the uncertainty caused by the contemporary financial crises.

Finally, a cross-industry comparison involving the automotive industry and the paper and pulp industry was carried out. The hypothesis behind the comparison was formulated as a tendency for companies with more heterogeneous products to release more relevant information. The hypothesis was assumed to reflect the delicate balance between supplying outside shareholders with relevant information, and putting the competitiveness of the firm at risk by supplying competitors with the very same information. However, the paper and pulp industry, characterized by fairly homogeneous products, provides no less information than the automotive industry. No statistically significant differences exist between the two distributions. Moreover, neither of the distributions shows any significant pattern regarding the nationality of the reporting firm.

## 11.5 ILLUSTRATION OF AN INFORMATION RELEASE THAT SATISFIES THE DEMANDS OF THE OUTSIDE SHAREHOLDER

What, then, should the information release look like in order to meet the demands of the outside shareholders as expressed in their desire to evaluate the company's strategy and performance in an adequate way? The information content of the release suggested here should not present the well-managed firm with no extra processing work. Rather, it should be seen as a subset or lower threshold for what could be used as relevant decision support by the company's own management and board of directors. What might call for a tougher demand on the part of the company's own management could be its need for more disaggregated information and for more frequent information updates.

Taking a Japanese company as an example, let us assume that the fundamental analysis has resulted in a limited number of variables. After the multivariate analysis the following have been found to be the most important: the JPY/EURO exchange rate, the Japanese long-term interest rate, and French producer prices. The sensitivity coefficients for these variables as reported in Table 11.3 make it possible to translate scenarios into statements about the magnitude of profits or cash flows, as well as to filter out the macroeconomic impact on the performance for the latest reporting period. The outside shareholder needs additional information about the strategy formulation of the firm regarding the current as well as future handling of

**Table 11.3** Reporting according to alternative (4) involving information about the macroeconomic impact on the company.

*Forecast:* The profit will increase next quarter by 15 percent compared with the preceding quarter. The seasonal effects represent 3 percentage points of that increase. The company's policy is not to work with hedging operations of any kind on external financial markets.

| | The forecast is based on the following changes in key variables | Sensitivity coefficients: one percentage point increase as compared to the anticipated change will impact the profit by |
|---|---|---|
| JPY/EURO | 2% | 3% |
| Japanese long-term interest rate | 2% | –2% |
| French producer prices | 1% | 3% |

influences from the identified macro-price variables. Moreover, the sensitivity coefficients form the basis for the risk assessment by the outside shareholder, since they also constitute the exposure coefficients of the company.

The sensitivity measurements in the example express the change in the target variable due to a change in each one of the three identified macroeconomic variables. In accordance with the figures in Table 11.3, a one percentage point increase in the JPY/EURO exchange rate (i.e., a depreciation of the Japanese yen against the euro) leads to a three percent increase in the profit. In this example, the profit is set as the target variable, but the analysis in other cases may refer to sales proceeds, cash flow, and soon. The measurement contains competitive aspects and, thus, provides an expression for the company's advantage vis-à-vis competitors when the JPY/EURO exchange rate changes.

A common mistake among companies that try to give the most important macroeconomic variables for the company without conducting a comprehensive multivariate analysis is to point to the exchange rate between the home currency and the currencies of the company's greatest sale and purchasing markets respectively. To look only at the currency distribution in the actual flows often leads to erroneous conclusions. Thus, the major competitor in the company's most important market, in this example the U.S. market, may be a French company with a manufacturing site in France. A comprehensive analysis like the MUST analysis would, as in this case, probably point to the fact that the euro is more important than the U.S. dollar.

The information can be given with or without forecasting. Table 11.3 shows an example in which the result of a comprehensive analysis based on a multivariate identification technique is presented in connection with a forecast in the company discussed above.

Assume that at the beginning of the quarter an outside shareholder believes in a different macroeconomic scenario from the one on which the company has built its forecast. The information content of Table 11.3 now allows a re-calculation of forecasted profits in light of the "new" scenario. Excluding macroeconomic influences of 5% (6% from the depreciation of the Japanese yen against the euro, –4% from the increase of the Japanese long-term interest rate and 3% from the increase in French prices), and the seasonal effect of 3%, reveals that the company's own forecast is built upon an assumption of a growth of 7% (15%–5%–3%).

On the basis of this assumed growth, the shareholder mentioned above could now make a new forecast reflecting his or her own macroeconomic scenario. Thus, if the shareholder believes that the JPY/EURO exchange rate will increase by 5 percentage points instead of the assumed 2 percentage points, that the Japanese long-term interest rate will remain unchanged (i.e., a change of zero percentage points), and that French producer prices will increase by 3 percentage points, the shareholder's own forecast will be an adjustment of the company's forecast, such that the result compared with the preceding period increases by $(3+7+15+0+9)\%=34\%$.

Likewise, and very importantly, at the end of the quarter access to information of the kind presented in Table 11.3 will allow an analysis of what has happened regarding the intrinsic profits, with the latest actual result and the forecasted result as benchmarks. The filtering conducted here is the key issue in the *ex post* evaluation of corporate performance. It improves the opportunities to make intertemporal comparisons and to obtain "early warning" signals. Apart from the reporting problem, no management or board of directors should afford not to pay attention to these signals.

Assume that the actual outcome was a 22% increase in the result relative to the previous period, and the macroeconomic scenario outlined by the shareholder came true. Disregarding the new macroeconomic scenario, management should have gotten credit for an extra 7% increase. The implicit but erroneous conclusion would be that the competitiveness of the firm was improving. The 7% increase might even lead to raises in bonuses, wages, and/or dividends. But if the change in the macroeconomic environment is adequately allowed for, the conclusions point in the opposite direction. The result is 12% lower than it appears when supported by the macroeconomic environment. Thus shareholders should call for a detailed examination of the company's performance. The outside shareholders would now want an explanation of the 12%—a figure that should be taken as a benchmark. Some explanations may be acceptable, for instance, that a major competitor has been running a campaign during the period. But if there are no acceptable explanations, the shareholders would like to be told how management intends to handle the loss of competitiveness. Instead of enjoying the comfort of a 7% rise in results, given concrete form in the increases in bonuses, wages and/or dividends mentioned above, the management should now present a plan about how it intends to catch up again in terms of competitiveness by enhancing its support for innovations in the product and production processes.

## 11.6 CONCLUDING REMARKS ON THE REPORTING OF THE IMPACT OF MACROECONOMIC FLUCTUATIONS ON CORPORATE PERFORMANCE

The importance of paying attention to the impact of a volatile macroeconomic environment on the competitiveness of the firm should be clear to most managers with experience of the economic turbulence of recent years—an experience that should make most companies willing to carry out analyses according to a comprehensive analysis built on a multivariate framework. Here, it has been argued that inside the firm most of the technical problems related to the measurement of the macroeconomic impact should and can be resolved.

The revised IAS 1 included in IFRS contains only minor changes with relevance for the topic of this book, as compared to IAS (rev. 1997). Paragraph 8 in IAS (rev. 1997) has been replaced by Paragraph 9. However, the reading of the new paragraph is very similar except on two points. The new paragraph states that "Many enterprises present....," whereas the former version had a somewhat more positive reading in "Enterprises are encourage[d] to present...." The only change in Paragraph 8a is that "performance" now has become "financial performance." Paragraphs 8b-c are changed, but the only thing that matters here is that the disclosure of risk management policies are no longer asked for or explicitly "encouraged." However, later paragraphs of IAS 1 may compensate for this somewhat weaker start of the new IAS 1.

Paragraph 116 states that "An entity shall disclose in the notes information about the key assumptions concerning the future and other key sources of estimation uncertainty at the balance sheet date that have a significant risk of causing a material adjustment to the carrying amounts of assets and liabilities within the next financial year." Paragraphs 117–124 then provide detailed instructions but also a loophole. Paragraph 120 provides maybe the most important instruction by making sure that "the disclosure of Paragraph 116 are presented in a manner that helps the user of financial statements to understand the judgements management makes about the future and about key sources of estimation uncertainty." Paragraph 121 may then be seen as providing something of a loophole by stating "It is not necessary to disclose budget information or forecast in making the disclosure of Paragraph 116."

The weakness of IAS (rev. 1997) and the target of our criticism in this chapter remain; there is no explicit requirement of having the macroeconomic impact disclosed in a *quantitative* way. However, Paragraphs 116 and 120 may be interpreted as containing an implicit requirement of such a quantification. Thereby, they may be interpreted as taking a step forward towards the disclosure of macroeconomic effects at a higher level of transparency.

An open question, however, is whether the results of these analyses will be passed on to the outside shareholders via corporate external reporting. Measurement problems and the risk of exposing a weakness that can be exploited by competitors are two arguments that will be raised against presenting shareholders with a detailed analysis of the company's development of a multivariate kind offered by the MUST analysis.

However, seven compelling factors—in addition to the momentum of the development of information technology—suggest that within the not-too-distant future there will be a shift of information paradigm. The new reporting practice should have come close to alternative (4) above, implying a complete specification of the most significant macroeconomic variables, of the sensitivity coefficients for these variables estimated within a multivariate framework, and of the company's strategy for handling fluctuations in these variables over the past period and in the future. These factors are:

(1) the mere presence of IAS 1 (rev. 1997 and 2005 as part of IFRS) and similar recommendations
(2) the great increase in competence among financial analysts and the accompanying demand for relevant information for determining the value of the company
(3) the presence of analytical tools like the MUST analysis, which now allows a proper analysis of the way the company is affected by changes in its macroeconomic environment and the resulting opportunities for adequate information release
(4) the avid and growing interest in shareholder value analysis (SVA, EVA, etc.), and the accompanying need to distinguish between what is temporarily created by macroeconomic fluctuations and what is intrinsic value
(5) the demand by banks and financial institutions for information that enables an analysis of the sustainability of profits and the resulting determination of the appropriate credit rating of the company
(6) the demand by prestigious international capital market authorities for information in prospectuses in connection with equity and bond issues on the vulnerability of the issuing company to macroeconomic fluctuations
(7) the adoption by the Securities and Exchange Commission of new rules (Regulation FD, effective as of October 2000) against selective disclosure of material information by public companies, and the greater importance today of information about the impact of macroeconomic variables on corporate performance in traditional reporting channels such as annual reports.

While waiting for reporting on the influence of the macroeconomic factors to fall in line with IAS 1 (rev. 1997 and 2005 as part of IFRS), alt. 4), outside shareholders and those engaged in servicing them will attempt as well as they can to conduct something corresponding to a MUST analysis. The most "ambitious" of these groups—the financial analysts—have of course the technical possibility to carry out the analysis, provided the company reports the most necessary pieces of the information puzzle. If reporting occasions are more frequent, there will be a greater temptation to perform the analysis even without this information. However, without the company's cooperation—in providing the required information pieces or the final result of a comprehensive analysis as part of its external reporting—the prospects are limited for the outside shareholders and financial analysts to obtain any idea of what is really going on regarding the performance of the company. An interpretation of IAS 1 (rev. 1997 and 2005 as part of IFRS) in terms of alternative (4) is the only way to make progress, and to give meaning to the two major goals of external reporting.

## NOTES

1 This chapter is adapted from Oxelheim (2003).
2 International Accounting Standards Committee (IASC) issued International Accountings Standards (IAS) from 1973 to 2000. The International Accounting Standards Board (IASB) replaced the IASC in 2001. Since then the IASB has amended some IASs, has proposed to amend other IASs, has proposed to replace some IASs with new International Financial Reporting Standards (IFRSs) and has adopted or proposed new IFRSs on topics for which there were no previous IASs.
3 Moreover, the usefulness of separating business risk from macroeconomic risk is further underlined by the fact that a number of countries already have or soon will issue regulations concerning business risks and their disclosure (IFAC, 1999). Assuming that the different standard-setting bodies' demand reflects different categories of stakeholders of firms, there is obviously a broad interest in an improved quality of information releases.
4 In the analysis of the "true" performance, changes in the magnitude of period-to-period deviations from PPP and IFP need to be measured. By focusing on changes rather than levels the problem of determining long-term equilibrium exchange rates, interest rates and inflations rates is circumvented.
5 "Among the disclosures that investors find most useful is analysis of the sensitivity of financial statement measurements to underlying assumptions and modelling methods" (CFA Institute, 2005).
6 Where the location of foreign production reflects the weights in the PPP calculation.
7 Expectations play a key role in PPP and IFP. "Deviation" and "excess" then become relative terms.
8 Due to the merger, Chrysler, Mercedes Benz and Daimler Chrysler are not included in the test.
9 A McNemar test of the information content before and after July 1, 1998 has been conducted under the assumption that the automotive industry can be seen as a representative sample from a "superpopulation." The material has been divided into a 2×2 matrix with columns 1+2 representing no valuable information at all and columns 3+4 information of at least some value to the shareholders.

# Chapter 12

# Macroeconomic Uncertainty
Strategy (MUST) Analysis:
A Summary

## 12.1 INTRODUCTION

The search for an adequate assessment of the sensitivity of the firm to changes in its macroeconomic environment has not been placed on the corporate agenda until recently. One very simple reason is that economics and management are not usually happily married at universities and business schools. Hence, many managers have not realized the importance of seeing the two as inseparable. Too many managers simply take the numbers produced by accounting systems as *the* truth. The situation has improved somewhat, however, and there is now an increased demand for information about the relationship between the individual firm and changes in macroeconomic conditions.

One reason for the increased "demand" for broader measures of sensitivity is the relative importance of macroeconomic uncertainty in a corporate perspective as expressed by the increasing volatility of exchange rates, interest rates, and inflation. Although there are many variables competing for the role of being major explanatory macroeconomic variables, we have argued that these three categories jointly capture most macroeconomic shocks.

A second reason is the growing influence of stakeholders, other than management, and their growing awareness of the importance of macroeconomic factors as explanations of corporate performance. The interest of these stakeholders' groups—shareholders, lenders, financial analysts, employees, customers, subcontractors, and government authorities—may soon make this kind of information mandatory in corporate external reporting (see Chapter 11).

Managers relying on accounting information have long neglected the possibility of capturing the influence of macroeconomic shocks, refusing to go beyond traditional methods. However, since research has made progress in this area, managers should today realize that reliable measures are available. It must be said that, in the past, managers may have appreciated the degrees of freedom offered by the lack of information available to outside stakeholders. Who would not like to take the credit for profit increases following from a positive change in the macroeconomic environment while transferring the blame for losses to the general unpredictability of the macroeconomic environment? In Chapter 6 we affirmed that, indeed, there are incentives for management not to be too clear about exposure unless mark-to-market accounting is implemented.

Many small firms and firms concentrating on domestic operations still regard themselves as unexposed to most macroeconomic fluctuations. We have argued that all firms have reason to be concerned about exchange rates as well as other changes in the macroeconomic environment. Such changes affect the competitiveness of a firm as measured by long-term intrinsic profits. In order to find these long-term profits, short term macroeconomic "noise" must be filtered away. Coefficients of sensitivity to macroeconomic shocks help firms accomplish this task. Most corporate performance measures in use ignore the need for "filtering" the impact of macroeconomic conditions. The use, for example, of a cross-border benchmarking procedure without considering the impact of differences in the macroeconomic environment of the firms is bound to be misleading.

Risk-averse firms have still greater reason to grasp how shocks in the macroeconomic environment affect them. This environment is a source of risk and for management purposes risk must be measured.

## 12.2 SHORTCOMINGS OF TRADITIONAL METHODS

Firms concerned with exchange rate and interest rate risks have had, and still have, many alternative exposure measures to use as a basis for hedging decision. We have argued that traditional transaction and translation exposures have many shortcomings, most notably that they are partial in terms of risks as well as in terms of cash flows considered. Even recently developed economic exposure measures are partial in terms of risks considered because they pay no attention to the simultaneous impact of exchange rates and other macro price variables.

Interest rate risk measures are all geared to estimating risks on the liability side of the firm. They do not capture such business effects as, for example, interest rate effects on the demand for a company's products. They also fail to capture the interdependence between interest rates on the one hand and exchange rates and inflation rates on the other. "Value at Risk" (VaR) has been implemented as a way of capturing risk on the liability side and this measure can easily be extended to include commercial risk using the sensitivity coefficients discussed in this book. "Cash-Flow at Risk" (CFaR) is a first step for non-financial firms. However, a successful use of CFaR requires exposure coefficients from a MUST analysis, as described in Chapter 7.

An additional problem with traditional exposure measures is that they do not contain inflation exposure measures; perhaps this is because accounting figures are rarely inflation adjusted.

Furthermore, existing performance measures such as Economic Value Added (EVA), Shareholder Value Analysis (SVA), and benchmarking, can all be criticized for not explicitly taking into consideration changes in the macroeconomic environment. Efforts to do so during the phase of implementation are often based on accounting data and principles embedded in the traditional exposure measures.

## 12.3 MEASURES OF CORPORATE PERFORMANCE AND EXPOSURE ASSESSMENT

An important part of both performance analysis and risk management (together constituting the MUST analysis) is to obtain good measures of the effects of macroeconomic events on the firm. Exposures to macroeconomic variables should be measured as sensitivity coefficients for cash flows or for a firm's economic value, taking into account the interdependence among macroeconomic variables. This interdependence implies that coefficients in a multiple regression equation are appropriate exposure measures. Lacking possibilities to carry out the statistical analysis one can measure exposures by scenario analysis. Exposures can be estimated either for a group of macroeconomic market price variables such as exchange rates, price levels, and interest rates, or for a group of policy and non-policy disturbances such as money supply changes, changes in budget deficits, and oil price changes. The two approaches require different kinds of information as inputs. Therefore, the relative advantage of each depends partly on the availability of relevant information. We argued in favor of measuring exposures to the market price variables on the grounds that these variables are easily observable for firms at the time macroeconomic disturbances occur. Thus, firms can respond directly to changes in these variables. Furthermore, there exist financial instruments for hedging exposures to most market price variables.

Given the sensitivity coefficients for exchange, interest, and inflation rates, information about the volatility of these variables and their interdependence (correlation) enables a firm to estimate the volatility of cash flows and the VaR/CFaR, that is, the maximum losses that will be sustained with a certain probability. The VaR measure of the firm's risk can be translated into the probability of bankruptcy while the CFaR measure captures a form of liquidity risk. We argued in Chapter 2 that these measures of risk are the most relevant in a general stakeholder perspective.

Regression analysis requires the availability of historical cash flow data. These data should be detailed cash flow figures for commercial and financial cash flows by product line, country of sales, currency of denomination, and other characteristics. They should exist on a quarterly or shorter basis for a minimum of five years. If such data are not available, internal knowledge about the structure of cash flows and the impact of macro-events on these flows can be applied in a scenario analysis.

For risk management, estimated exposure coefficients must be applicable to future periods. The structure of the firm as well as the behavior of policy authorities must not be very different in the period when the exposure is to be managed relative to the period over which exposure was estimated. The addition, for example, of a new product line, a major acquisition on the part of the firm, or a change in exchange rate regime in the macroeconomic environment would call for new estimates. Uncertainty about policy regime with respect to exchange rates and interest rates are important aspects of political risk. When political risk is substantial, regression analysis must be supplemented with current information of relevance for exposure coefficients.

Even in cases when regression analysis is not directly applicable or reliable, the definition of exposure coefficients within regression equations provides useful guidance for the exposure measures a firm should try to arrive at by any method. Regression coefficients are summary figures for the economic impact on cash flows of different disturbances through a whole variety of more or less obvious channels. The coefficients include valuation effects as well as price and quantity effects on cash flows. When a scenario analysis is to be conducted, internal knowledge about the impact of different kinds of disturbances on cash flows must be utilized. This knowledge may be based on judgment and experience or it may be based on the explicit formulation of macroeconomic relationships among disturbances and relative prices, as well as on the market conditions of relevance for a firm. If explicit formulations can be specified for the relationships between macroeconomic variables, and if the impact of these variables on a firm can be identified, then a scenario analysis of the type discussed in Oxelheim and Wihlborg (1987) is useful.

Exposure coefficients are a useful tool for sensitivity analysis in the budget process as well. Events of particular importance for cash flows can be identified and budget alternatives can be analysed under different forecasts about macroeconomic events. Such an analysis in the budget process is essential for the evaluation in hindsight of what might be regarded as temporary developments caused by an unforeseeable macroeconomic event.

Although we have presented the different methods for estimating exposure as substitutes, it is obvious that, from management's perspective, they are complementary. Ideal methods are hard to obtain. Political risk, data problems, and other econometric problems are reasons for scepticism about any measure. By obtaining measures of exposure using different methods, the uncertainty about exposure measures can be reduced. If different methods give similar results, then the exposure measures are credible. However, if results are different, then there is reason to check the underlying assumptions of each method.

## 12.4 ELEMENTS OF MUST ANALYSIS

We summarize the different parts of the book in Table 12.1. It contains the elements that should enter into a comprehensive analysis and formulation of a Macroeconomic Uncertainty Strategy (MUST). The table lists the inputs necessary to create a strategy. The first input (1) is a fundamental analysis of how cash flows of different kinds depend on price levels, exchange rates, and interest rates. An important step here is to identify a set of macro price variables that capture the impact of macroeconomic disturbances on the firm. We emphasized that the real effects should be analysed. In order to select these relevant variables we must first answer the following questions: (a) in which countries does the firm produce? (b) from which countries does it buy its inputs? (c) where are these inputs produced? (d) which are the major geographical markets for the products and services? (e) how differentiated is the firm's product? (f) which firms are the major competitors? (g) in which countries do the competitors produce? (h) from which countries do they buy their inputs? (i) in which countries are these inputs produced? And in the case of financial cash flows: (j) in which currencies are the firm's financial positions denominated?

**Table 12.1  Elements of Macroeconomic Uncertainty Strategy (MUST) analysis.**

**Inputs for analyzing performance and determining exposure management strategy**
1. Character of cash flows and identification of important macro price variables.
2. Firm objective, target variable, risk attitude, time perspective.
3. Goods and financial market pricing relationships (PPP, IFP, Expectations hypothesis, Inflation indexation).

**Information**
4. Current organization and information system.
5. Availability of information and expertise to implement the desired strategy and performance analysis at different levels (exposure measures determined within a multivariate framework and forecasts).

**Operational management**
6. Possible reorganization and information system development; creating flexibility.
7. Specification and delegation of responsibilities to tactical and operational decision levels.

**Evaluation and feedback**
8. Accounting and reporting systems.
9. Evaluation of Macroeconomic Uncertainty Strategy.

The second input (2) is the specification of the firm's objective relative to stakeholders. Thereby, the target variable can be selected. This variable may be near-term cash flows, economic value, market value, or accounting value. We argue that real cash flows or economic value should be chosen. The time perspective of the firm is one aspect of the choice between these two variables. The risk attitude of management on behalf of the stakeholders determines whether the variance of the target variable should be part of the objective. Finally, the third input (3) is the management's view on pricing relationships in international goods and financial markets, or rather on the firm's ability to exploit deviations from them. For example, if Purchasing Power Parity (PPP) holds, then there is no (real) exchange rate risk. If International Fisher Parity (IFP) holds, then the expected costs of borrowing in different currencies are equal. The validity of the latter relationship enables the firm to select highly simplified strategies even when variance of cash flow and value are considered important. Sales and purchase divisions can then be run with the objective of maximizing cash flows or value, while the responsibility of minimizing variance is taken over by the finance function. The Expectations hypothesis for the term structure of interest rates has implications for interest rate exposure similar to the implications of IFP for exchange rate exposure. Inflation indexation in contracts determines the concern with inflation exposure.

Next we turn to information available to implement performance evaluation and a risk management strategy. The current organization and information system (4) could constrain the implementation of a desired strategy. Furthermore, the relevant information and expertise for estimating exposure and obtaining a forecast may not exist (5). One of the important features of the MUST analysis is the identification of sensitivity coefficients within the multivariate framework outlined in this book.

To operationalize the desired strategy, reorganization and new information systems may be required (6). The minimum step is to acquire the information needed to pursue filtering operations. If the strategy includes flexibility of sales and purchasing, then it may be necessary to make investments and changes in organization that enable the firm to shift sales among markets and purchases among origins in response to changes in relative profitability and costs. The information requirements for the desired strategy may be overwhelming. In this case management must decide what is feasible and the extent to which desired objectives are compromised by a feasible strategy. Thereafter, responsibilities must be delegated to tactical and operational levels in the firm (7). The specific tasks of head of sales, head of purchase, and head of finance on the tactical level vary depending on the strategy. For example, if IFP is considered valid, and a minimize variance strategy has been selected, then exposure of commercial cash flows can easily be handled by the finance department because hedging is essentially costless.

The incentives of management on different levels to fulfil the firm's objective depend strongly on performance evaluation systems. It is therefore necessary that the delegation of authority is consistent with the evaluation system and with overall objectives. In order to perform evaluation and to obtain information feedback among different levels of authority, accounting and reporting systems (8) must be developed for the chosen strategy. Managers must be evaluated using the relevant information. For instance, when evaluating loans in different currencies, it is an important issue to determine how a specific exchange rate change should be allocated over the loan period. The effects on sales of changes in exchange rates or interest rates should be reported as related to these variables. If not, managers are evaluated on circumstances beyond their control. The MUST analysis is also of crucial importance in evaluating the "true" performance of foreign subsidiaries of a multinational firm as well as in understanding the "intrinsic" creditworthiness of a firm (Oxelheim and Wihlborg 2008).

We foresee that accounting systems in the future will be developed to answer questions of a "what if" character. In such a system, the sensitivity coefficients discussed in this book will, as discussed in Chapter 11, play an important role. Whenever a company publishes profit and sales forecasts, they should be accompanied by information about the assumptions on which they are based. In addition, the sensitivity coefficients should be made public, thus allowing outside stakeholders to update a forecast which may already be outdated when it is published. This information also allows the outside stakeholder to modify the published forecast to reflect his or her own macroeconomic scenario. In most cases, the sensitivity coefficients for profit filtering are the same as those for exposure measurement. If not, they should also be given in the reports from the company as an integrated part of the analysis of competitiveness.

Finally, a plan for the overall evaluation of the Macroeconomic Uncertainty Strategy is called for (9). A selected exposure strategy within this strategy framework can be compared with alternative strategies in order to determine, for example, the actual costs of obtaining a desired decrease in the variance of cash flows. This type of evaluation would show whether assumptions made about goods and financial market relationships were correct. It may then be revealed to a risk-averse firm that deviations from, say, IFP are not large enough to justify the firm's expense on variance reduction of both commercial and financial cash flows, or that real exchange rate fluctuations are so predictable or unimportant that a strategy of never hedging would lead to substantial savings without a substantial increase in the variance of cash flows.

Part of an evaluation programme should naturally include an evaluation of its organization, and how objectives are best met with different degrees of centralization, as discussed in Chapter 10. The advantages of centralization of exposure management from the point of view of the firm's objective may be offset by decreased motivation when responsibilities are removed from local decision-makers. The pros are found in having scale advantages in financial markets, that is, opportunities to put pressure on transaction costs and advantages within global tax planning and exchange control avoidance at a centralized level. In addition to reduced motivation, the cons include the argument that in a decentralized system relevant information is available faster and with a higher quality than in a system where subsidiaries are unable or unwilling to report relevant information on time.

A coherent strategy for managing under macroeconomic uncertainty requires that incentives on all levels are made consistent with the firm's general objectives. Internally, the incentives are determined by performance assessment by top management. Thus, the incentives of top management provide the foundation for incentives on lower levels. For this reason the two legs of the Macroeconomic Uncertainty Strategy—performance assessment and exposure management—are inseparable and they depend ultimately on information enabling stakeholders to evaluate management after filtering out macroeconomic influences.

Hence the "MUST" analysis is really a must for all stakeholders involved.

# REFERENCES

Adams, J. B., and C. J. Montesi (1995), *Major Issues Related to Hedge Accounting*, International Accounting Standards Board, Stamford.

Adler, M., and B. Dumas (1980), "Accounting Standard and Exposure Management," in B. Antl (ed.), *Currency Risk and the Corporation*, Euromoney Publications, London.

Adler, M., and B. Dumas (1983), "International Portfolio Choice and Corporation Finance: A Synthesis," *Journal of Finance*, vol. 38, no. 3 (June): 925–984.

Adler, M., and D. Simon (1986), "Exchange Risk Surprises in International Portfolios," *Journal of Portfolio Management*, vol. 12, no. 2 (Winter): 44–53.

Aggarwal, R., and L. A. Soenen (1989), "Managing Persistent Real Changes in Currency Values: The Role of Multinational Operating Strategies," *Columbia Journal of World Business*, vol. 24, no. 3 (Fall), 60–67.

Aliber, R. Z., and C. P. Stickney (1975), "Accounting Measures of Foreign Exchange Exposure: The Long and Short of It," *Accounting Review*, vol. 50, no. 1 (January): 44–57.

Amihud, Y. (1993), "Exchange Rates and the Valuation of Equity Shares," in Y. Amihud and R. M. Levich (eds.), *Exchange Rates and Corporate Performance*, Lexington Health, Lexington, MA.

Amram, M., and N. Kulatilaka (1991), *Real Options: Managing Strategic Investment in an Uncertain World*, Oxford University Press.

Andrén, N., H. Jankensgård, and L. Oxelheim (2005), "Exposure-based Cash-Flow-at-Risk under Macroeconomic Uncertainty," *Journal of Applied Corporate Finance*, vol. 17 (Summer).

ASC (1976), *Guidance Manual on Current Cost Accounting Including the Exposure Draft 18*. London.

ASC (1977), *Accounting for Foreign Currency Translation, Exposure Draft 21*. London.

ASC (1980), *Accounting for Foreign Currency Translation, Exposure Draft 27*. London.

ASC (1983), *Foreign Currency Translation*. London.

Barnea, A., J. Ronen, and S. Sadan (1975), "The Implementation of Accounting Objectives: An Application to Extrordinary Objective," *Accounting Review*, vol. 50, no. 1 (Jan): 56–68.

Bartov, E., and G. M. Bodnar (1994), "Firm Valuation, Earnings Expectations and the Exchange Rate Exposure Effect," *Journal of Finance*, vol. 49, no. 5 (Dec.): 1755–1785.

Beaver, W. H., and M. A. Wolfson (1982), "Foreign Currency Translation and Changing Prices in Perfect and Complete Markets," *Journal of Accounting Research*, vol. 20, no. 2 (Autumn): 529–542.

Bhandari, J. S., and H. Genberg (1989), "Exchange Rate Movements and the International Interdependence of Stock-Markets," *Kredit und Kapital*, vol. 23, no. 4: 490–532.

Bierman, H., T. Johnson, and S. Peterson (1991), *Hedge Accounting: An Exploratory Study of the Underlying Issues*, FASB: Norwalk.

Black, F., and M. Scholes (1973), "The Pricing of Options and Corporate Liabilities," *Journal of Political Economy*, vol. 81, no. 3 (May/June): 637–654.

Boyd, W. (1801), *A Letter to the Rt. Hon. William Pitt on the Influence of the Stoppage of Specie*, London.

Bromwich, M. (1975), "Individual Purchasing Power Indices and Accounting Reports," *Accounting and Business Research*, vol. 5, no. 2 (Spring): 188–222.

Bromwich, M. (1977), "The General Validity of Certain Current Value Asset Valuation Bases," *Accounting and Business Research*, vol. 7, no. 3 (Summer): 242–249.

Bushman, R., J. D. Piotroski, and A. J. Smith (2004), "What Determines Corporate Transparency," *Journal of Accounting Research*, vol. 42, no. 2: 207–250.

Cahan, S. (1992), "The Effect of Antitrust Investigations on Discretionary Accruals: A Refined Test of the Political Costs Hypothesis," *Accounting Review*, vol. 67, no.1 (Jan.): 77–95.

Campbell, J. Y. (1987), "Stock Returns and the Term Structure," *Journal of Financial Economics*, vol. 18, no. 2 (June): 373–399.

Capel, J. J. (1992), "How to Service a Foreign Market under Uncertainty," *European Journal of Political Economy*, vol. 8, 455–476.

Capel, J. J. (1997), "A Real Option Approach to Economic Exposure Management," *Journal of International Financial Management and Accounting*, vol. 8, no. 2 (Summer): 87–113.

Cassel, G. (1922), *Money and Foreign Exchanges After 1914*, Constable, London.

CFA Institute (2005), *A Comprehensive Business Reporting Model: Financial Reporting for Investors*, CFA Center for Financial Market Integrity, New York.

Chambers, R. (1966), *Accounting, Evaluation and Economic Behavior*, Prentice Hall, Englewood Cliffs, NJ.

CICA (1978), *Translation of Foreign Currency Transactions and Foreign Currency Financial Statements*. Toronto.

CICA (1982), *Translation of Foreign Currency Transactions and Foreign Currency Financial Statements*. Toronto.

CICA (1983), *Foreign Currency Translations, Section 1650*. Toronto.

Copeland, T., and V. Antikarov (2003), *Real Option: A Practitioners Guide*, Thomson Texere, New York.

Cornell, W. B. (1980), "Inflation, Relative Prices and Exchange Risk," *Financial Management*, vol. 9, no. 9 (Autumn): 30–34.

Cornell, B., and A. Shapiro (1988), "Managing Foreign Exchange Risks," in J. Stern and D. Chew (eds.), *New Developments in International Finance*, Basil Blackwell, New York.

Craig, R., and P. Walsh. 1989. "Adjustments for Extraordinary Items in Smoothing Reported Profits of Listed Australian Companies: Some Empirical Evidence," *Journal of Business Finance and Accounting*, vol. 16, no. 2 (March): 229–245.

Dempsey, S. J., H. G. Hunt III, and N. W. Schroeder (1993), "Earnings Management and Corporate Ownership Structure. An Examination of Extraordinary Items Reporting," *Journal of Business Finance and Accounting*, vol. 20, no. 4 (June): 479–500.

Dixit, A. (1989a), "Hysteresis, Import Penetration, and Exchange Rate Pass-Through," *Quarterly Journal of Economics*, vol. 104, no. 2 (May): 205–228.

Dixit, A. (1989b), "Entry and Exit Decisions under Uncertainty," *Journal of Political Economy*, vol. 94, no. 3 (June): 620–638.

Dixit, A., and R. S. Pindyck (1995), "The Option Approach to Capital Investment," *Harvard Business Review*, vol. 73, no. 3 (May/June): 105–115.

Dornbusch, R., and P. Krugman (1976), "Flexible Exchange Rates in the Short Run," *Brookings Papers on Economic Activity*, no. 3, 537–584.

Dufey, G., and I. Giddy (1978), "International Financial Planning: The Use of Market Based Forecasts," *California Management Review*, vol. 21, no. 1 (Fall).

Dufey, G., and S. L. Srinivasulu (1983), "The Case for Corporate Management of Foreign Exchange Risk," *Financial Management*, vol. 12, no. 4 (Winter): 54–62.

Dukes, R. (1978), *An Empirical Investigation on the Effects of Statement of Financial Accounting Standards*, no. 8, Financial Accounting Standards Board, Stamford.

Dumas, B., and B. Solnik (1995), "The World Price of Foreign Exchange Risk," *Journal of Finance*, vol. 50, no. 2 (June): 445–479.

Durham, J. B. (2001), "Sensitivity Analyses of Anomalies in Developed Stock Markets," *Journal of Banking and Finance*, vol. 25, no. 8 (August): 1503–1541.

Einzig, P. (1962), *The History of Foreign Exchange*, Macmillan, London.

Evans P., M. Folks Jr., and M. Jilling (1978), *The Impact of Statement of Financial Standards No. 8 on the Foreign Exchange Risk Management Practices of American Multinationals*, Financial Accounting Standards Board, Stamford.

Fama, E. F. (1981), "Stock Returns, Real Activity, Inflation, and Money," *American Economic Review*, vol. 71, no. 4 (September): 545–565.

Fama, E. F. (1984), "Forward and Spot Exchange Rates," *Journal of Monetary Finance*, vol. 54, 319–338.

Fama, E. F., and G. W. Schwert (1977), "Asset Returns and Inflation," *Journal of Financial Economics*, vol. 5, no. 2 (Nov.): 115–146.

FASB (1975), *Statement of Financial Accounting Standards No. 8, Accounting for the Translation of Foreign Currency Transactions and Foreign Currency, Financial Statements*. Stamford.

FASB (1981), *Statement of Financial Accounting Standards, No. 52*, Foreign Currency Translation. Stamford.

FASB (1994), *Statement of Financial Accounting Standards, No. 119, Disclosure about Derivative Financial Instruments and Fair Value of Financial Instruments*, Stamford.

FASB (1998), *Statement of Financial Accounting Standards, No. 133, Accounting for Derivative Instruments and Hedging Activities*, Stamford.

FASB (1999), *Statement of Financial Accounting Standards, No. 137, Accounting for Derivative Instruments and Hedging Activities*, Deferral of the effective date of FASB Statement No. 133. Stamford.

Fisher, I. (1896), "Appreciation and Interest," *Publications of the American Economic Association 11*.

Francis, J. (1990), "Accounting for Futures Contracts and the Effect on Earnings Variability," *Accounting Review*, vol. 65, no. 4 (October): 891–910.

Frenkel, J. (1981), "The Collapse of Purchasing Power Parities During the 1970s," *European Economic Review*, vol. 16, no. 1 (May): 145–165.

Friberg, R. and F. Wilander (forthcoming), "The Currency of Denomination of Exports: A Questionnaire Study," *Journal of International Economics*.

Froot, K. A., D. S. Scharfstein and J. C. Stein (1994), "A Framework for Risk Management," *Harvard Business Review*, vol. 71 (Nov.–Dec.): 91–102.

Garner, K., and A. Shapiro (1984), "A Practical Method of Assessing Foreign Exchange Risk," *Midland Corporate Finance Journal*, vol. 2, no. 3 (Fall): 6–17.

Geske, R., and R. Roll (1983), "The Fiscal and Monetary Linkage between Stock Returns and Inflation," *Journal of Finance 38* (March): 1–33.

Godfrey, J. M., and B. Yee (1996), "Mining Sector Currency Risk Management Strategies: Responses to Foreign Currency Accounting Regulation," *Accounting and Business Research*, vol. 26, no. 3 (Summer): 200–214.

Goodwin, T., F. Farsio, and T. Willett (1992), "The Dollar and the DOW," *Rivista Internazionale di Scienze Economiche e Commercialli*, vol. 39, no. 10–11 (Oct.): 899–906.

Han, J. C. Y. and S. W. Wang (1998), "Political Costs and Earnings Management of Oil Companies during the 1990 Persian Gulf Crisis," *Accounting Review*, vol. 73, no. 1 (January): 103–117.

Hekman, C. R. (1985), "A Financial Model of Foreign Exchange Exposure," *Journal of Portfolio Managment*, vol. 12 (Winter): 44–53.

Hodder, J. E. (1982), "Exposure to Exchange Rate Movements," *Journal of International Economics 13*, (Nov.): 375–386.

Huefner, R. J., J. E. Ketz, and J. A. Largay III (1989), "Foreign Currency Translation and the Cash Flow Statement," *Accounting Horizons*, vol. 3, no. 1 (March): 66–75.

IASC (1983), *International Accounting Standard 21, Accounting for the Effects of Changes in Foreign Exchange Rates*, London.

IASC (1994), *International Accounting Standard 30, Disclosure in the Financial Statements of Banks and Similar Financial Institutions Standard 30*, London.

IASC (1995), *International Accounting Standard 32, Financial Instruments: Disclosure and Presentation*, London.

IASC (1997), *International Accounting Standard 1, Presentation of Financial Statements*, London.

IASC (1998), *International Accounting Standard 39, Financial Instruments: Recognition and Measurement*, London.

Ibrahimi, F., L. Oxelheim, and C. Whilborg (1995), "International Stock Markets and Fluctuations in Exchange Rates and Other Macroeconomic Variables," in R. Aggarwal and D. C. Schirm (eds.), *Global Portfolio Diversification. Risk Management, Market Microstructure, and Implementation Issues*, Academic Press, San Diego, CA.

IFAC (1999), *Enhancing Shareholder Wealth by Better Managing Business Risk*, FMAC, New York.

Ijiri, Y. (1975), "Theory of Accounting Measurement," AAA Research Study 1975, no. 10, Menastra.

Ijiri, Y. (1976), "The Price-level Restatement and Its Dual Interpretations," *Accounting Review*, vol. 51, no. 2 (April): 227–243.

Jilling, M. (1979), *Foreign Exchange Risk Management in U.S. Multinational Corporations*, UMI Research Press, Stamford.

Jones, J. (1991), "Earnings Management during Import Relief Investigations," *Journal of Accounting Research*, vol. 29, no. 2 (Autumn): 193–228.

Jorion, P. (1990), "The Exchange-rate Exposure of US Multinationals," *Journal of Business*, vol. 63, no. 3 (July): 331–345.

Jorion, P. (1991), "The Pricing of Exchange Rate Risk in the Stock Market," *Journal of Financial and Quantitative Analysis*, vol. 26 (Sept.): 363–376.

Jorion, P. (2006), *Value at Risk: The New Benchmark for Measuring Financial Risk,* 3rd ed., McGraw-Hill, New York.

Jorion, P. and R. J. Sweeney (1996), "Mean Reversion in Real Exchange Rates: Evidence and Implications for Forecasting," *Journal of International Money and Finance*, vol. 15 (August): 535–550.

Keim, D. B, and R. F. Stambaugh (1986), "Predicting Returns in the Stock and Bond Markets," *Journal of Financial Economics*, vol. 17: 357–390.

Kennedy, C. (1978), "Inflation Accounting: Retrospect and Prospect," *Economic Policy Review*, vol. 4, no. 78 (March): 58–64.

Keynes, J. M. (1923), *A Tract on Monetary Reform*, Macmillan, London.

Kogut, B., and N. Kulatilaka (1994), "Operating Flexibility, Global Manufacturing and the Option Value of a Multinational Network," *Management Science 40* (Jan.): 123–139.

Lessard, D. R. (1986), "Finance and Global Competition: Exploiting Financial Scope and Coping with Volatile Exchange Rates," *Midland Corporate Finance Journal* (Fall): 6–29.

Lessard, D. R., and J. B. Lightstone (1986), "Volatile Exchange Rates Can Put Operations at Risk," *Harvard Business Review 64* (July–Aug.): 107–114.

Lessard, D., and P. Lorange (1977), "Currency Changes and Management Control: Resolving the Centralization/Decentralization Dilemma," *Accounting Review*, vol. 52, no. 3 (July): 628–637.

Levi, M. (1983), *Financial Management and the International Economy*, McGraw-Hill, New York.

MacDonald, R. (1988), *Floating Exchange Rate Theories and Evidence*, Unwin Hyman, London.

Madden, B. J. (1999), *A Total System Approach to Valuing the Firm*, Butterworth-Heinemann.

Mahdavi, S., and S. Zhou (1994), "Purchasing Power Parity in High-inflation Countries: Further Evidence," *Journal of Macroeconomics*, vol. 36, no. 5 (Summer): 403–422.

Makar, S. D., B. B. Stanko, and T. L. Zeller (1996), "Foreign Currency Translation under the Temporal Rate Method," *International Advances in Economic Research*, vol. 2, no. 4 (Nov.): 444–454.

Marston, R. C. (1990), "Pricing to Market in Japanese Manufacturing," *Journal of International Economics*, vol. 29, no. 3–4 (November): 217–236.

McCormack, J., and I. D. Gow (2001), "EVA in E&P Industries: The Case of Nuevo Industries," *Journal of Applied Corporate Finance*, vol. 13, no. 4.

McNown, R., and M. S. Wallace. (1989), "National Price Levels, Purchasing Power Parity and Cointegration: A Test of Four High Inflation Economies," *Journal of International Money and Finance*, vol. 8, no. 4 (Dec.): 533–535.

Milgrom, R., and J. Roberts (1992), *Economics, Organization and Management*, Prentice-Hall, New York.

Miller, M. (1992), "A Framework for Integrated Risk Management in International Business," *Journal of International Business Studies*, vol. 23, no. 2, 311–331.

Miltz, D., and P. Sercu (1993), "Accounting for New Financial Instruments," *Journal of Business Finance and Accounting*, vol. 20, no. 2 (Jan.): 275–290.

O'Byrne, S. (1997), "EVA and Shareholder Return," *Financial Practice and Education*, vol. 7, no. 1 (Spring–Summer): 50–54.

Officer, L. (1982), *Purchasing Power Parity and Exchange Rates: Theory, Evidence and Relevance*, JAI Press, New York.

OPTICA Report 2 (1977), "Inflation and Exchange Rates," *Evidence Guidelines for the European Community*, Brussels, February.

Ottosson, E., and F. Weissenrieder (1996), "Cash Value Added (CVA): A New Method for Measuring Financial Performance," *Gothenburg Studies in Financial Economics*, 1996: 1, Department of Economics, Gothenburg University.

Oxelheim, L. (1983), "Proposals for New Accounting Standards for Monetary Items," *Journal of Business Finance and Accounting*, vol. 10, no. 2 (March): 257–288.

Oxelheim, L. (1985), *International Financial Market Fluctuations*, Wiley, Chichester and New York.

Oxelheim, L. (1990), *International Financial Integration*, Springer-Verlag, Heidelberg and New York.

Oxelheim, L. (1996), *Financial Markets in Transition: Globalization, Investment and Economic Growth*, Routledge, London.

Oxelheim, L. (2003), "Macroeconomic Variables and Corporate Performance," *Financial Analysts Journal*, vol. 59, no. 4: 36–50.

Oxelheim, L. (2006a), "IFRS Transparency and Economic Growth," *Journal of Finnish Economic Society*, vol. 2.

Oxelheim, L. (ed.) (2006b), *Corporate and Institutional Transparency for Economic Growth in Europe*, Elsevier, Oxford.

Oxelheim, L., A. Stonehill, T. Randøy, K. Vikkula, K. Dullum and K.-M. Modén (1997), *Corporate Strategies to Internationalize the Cost of Capital*, Copenhagen Business School Press, Copenhagen.

Oxelheim, L., and C. Wihlborg (1987), *Macroeconomic Uncertainty: International Risks and Opportunities for the Corporation*, John Wiley and Sons, Chichester and New York.

Oxelheim, L., and C. Wihlborg (1991a), "Corporate Strategies in a Turbulent World Economy," *Management International Review*, vol. 31, no. 4: 293–315.

Oxelheim, L., and C. Wihlborg (1991b), "Accounting for Macroeconomic Influences on the Firm," *Journal of International Financial Management and Accounting*, vol. 3, no. 3 (Autumn): 258–252.

Oxelheim, L., and C. Wihlborg (1995), "Measuring Macroeconomic Exposure: The Case of Volvo Cars," *European Financial Management*, vol. 1, no. 3 (Autumn): 241–263.

Oxelheim, L., and C. Wihlborg (1997), *Managing in the Turbulent World Economy: Corporate Performance and Risk Exposure*, John Wiley and Sons, Chichester and New York.

Oxelheim, L., and C. Wihlborg (2003), "Recognizing Macroeconomic Fluctuations in Value-Based Management," *Journal of Applied Corporate Finance*, vol. 15, no. 4: 104–110.

Oxelheim, L., and C. Wihlborg (2008), "Measures of Creditworthiness with Macroeconomic Fluctuations," *Mimeo*, Lund University.

Oxelheim, L., C. Wihlborg, and D. Lim (1990), "Contractual Price Rigidities and Exchange Rate Adjustments," *The International Trade Journal*, vol. 5, no. 2: 53–76.

Oxelheim, L., C. Wihlborg, and J. Zhang (2008), "Executive Compensation and Macroeconomic Fluctuations," in L. Oxelheim and C. Wihlborg (eds.), *Markets and Compensation for Executives in Europe*, Emerald Group Publishing, Bingley.

Pigott, C., and R. J. Sweeney (1985), "Purchasing Power Parity and Exchange Rate Dynamics: Some Empirical Results," in S. W. Arndt, R. J. Sweeney, and T. D. Willett (eds.), *Exchange Rates, Trade and the U.S. Economy*, Ballinger, Cambridge, MA.

Pindyck, R. S. (1988), "Risk Aversion and Determinants of Stock Market Behaviour," *Review of Economics and Statistics*, vol. 78, no. 2: 183–190.

Prakash, P., and S. Sunder (1979), "The Case Against Separation of Current Operating Profit and Holding Gains," *Accounting Review*, vol. 54, no. 1 (Jan.): 1–22.

Rappaport, A. (1986), *Creating Shareholder Value*: *The New Standard for Business Performance*, Free Press, London.

Roll, R. (1979), "Valuations of Purchasing Power Parity and Their Implications for Efficient International Commodity Markets," in M. Sarnat and G. P. Szegö (eds.), *International Finance and Trade*, Ballinger, Cambridge, MA.

Rosenfeld, P. (1972), "Confusion between General Price-level Restatement and Current Value Accounting," *Journal of Accountancy*, vol. 140, no. 4 (Oct.): 63–68.

Samuelson, R. A. (1980), "Should Replacement Costs Changes Be Included in Income," *Accounting Review*, vol. 55, no. 2 (April): 254–287.

Schmidt, F. (1930), "The Impact of Replacement Value," *Accounting Review*, vol. 5, no. 2 (Sept.): 235–242.

Securities and Exchange Commission (2000), *Regulation FD, Selective Disclosure and Insider Trading*, Washington, DC.

Shank, J., J. Dillard, and R. Murdoch (1979), *Assessing the Economic Impact of FASB No. 8*, Financial Executives Research Foundation, New York.

Shapiro, A. C., and S. Titman (1984), "An Integrated View of Risk Management," *Midland Corporate Finance Journal* (Summer).

Solnik, B. (1983), "The Relation between Stock Prices and Inflationary Expectations: The International Evidence," *Journal of Finance*, vol. 38, no. 1 (March): 35–48.

Solnik, B. (1984), "Stock Prices and Monetary Variables: The International Evidence," *Financial Analysts Journal*, vol. 40.

Srinivasulu, S. (1981), "Strategic Responses to Foreign Exchange Risks," *Columbia Journal of World Business*, vol. 16 (Spring): 13–23.

Staubus, G. (1975), "Price-level Accounting: Some Unfinished Business," *Accounting and Business Research*, vol. 5, no. 1 (Winter): 42–47.

Stein, J., S. Usher, D. LaGatutta, and J. Younger (2001), "A Comparables Approach to Measuring Cash Flow at Risk for Non-Financial Firms," *Journal of Applied Corporate Finance*, vol. 13, no. 4, 100–109.

Sterling, R. R. (1975), "Relevant Financial Reporting in an Age of Price Changes," *Journal of Accountancy*, vol. 143, no. 1 (Feb.): 42–51.

Stewart, B. (1983), "Normalizing Exchange Rates for Purchasing Power Parity," *Midland Corporate Finance Journal*, vol. 1, no. 2 (Summer).

Stewart, B. (1990), *The Quest for Value: The EVA-TM Management Guide*, Harper Business, New York.

Stonehill, A., N. Ravn, and K. Dullum (1982), "Management of Foreign Exchange Economic Exposure," in Bergendahl, G. (ed.), *International Financial Management*, Norstedts, Stockholm.

Sweeney, H. W. (1927), "Effect of Inflation on German Accounting," *Journal of Accountancy*, vol. 95, no. 3 (July): 180–191.

Trigeorgis, L. (1996), *Real Options: Managerial Flexibility and Strategy in Resource Allocation*, MIT Press, Cambridge, MA.

Walsh, P., R. Craig, and F. Clark (1991), "Big Bath Accounting: Using Extraordinary Items Adjustment: Australian Empirical Evidence," *Journal of Business Finance and Accounting*, vol. 18, no. 2 (Jan.): 173–189.

Watts, R., and J. Zimmerman (1986), "Toward a Positive Theory of the Determination of Accounting Standards," *Accounting Review*, vol. 54, no. 2 (Jan.): 112–134.

Westwick, C. A. (1980), "The Lessons to Be Learned from the Development of Inflation Accounting in the UK," *Accounting and Business Research*, vol. 10, no. 4 (Autumn): 357–373.

Wharton/CIBC (1995), Survey of Derivatives Usage by U.S. Non-Financial Firms, *Financial management.*

Vickrey, D. W. (1976), "General Price-level Adjusted Historical Cost Statements and the Ratio-scale View," *Accounting Review*, vol. 51, no. 1 (Jan.): 31–40.

Wihlborg, C. (1978), "Currency Risks in International Financial Markets," *Princeton Studies in International Finance 44*, Princeton University.

Ziebart, D. A., and J.-H. Choi (1998), "The Difficulty of Achieving Economic Reality Through Foreign Currency Translation," *International Journal of Accounting*, vol. 33, no. 4 (Oct.): 403–414.

# Index

Note: Information presented in figures and tables is denoted by *f* and *t*. Information in endnotes is denoted by n following the page number and preceding the note number.